D1612227

Personal Effectiveness in Project Management

**Tools, tips and strategies
to improve your
decision-making, influence,
motivation, confidence,
risk-taking, achievement
and self-sustainability**

Zachary Wong, Ph.D.

Author Photo by Maksim Yankovskiy

Library of Congress Cataloging-in-Publication Data

Wong, Zachary.
 Personal effectiveness in project management : tools, tips and strategies to improve your decision-making, influence, motivation, confidence, risk-taking, achievement and self-sustainability / Zachary Wong, Ph.D.
     pages cm
 Includes bibliographical references and index.
 ISBN-13: 978-1-62825-029-9 (alk. paper)
 ISBN-10: 1-62825-029-1 (alk. paper) 1. Project management. 2. Teams in the workplace.
3. Employee motivation. 4. Interpersonal relations. I. Title.
 HD69.P75.W657 2013
 658.4'04--dc23

                        2013035974

ISBN: 978-1-62825-029-9

Published by: Project Management Institute, Inc.
                   14 Campus Boulevard
                   Newtown Square, Pennsylvania 19073-3299 USA
                   Phone: +610-356-4600
                   Fax: +610-356-4647
                   Email: customercare@pmi.org
                   Internet: www.PMI.org

PMI Publications welcomes corrections and comments on its books. Please feel free to send comments on typographical, formatting, or other errors. Simply make a copy of the relevant page of the book, mark the error, and send it to: Book Editor, PMI Publications, 14 Campus Boulevard, Newtown Square, PA 19073-3299 USA.

To inquire about discounts for resale or educational purposes, please contact the PMI Book Service Center.

        PMI Book Service Center
        P.O. Box 932683, Atlanta, GA 31193-2683 USA
        Phone: 1-866-276-4764 (within the U.S. or Canada) or +1-770-280-4129 (globally)
        Fax: +1-770-280-4113
        Email: info@bookorders.pmi.org

In memory of my parents,
Wilfred and Margaret

To my love and joy,
Elaine

To my hope and happiness,
Amy and Sarah

Acknowledgments

I wish to thank my family and friends who made this book possible. To my wife, Elaine, whose love, support and encouragement inspired me to write this book. In addition to being an extraordinary wife, mother and teacher, she is the best person I have ever met in my life.

I am grateful to my two daughters, Amy and Sarah, for fulfilling my dream of being a dad and giving me a lifetime of unforgettable experiences. Amy gives me kindness, compassion and a positive attitude; Sarah instills courage, resourcefulness and passion.

My book wouldn't have had a starting point without my mom and dad, Margaret and Wilfred; sister, Pamela; brothers, Reynold and Gary. Thanks to my extended family: Bob, Marilyn, Tom and Marguerite Almond, and my nieces and nephews, Angie, Ashley, Cassandra, Christie, Christopher, Courtney, Kevin, Lindsay, Madeleine and Nicole. Special thanks to Reynold for his lifelong mentorship and Gary for helping me design the personal effectiveness diagram.

My sincere gratitude to my friends for their contributions: Rich Clark for reviewing and improving my book and helping me find the joy in writing; Judith MacGregor, who launched and championed my career at Chevron, which eventually lead to a second career in teaching and writing; Maria Marquez, who invited me over to East Bay Municipal Utility District (EBMUD) when I retired from Chevron and gave me a second home to develop my work; Rob Judd and Tom Kendrick for sponsoring my course at U.C. Berkeley Extension that gave me a venue to test and hone this book; Ray Ju and Neal Maillet for their continued friendship and professional support and final thanks to all my students in *Human Factors* who I have had the honor and privilege of teaching. Nothing beats a live classroom for learning, growing and connecting with other people—I hope the classroom never dies.

Lastly, I want to acknowledge all the mentors, coaches and teachers in my life whose knowledge, guidance and generosity have enabled me to find who I am and to express myself in the best possible way. Whether it's family, friends, colleagues or the classroom, I have learned that it's people who always bring out the best in me.

Contents

Introduction

PERSONAL EFFECTIVENESS IN PROJECT MANAGEMENT

Successful project management requires a well-organized, well-structured, disciplined approach in completing project tasks, schedules, work plans and goals. It involves the expert application of knowledge, experience, skills and tools to project tasks and activities. These project activities do not operate separately but work together as a project management system to ensure that all processes, resources and assets are used efficiently. Planning, budgeting, procurement, quality, risk, project execution, human resources, monitoring and control are systematically and explicitly managed. But what is not as explicitly understood and managed are the human *behaviors* behind the tasks and activities; yet human behaviors determine whether people are motivated to perform, activities are completed on time, tools are used properly, information is communicated clearly and whether projects succeed or fail. Managing behaviors on a project is not a "soft" skill but an *essential* skill in project management.

A project is a planned undertaking of human tasks and activities toward achieving a common goal. Good planning, execution and completion of a project rely on the collective effectiveness of people. Success depends on people—and their ability to utilize information, processes and tools. How well they apply their knowledge, experience and skills to problems and tasks depend on human behaviors; and the underlying elements that motivate human behaviors are called *human factors*. Human factors are the values, experiences, diversity, knowledge, skills, personality, ambitions, emotions and attitudes that make people unique, extraordinary and accomplished. Human factors affect people's thinking, behaviors and performance. These factors are internal and how well they work together as a system in helping people think, create and achieve is called *personal effectiveness*—the inherent ability to make great decisions, perform at a high level, achieve challenging goals and sustain success.

Project management has a strong foundation of excellent, well-proven concepts, tools and techniques (Project Management Institute, 2013), but project managers and professionals desire more skills in behavioral tools, techniques and strategies for managing people and motivating higher performance. For project management, there are four major functions in personal effectiveness—*decision-making, motivation, achievement and sustainability*—and this book will help you measure, assess and diagnose how well you are functioning in these four areas and what your greatest opportunities are for personal improvement. This book will demonstrate how human factors shape your thinking, behaviors, motivation, influence, self-confidence, risk-taking, achievements, personal goals, work-life balance and self-esteem.

Personal effectiveness includes both *inter*personal and *intra*personal skills. Interpersonal effectiveness is the ability to build positive relationships and motivate team success (Wong, 2007), while intrapersonal effectiveness is the ability to motivate and inspire personal success from within. People's *inter*personal skills are only as strong as their *intra*personal skills. This book presents practical concepts, cases, tools and techniques to strengthen your personal effectiveness and increase your skills in managing projects.

Unlike many "personal success" books that favor a certain way of thinking or behaving (Covey, 1989, 1990, 2006; Luciani, 2004; Goldsmith, 2007), human factors deal with the root elements behind your thinking and behaviors and how they influence your personal performance. There is no right or wrong way to think or behave when it comes to success because people are unique, diverse and have different definitions of success. Your individual diversity defines your values, beliefs and behaviors and everyone has a different work style in managing projects. Although most people and organizations recognize that diversity is important, they struggle to find its connection to one's ability to successfully manage and execute a project.

In the human resource aspects of project management, people are saturated with "buzz" words, such as diversity, culture, leadership, integrity, accountability, achievement, inclusiveness, performance, values, behaviors, self-esteem, motivation, self-confidence, passion and fulfillment. Unfortunately, these words have been overrated, oversold and overused for so long that they have lost meaning. For many people, these words start to sound like the "flavor of the month" or they run together, sounding redundant and delusional. For these words to have practical meaning and application to project management, *they need to be better defined, organized and structured into a coherent system* of tools, techniques and strategies that project managers can understand and apply to their personal performance. This book provides a simple, unified model for putting these "soft" terms into a "hard" framework to help project managers improve their personal effectiveness.

In projects, one of the basic human elements for individual and team achievement is motivation. Motivation is the inner drive behind human behaviors and actions in meeting personal needs. "Achievement motivation" is the innate drive to reach success and achieve higher goals. According to Fred Luthans (2008), the most important human motives are "power and achievement." Achievement stems from the need to compete against others, meet goals, solve problems and an inner drive to do things better. This is consistent with the project management concepts of continuous improvement, quality management, employee empowerment, problem-solving and behavioral reinforcement.

Project success depends on the management of human factors that enables people to make the *right decisions*, take the *right actions*, achieve the *right goals* and *feel right* about the outcome. This means that personal success is dependent on your ability to develop the *right* strategies, goals and actions that fit the objectives of the project and your human factors—beliefs, expectations, strengths, weaknesses, work styles, motivations, attitude and passions. This book will help you identify and assess your key human factors and improve your personal performance.

CONTENTS OF THIS BOOK

Just as project life cycles provide a basic framework for managing the "hard" skills in project management, this book provides a basic framework for managing the "soft" skills called the "personal effectiveness cycle," which has four functions—decision-making, motivation, achievement and sustainability—and they are powered by four pairs of human factors: *diversity and values, space and set point, fear and inclusion, and passion and goals.*

Personal effectiveness is determined by one's ability to make good decisions, perform well, get results and achieve success. This model is based on the author's thirty-five years of experience as a project manager, mentor, coach and teacher in private industry, academia and consulting. The concepts in the model were derived from his experiences in leading team projects, working on global teams, teaching and mentoring project managers, consulting and conducting surveys. The eight human factors for personal effectiveness are critical for decision-making, influence, self-confidence, risk-taking, accountability, conflict management, motivation, self-esteem, inner strength and self-sustainability. *Managing human*

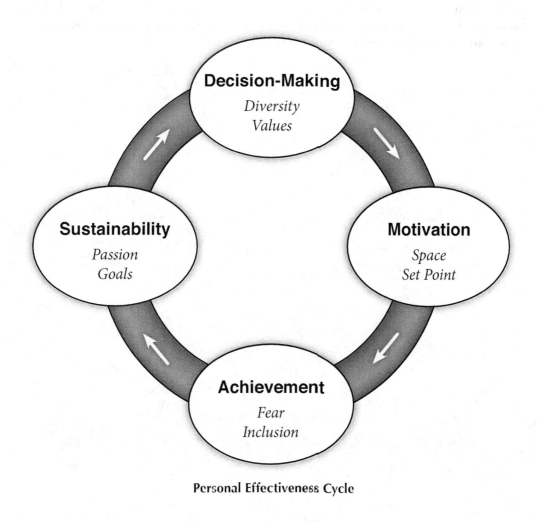

Personal Effectiveness Cycle

factors is a skill and it should be treated in the same manner as any skill in project manage-ment—it requires knowledge, training, development and experience. This book provides valuable strategies, techniques, tools and self-assessments to raise one's awareness and competency in human factors.

Personal Effectiveness in Project Management is based on real examples, research, practical concepts and useful tools to help develop and accelerate your personal success. What makes this book unique is that it *works with you* to clarify and optimize your decision-making, motivation, achievement and sustainability. The true measure of project success is not doing *a* project well but to do many projects well over a long time and feeling personally satisfied—to achieve *self-sustainability*—the capacity to achieve continuous success. This book is meant to strengthen your inner skills to achieve sustainable project and personal success.

The definitions, concepts and methodologies for identifying and assessing your eight human factors are presented in twelve chapters. As you go through each chapter, different factors and assessments will be presented and your answers are fed into an overall model, like building blocks, to reveal your personal effectiveness. Hopefully by the end of this book, you would have learned new concepts, skills and techniques for vastly improving your personal effectiveness in project management.

1

Personal Effectiveness Cycle

Everyone has one. People are born with one and it stays with them for life. It is the essence of who you are, what you are and why "you do the things you do." It's an internal subconscious process that gives you continuous direction, motivation, feedback and energy to accomplish wonderful things in life, and it's an incredible source of personal power and achievement. This internal process is called the "personal effectiveness cycle."

Just as there are project life cycles that help guide and control the "hard" skills in project management, people have psychological processes that help regulate their "soft" skills or personal effectiveness. This personal effectiveness cycle is a set of subconscious processes that controls the critical mental functions in project management: decision-making, motivation, achievement and sustainability. These mental functions give you knowledge, energy, drive and intuition. You don't have to see this cycle to know it's there—you feel it and it enables you to do special things in your career and personal life. How many times have you achieved things that you initially thought were too difficult? How many of your successes were driven by your natural inclination or a belief in yourself? How many times have you trusted your gut feeling and it turned out right? How often have you felt that your successes were somehow "meant to happen?" All your achievements and successful decisions were derived from and supported by subconscious factors in your personal effectiveness cycle that were either in-born or developed during your life.

The personal effectiveness cycle contains many interdependent components that control and power your motivation and behaviors. The most important elements are called *human factors* and they are the underlying factors that drive your personal effectiveness.

HUMAN FACTORS

Human factors are the underlying elements that define who you are and what you do. They are your values, personality, genetics, culture, experiences and emotions that motivate your behaviors and relationships with other people. Human factors are the things that shape your thinking, give meaning to your actions, create your goals and motivate you to succeed. The management of human factors is the single most important determinant of project success—projects are run by people and it takes a highly motivated and skilled team to successfully complete projects.

Human factors are the underlying elements of personal effectiveness, affecting decision-making, motivation, achievement and sustainability.

Human factors constantly influence how people perceive themselves and the world around them. Everything that they see, hear or feel is processed through their human factors. They help people interpret and respond to their environment, and they help people judge what's good and bad, right and wrong, and what's true and false. When people make a decision or engage in an activity, their human factors are the things that make them feel happy, sad, indifferent or excited. They provide confidence, hope, courage and motivation as well as self-doubt, despair, fear and reluctance. There are no good and bad human factors (though they are all essential for thinking, behavior and survival), only good and bad *effects* from human factors that appear in the outcomes and consequences of one's behaviors.

"Human Factors" is not a philosophy or a set of behaviors. They are the underlying elements of personal effectiveness, affecting *decision-making, motivation, achievement* and *sustainability*. Personal effectiveness requires good thinking (decision-making), positive behaviors (motivation), high performance (achievement) and continuous success (sustainability). Thinking refers to judgment, perception and intent; behaviors are the things that people do and say (actions); achievement is the desired consequence, and sustainability is the ultimate outcome.

If people know what they want and believe in it, their actions and achievements will flow from it. However, success doesn't materialize from good thinking and behaviors; it also requires the right opportunities and an external environment that supports one's actions and goals. Thus, personal success is a lifelong cycle that requires internal and external synchronization of one's human factors with his or her decision-making, motivation, achievement and sustainability (Figure 1.1). A cycle is a series of internal actions and factors that loop continuously. The personal effectiveness cycle is a simple, dynamic, unified model for personal success in project management and it controls many important mental processes, such as judgment, self-confidence, fear and self-esteem. *The personal effectiveness cycle models how the subconscious works.* By understanding and improving one's cycle, people can greatly increase their personal effectiveness as project leaders, managers, team members, colleagues, employees and career professionals.

The personal effectiveness cycle is comprised of four functional areas with each area supported by two critical human factors.

- **Decision-making** (thinking) is a mental process that requires an understanding of who you are (diversity) and what you believe in (values). Decision-making is

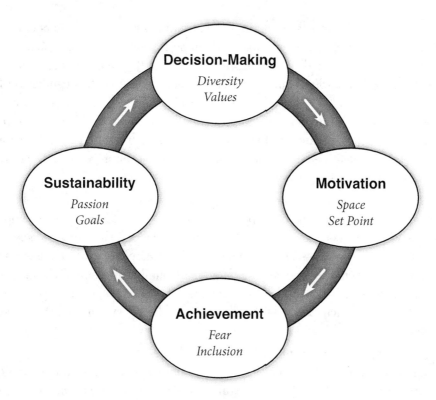

Figure 1.1 Personal Effectiveness Cycle

an essential skill in project management. You want to use your best thinking to make judgments, perceptions and good decisions and to determine what is "right." Diversity and values are critical human factors for decision-making.

- **Motivation** (behavior) is an internal feeling or desire that is both self-generated (set point) and externally induced (space) that leads to the "right" actions and behaviors. Project success depends on the collective motivation and behaviors of the project team. Space and set point are major human factors that determine motivation.

- **Achievement** (performance) is a desired output of your actions, opportunities and abilities (skills, knowledge and experience) and it entails performing at a high level in solving problems, creating new ideas, satisfying customers, meeting project goals and getting the "right" results. Fear (worry and anxiety) and inclusion (engagement) are key human factors that affect achievement.

- **Sustainability** (success) is reached when you consistently and continuously do the right things, in the right way, with the right results and feel right about it—this is the essence of project management. Success means feeling positive and "right" about your achievements in life. Passion and goals are essential human factors for sustainability. (In this book, *sustainability and self-sustainability* are synonymous.)

The personal effectiveness cycle is your internal engine and for it to operate well, it requires energy, timing, balance, input and support from your human factors. Human factors, such as fear and diversity, are not static but they continuously develop and change as you gain knowledge and experience. These human factors can help or hinder you depending on how well you understand, control and use them. Unfortunately, people assume these internal, subconscious factors can't be controlled, which is not true. This book provides tools, tips and strategies for assessing, improving and optimizing your human factors to make better decisions, raise motivation, improve project performance and increase personal satisfaction.

In any given project, project managers are expected to oversee and control hundreds of behaviors in themselves and other people. This is not only difficult but also impossible and that's why behaviors are rarely addressed in projects. However, because human factors are the root elements of all behaviors, project managers can manage hundreds of behaviors by leveraging and managing a small number of key human factors. And eight human factors have been identified that are critical for project managers and these eight "soft" human factors can be managed in a "hard" system called the personal effectiveness cycle.

In one's lifetime, achievements occur during special moments and opportunities over time, like snapshots, and the timing has to be *in sync*. You need to be ready with your skills and strengths when opportunities arise in your external environment, and you need to be confident enough to go after it. If you wish to maximize the chances for success, your goal is to pursue as many opportunities as possible and as efficiently as possible. To do this, you need to optimize the things that control the synchronization and effectiveness of your personal effectiveness cycle—the eight human factors.

How Do You Know if Your Cycle is Working Well?

When your cycle is running smoothly, you are "doing the right things, in the right way, getting the right results and feeling right about it." However, when your cycle isn't working well, you feel "over" or "under" pressured—you feel overstressed, overworked or overwhelmed, or you feel undervalued, underutilized, unappreciated or unsatisfied. When these feelings exist, decision-making, motivation, initiative and self-esteem are diminished. Project management is a challenging endeavor and at times everyone feels a bit stressed or unappreciated but when that feeling lowers your self-confidence, motivation and attitude, project performance and personal satisfaction both suffer. The state of your internal human factors is manifested in your external behaviors and relationships. Having a "bad cycle" is costly, not in terms of promotions and money but in terms of relationships, energy and happiness. If you feel dissatisfied with your current job, you're not alone. A high percentage of U.S. workers feel the same way and less people are feeling satisfied with their jobs and careers (Franco, Gibbons and Barrington, 2010).

When people have a bad cycle, they tend to live with it, feeling dissatisfied and powerless to improve it. However, during these times, people fail to appreciate three factors:

- First, you have more power and control of your human factors than you think;
- Second, inaction has consequences—rarely do problems correct themselves and the longer you wait or rely on others to do something, the longer the problem will persist; and
- Third, time is precious and if you're not achieving and succeeding, you are just filling and wasting time. It's like working in a job that you hate year after year but still do it day after day. You don't have to accept the status quo—you have the power to change.

In the following chapters, each functional area of the personal effectiveness cycle (decision-making, motivation, achievement and sustainability) is presented in a series of four modules with three chapters each:

Module 1: Diversity, Values and Decision-Making
Module 2: Space, Set Point and Motivation
Module 3: Fear, Inclusion and Achievement
Module 4: Passion, Goals and Sustainability

Module I

Decision-Making

2

Diversity
What makes you unique and successful?

The personal effectiveness cycle begins with decision-making and diversity. Diversity is a vital human factor that makes people unique, distinguished and independent. Fundamentally, diversity means respecting individual differences, accepting others regardless of ethnicity, race, culture, language, education, experience and work styles, and not tolerating discrimination, profiling or stereotyping of people. In a diverse project team, the goal is to create an inclusive work environment where everyone feels mutually valued, respected and accepted. But how does diversity help teams make better decisions or achieve project goals? Diversity is an important concept in project management but how does it help get the job done?

The workplace has become more diverse, globally interactive and team-based, and these changes have required a greater understanding and cooperation among workers of different cultures, languages and work styles. Many organizations manage diversity as a policy and they expect people to be culturally sensitive, legally compliant and socially tolerant. Companies recognize that well-managed, diverse teams offer great flexibility, creativity and motivation. From this "top-down" structure of policy and teams, they assume that diversity will be valued, and somehow people will "get it" because it is extolled and expected by the organization. But diversity doesn't happen on its own; it needs to be "operationalized"—to translate this idealistic concept into a real practice for improving project management. But how is that done? The first step is to stop treating diversity as a *workforce* issue and start appreciating diversity as an *individual* issue. Diversity is not a process or policy but a crucial human factor in teamwork and decision-making.

Instead of valuing individual diversity, organizations tend to do the opposite. They create work environments that suppress individuality, such as excessively standardizing processes, limiting decision-making, micro-managing, providing little or no personal development, and discouraging new ideas, risk-taking and independent-thinking. In many companies, instead of integrating diversity, they segregate it—they form intra-company communities and networks, such as the Generation X Network, the African American Network, the Asian American Network and others. Celebrating different ethnic cultures and establishing employee networks

---

are wonderful and they should be encouraged, but when networks become primarily a social engagement, diversity loses its value. It's unfortunate that few organizations take the bigger step in appreciating and understanding how diversity can increase organizational performance, such as:

- What can be learned from these networks and diversity activities that can be applied across the organization for improving teamwork and success?
- What cultural or diversity characteristics are most important for motivating greater organizational and project performance?
- What are the links between cultural values and motivation?

Diversity is a huge opportunity for organizations; there's so much more to be gained if companies can learn to convert this tremendous human resource into organizational and project performance. Where does one start? It begins by understanding how individual diversity contributes to project success. Each person possesses a unique blend of skills, knowledge and experiences that help create new ideas, solve problems, improve processes and manage projects. Individual diversity contributes knowledge, creativity, will power and energy to teams and organizations. For example, people apply their individual competencies and imagination to develop new product ideas and services, and they use their individual knowledge and communication skills to facilitate change across the organization. Success depends on how effective people are in building and contributing their *individual* knowledge and skills to project teams and organizations.

The most successful skills are those that you do the best and/or enjoy the most, and when those particular skills are recognized and revered, it becomes a talent. Everyone has a special talent or gift in life. Your talent may be in mathematics, writing, critical thinking, sciences, leadership or languages. It may not be a single spectacular talent but a subtle one that is drawn from multiple personal attributes and skills. For example, teaching is a profession that requires skills in communications, organization and psychology combined with a broad knowledge of educational methods and academic subjects. Teachers are also caring and have a natural inclination to help others learn and grow. Thus, talents are in-born as well as learned thereby making each person unique—it's your unique diversity that makes you successful.

VALUING YOUR DIVERSITY

Some people may not know their true gifts and talents yet because it takes time and opportunity to discover one's special abilities and diversity. Too often people limit diversity to cultural and ethnic factors, when in fact it is more useful and valuable to view diversity as an individual-based set of unique strengths and weaknesses that continues to develop and improve over time. Everything you do, experience and learn is to create individual variation and diversification, and your ability to differentiate yourself enables you to accomplish great things in life. *Personal success comes from your diversity, which reflects your ability to differentiate yourself.*

Do you know what aspects of your diversity are most important to you? Diversity is made up of innumerable things—race, culture, religion, beliefs, education, family, socioeconomic background, occupation, life experiences, gender, age, knowledge, personality styles, sexual orientation, language, physical abilities and more. All these elements of diversity are important, but which ones matter the most and make a *difference* in personal performance and success? Do you know your best diversity factors, those that make you unique, differentiated and successful?

The first step in personal effectiveness is to learn how to value your individual diversity, which *means recognizing and understanding those human factors that motivate you to perform at your best.* What do you feel are your greatest personal attributes that enable you to perform well as a project manager and achieve great things in your career? Your inherent diversity is a combination and culmination of many different things, such as:

- Knowledge
- Experience
- Education and training
- Socioeconomics
- Skills and deficiencies
- Strengths and weaknesses
- Physical and mental abilities and limitations
- Cultural factors—languages, customs, birthplace, heritage, religion
- Genetics—race, gender, physical attributes
- Temperament, character and personality type

Your Diversity is a Living Library

When you step back and look at your background, knowledge, skills, abilities, personality type and others, it tells a "story" about your life and personal characteristics. Like any good story, diversity is a personal narrative of five "Ws": *who* you are (genetics, culture and personality type), *what* you have learned and gained (education, skills and knowledge), *where* you have been and *when* (experiences and locations), and *why* you do the things you do (all diversity factors) (Figure 2.1). Your story is likely filled with great intrigue, mystery, action, adventure, thrills, drama and comedy. In fact, your memory and subconscious do not contain a single story but a large *"library of stories"* and it's a safe bet that no one else has that same library.

Diversity is a personal library of great variety and uniqueness, and it includes stories of good and bad experiences, strengths and weaknesses, skills and deficiencies, and abilities and limitations. The value of one's diversity lies in the range and balance of strengths and weaknesses cultivated from one's culture, experiences and genetics. Sometimes, the worst stories can be the best gifts as they instill wisdom, humility, hunger, motivation, restraint, creativity and compassion.

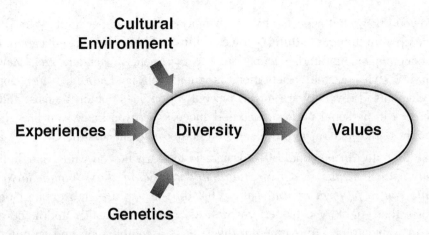

Figure 2.1 Personal Diversity Library

Essentially everything in a person's diversity is learned, even people's genetics are derived from centuries of "DNA learnings" from natural selection. Some of the best lessons learned come from mistakes, struggles and failures. Skills, knowledge, competencies and character don't just happen but are earned through trial and error, hard work, tough lessons and challenging experiences. These experiences are internalized and become a part of who you are. Life is a puzzle and every experience, whether good or bad, reveals a piece of yourself. New ventures are invaluable because every significant experience brings you closer to your authentic self. That's why people shouldn't be afraid to take some risks and experience different things in life. As a project manager, it is in the breadth of your culture, experiences and genetics that give power and strength to your diversity—that is the secret—building your library of knowledge and experiences to reveal who you are and what you want and then bringing that power to bear on solving problems, resolving conflicts, making decisions, taking risks and pursuing new opportunities. Having a rich culture and wide range of experiences, give you elasticity, adaptability, creativity and resilience—all key attributes in project management.

Your diversity is a "living library" of who you are and what you have achieved and experienced—that's why it's so important to understand your heritage, upbringing and cultural background. Both good and bad experiences contribute to your wisdom, thinking, behaviors and abilities, and your rich history and personal attributes make you different from other people. Diversity is a dynamic process where you are constantly learning, growing and changing. Your growth experiences and learnings are probably the most important part of your diversity.

Your stories and learnings are not internally stored for vanity. They are safely archived in your subconscious and utilized when you make decisions and judgments. They are utilized in your thinking, behaviors and interactions with others. The dynamics of your library are part of your natural growth and adaptation.

How would you describe your diversity? What are the key stories in your library? What things in your past and present have contributed most to your uniqueness, abilities and personal effectiveness? Using a chart such as Table 2.1 is a good way to capture your key diversity factors and the relative strengths and weaknesses of each one. In

Life is a puzzle and every experience, whether good or bad, reveals a piece of yourself.

addition, it is important to rate the relative benefit of each diversity factor and the degree in which that factor is being utilized in your current job.

Table 2.1 Diversity Library Example

Diversity Factor[a]	Range of Diversity Learnings		Diversity Rating Score 1 to 5 (1=Low, 5=High)	
	Strengths	Weaknesses	Value[b]	Utilization[c]
Education: B.S. degree in Biology	Strong knowledge of natural sciences	Weaker aptitude for humanities	4	1
Language: Fluent in English and Spanish	Multilingual	English second language	4	2
Culture: Ethnicity	Family values, education	Don't challenge authority enough	4	2
Skills	Analytical, mathematics, computers	Software programming, marketing	5	2
Family: Father, husband, mentor	Concern for others	Better work-life balance	5	3
Culture: Socioeconomics	Middle-class values, industrious	Struggle to gain social influence	3	2
Experience: Sports	Teamwork, discipline	Too competitive at times	3	3
Geography: Lived in U.S.	National pride, loyalty, service	Limited cultural diversity	4	1
Experience: Supervisor	Leadership skills	Need more people skills	4	3
Genetics: Rational personality type	Goal-oriented, independent	Too analytical and critical	5	5

(a) *Refers to culture, experiences and genetic traits*

(b) *Degree of worth to your career or personal effectiveness*

(c) *Your level of use and application in your current job*

Taking inventory of your diversity factors is a vital step in operationalizing your diversity—converting concept to practical value. Diversity has several important dimensions: (1) each person has a unique blend of diversity factors learned from their culture, experiences and genetics; (2) the wide range of strengths and weaknesses for each diversity factor gives you character, ability and opportunity; and (3) it's important to identify those factors that you value the most. People have so much range in their diversity that it isn't uncommon to underestimate the size of your library. It's easy to take certain knowledge or skills for granted or experiences that you may have forgotten. But they all have contributed in different ways to your career, versatility and successes.

By rating your factors in terms of perceived "value" and "utilization," it helps to identify those factors that you value the most and how active you are in using your diversity factors. Those factors that are rated higher for "value" but rated lower for "utilization" are career growth opportunities, while factors that are rated higher in "utilization" but lower in "value" are potential priorities for further personal growth and development. Both strengths and weaknesses have value and utility for building greater self-awareness, capacity, confidence, humility and motivation.

DIVERSITY AND HUMAN FACTORS

What is the difference between diversity and human factors? Diversity is recognizing, respecting and valuing the differences and similarities in people and how people value and differentiate themselves as individuals. Human factors are about understanding the motivators of human behaviors. In short, human factors deal with the behavioral aspects of diversity. Many elements of diversity are motivators of behaviors, such as values, personality type, culture, experiences, education, profession and language, and therefore diversity is a key human factor. No doubt, individual diversity plays a big part in behaviors, feelings, beliefs and personal performance. In fact, your best learnings about personal effectiveness and diversity can come from your culture and experiences.

In short, human factors deal with the behavioral aspects of diversity.

Life's Worst Experiences Reveal the Best Lessons

This story is about diversity, a young woman named Margaret and her dream of having a family and owning a home. Growing up in San Francisco, diversity was not an issue for Margaret; she was immersed in ethnic *diversity*—Chinatown, Japantown, the Italian North Beach district, Market Street, Haight-Ashbury and the Hispanic Mission district. These cultures were geographically separated but the city's municipal systems, such as public buses, shopping centers, schools, sports and parks, brought people together to form one large diverse community. Exposure to different people and cultures had a tremendously positive influence on her perspectives about people and family life.

In her younger years, Margaret attended grade school and successfully finished high school where she met and married her sweetheart, Wil, and they lived happily together in San Francisco Chinatown with her mother. They lived in a neighborhood of narrow streets, sidewalk markets, tiny shops, elegant banks and wonderful food. Her husband, Wil, started a small television repair business in the heart of Chinatown and he spent all his time developing the business. Margaret helped her mother who worked as a seamstress, six days a week, ten hours a day in a "sweatshop," sewing denim pants in small cramped quarters, getting paid by the piece, which was tracked using brightly colored tickets attached to each garment. Each week they got paid by the number of tickets they submitted. Sewing seams together and riveting small, metal studs into pockets were meticulous work. The denim was stiff and dirty, and the smell was inescapable. Not even the pleasant aroma of Peking duck, barbeque pork and soy sauce chicken from surrounding shops could mask the pungent odor. Working in the sweatshop was stuffy, smelly hard work that paid very little; but it did eventually help pay their way out of Chinatown.

Her family earned every dime they received and they all worked with great hunger and desperation for a higher standing or *set point* in life. They *valued* hard work, honesty, family and respect. She and her family saved like fiends and economized by living together in a small second floor communal apartment in Chinatown. There was only one bathroom on each floor, which they shared with several other families. But just outside their apartment was a bustling community with Chinese conversations that always sounded like people arguing constantly and small prominent churches that served as community centers and playground leagues. In the evenings, Margaret would work at the Chinese opera house and received tips of silver dollars from wealthy patrons and actors. She enjoyed the colorful and elaborate costumes, the actors with frightening make-up and the unusual sounds of clanging cymbals, stretched cat strings and rhythmic drums. The opera house was a cultural phenomenon—a social center and prominent symbol of the community.

One cultural human factor that stood out was *fear* or superstition. Most notably, shopkeepers would hire lion dancers who would light off loud fireworks to ward off evil spirits; families would eat "thousand-year-old eggs" to ensure good fortune for the year; and bitter melon soup was served in restaurants to help restore one's soul, balance and fertility in life. The diet must have been favorable for Margaret because she soon gave birth to two sons and a daughter and then had another son a few years later. Margaret and her family all lived together in this culturally rich community, immersed in work, food, music, superstition and commerce. They had a real *passion* for life, survival, learning and prosperity (Figures 2.2, 2.3 and 2.4).

Figure 2.2 Family Portrait
Margaret is in the middle on the lap of her mother; her father is the bespectacled man behind her (photo taken in S.F. Chinatown, 1928). Others are Margaret's aunts, uncles and their children. The children are third generation U.S.

In the early 1950s, Margaret fulfilled her dream and *goal* of owning a home in the newer west section of the city, known as the Richmond district. It was a beautiful part of the city and it was bordered by Golden Gate Park, Ocean Beach and the Presidio, creating a lovely landscape of people, nature and recreation. The community was comprised of two-story single family homes, with a one-car garage built beneath each house, pretty backyards, flowering trees, playgrounds, schools and corner grocery stores, all organized in parallel avenues. Margaret and her family finally had *space* in their lives. Each morning they could see the San Francisco fog roll in, with fog horns bellowing in the distance, and the fog would blanket the city until the sun emerged around lunchtime. The fog flowed into the Richmond like a tide, giving rise to the day and filling the air with soothing moisture. Although cold at times, the fog felt protective and warm—maybe because it surrounded her home like a soft blanket.

Not long after moving into their new home, their neighbors "welcomed" them by circulating a petition in the neighborhood, calling for the *expulsion* of her family.

Figure 2.3 Margaret at Home with Her Kids
Margaret with her family, Reynold, Pamela and myself (circa, 1951).

Figure 2.4 The "Boys of the Family"
Wil and his three sons: myself, Gary and Reynold (circa 1956).

They were the first non-white family to live in this area and there was great *fear* that "these Chinese people" were going to ruin the neighborhood and bring property values down. They were unfriendly and avoided all contact with Margaret and her family. Their message was clear: *you are not wanted here.* This was a surprising and disturbing experience because the neighbors were all well-educated, family-oriented and familiar with the diverse ethnicity of the city.

The neighbors had met secretly behind closed doors to try to expel her family by forcing the developer and local officials to bar them from taking residence in their neighborhood. It was emotional and upsetting to her and her family who anguished over this predicament. Here they were in this grand neighborhood, trying to *set a higher point* in their lives, away from the cramped alley quarters in Chinatown, yet they never felt so afraid, backward and inferior. They yearned for *inclusion*, yet feared exclusion and rejection from their community. They grew up believing that family, community and *inclusion* were shared *values* among all people.

After several weeks of worry and threats from their neighbors, a breakthrough occurred at one of the private neighborhood meetings. During this meeting one brave soul had stood up to voice strong disagreement over the petition and convinced his neighbors that *exclusion* was the wrong thing to do. He was a dentist who lived across the street from Margaret and he was well regarded in the neighborhood. He spoke in total opposition to the proposed action and vowed to support Margaret and her family even though he did not know them very well. He spoke on the principles of values, diversity and *inclusion*, and not on color, culture or friendship and he convinced the neighborhood to drop the petition. In that special moment, one person with clear principles successfully stood up against many and it subsequently allowed Margaret and her family to live happily in the neighborhood for over thirty years.

This story is not a random tale about social injustice but a true "good-bad" experience that contributed valuable lessons to Margaret's personal "library." What is more enlightening is that Margaret was my mother and her stories and "lessons learned" were *carried forward* into my "diversity library."

Lessons Learned

Looking back, this early family experience provided many important life lessons about diversity, human factors and their role in personal effectiveness and project management.

- Both good and bad experiences contribute to the depth and breadth of a person's "library" of knowledge, wisdom and values—that's why it's important to understand and appreciate one's heritage, upbringing and cultural background. They are important in the development of people's values and behaviors.

- Sometimes the worst experiences are the best gifts as they instill gratitude, humility, inner strength, resilience and compassion, which are all qualities needed to be a successful project manager.
- Neighbors and people do not fail because of bad intentions, processes or planning; failure results from narrow thinking, poor decision-making, wrong perceptions and bad behaviors that are motivated by certain human factors, such as *fear and exclusion.*
- Opportunities to do great things are not planned or predicted but occur in unexpected, spontaneous moments in time. Despite the negative *space* created by the neighbors, the dentist did the "right" thing, in the "right" way at the "right" moment. He had a positive, forward-looking, *inclusive* mindset and the right *set point* to make the "right" decision. Opportunities to do the "right" things occur in every project; the key is to make the right decision.
- My family had a *goal* for a better life that almost failed. Successes and failures in projects are determined by eight specific human factors that affect people's decision-making, motivation, achievement and success and those human factors are: *diversity, values, space, set point, fear, inclusion, passion and goals.*

The Eight Human Factors for Personal Effectiveness

The eight key motivators of human behavior that drive your personal effectiveness are:

- **Diversity.** The personal characteristics that make individuals unique and different from other people, which include one's genetics, background, experiences, education, personality type, skills, culture and work styles. Diversity reflects who you are and your ability to differentiate yourself. The strength of your "diversity library" affects your thinking and decision-making.
- **Values.** The things that you believe in; your assumptions, convictions and ethics that guide your thinking, judgments, decision-making and behaviors. Values are personal and formed from family, culture, experiences, religion, profession and other social factors. Success is meaningless unless it meets your values.
- **Space.** A group of environmental elements that affect your motivation and behaviors. Everyone lives in three distinct spaces—organizational space, team space and personal space—and they influence people's feelings, behaviors and actions. Success is highly dependent on how well people interact and manage their three spaces, especially personal space.
- **Set Point.** A state of mind in terms of temperament, attitude or mood and relative psychological state or outlook on life. It reflects a person's level of motivation and is tied to optimism, confidence, openness, engagement and transparency. Set point affects one's ability to take action, solve problems and perform at a high level.

- **Fear.** An emotional response to danger, risks and threats. Fear induces worry, anxiety and caution as well as energy, urgency and focus. Fear can both weaken and strengthen one's personal effectiveness, ability to take action and performance. When managed properly, fear is a powerful human factor for achievement—it motivates urgency and action.
- **Inclusion.** An act of including, accommodating and belonging. Inclusionary behaviors encourage, invite and draw people and ideas together. It is a mentality that embraces change, new challenges, risks and working with others toward achieving common goals.
- **Passion.** An intense emotional feeling of great excitement, enjoyment and enthusiasm for a subject, occupation or activity as well as a strong compelling interest for a cause or process. Passion is the energy behind great successes and sustainability.
- **Goals.** Personal desires and objectives in life that are motivated by passions, definition of success and other human factors. Goals provide purpose, power, control and sustainability.

People succeed when they express their *diversity*, live their true *values*, work in an inspiring *space*, achieve a high *set point*, manage their *fears*, ensure *inclusion*, find their real *passions,* and achieve their personal *goals* in life. These eight human factors are not visible, conscious traits but the invisible, subconscious aspects of oneself. They are not actions, behaviors or tangible elements that can be touched or measured. They are intrapersonal elements that affect feelings, emotions and motivations that are always present internally. They are personal, inherent and dynamic and they constantly affect personal effectiveness.

Revealing Your Human Factors

These eight human factors affect thinking by helping you process and interpret what you see, hear and feel. This processing and interpreting of information by your human factors form internal perceptions. For example, three people can meet the same person at the same time, yet each person can walk away with a much different impression because their human factors, perceptions and interpretations are all different—*each person controls and creates their own realities.*

You are at your best when you are yourself.

Human factors can cause people to over-process, overreact and overthink situations. At times people make "mountains out of mole hills," imagine conflicts that don't exist, stress over outcomes that never occur, or create false images and scenarios in their minds. People create their own paradigms and play "mind games" that can often lead to internal conflicts. People can talk themselves into doing things that they normally would not do or say things that are contrary to their own beliefs. Their values may tell them to think one way, but their passion and fears may tell them to behave differently. For example, their values may tell them to save money but their passion is to drive expensive cars, or their values may tell them to stand up to bullies but their fears tell them to sit down. The eight human factors are not always aligned and consistent with each other.

When human factors are mismanaged, bad behaviors can result due to personal insecurities and distrust. For example, people who have a need to control other people are usually insecure, distrustful and fearful. Controlling others does not alleviate insecurities or raise trust and confidence; it only perpetuates the problem. However, if people are more conscious of their human factors and how they influence their thinking and behaviors, they can begin to accept who they are and reduce their insecurities and need for controlling others.

Once you are "comfortable in your own skin," you can begin not only *accepting* who you are but also more important, begin *believing* and *acting* on who you are. Being true to oneself is called personal integrity and it's fundamental to your personal effectiveness in project management. Success begins internally and *you are at your best when you are yourself.* That's why individual diversity is so essential to your success—recognizing and understanding who you are, what you're all about, how you think, your strengths, weaknesses, desires and motivations. You can't bring out the best in yourself until you know what's truly there.

When people become aware of their eight human factors of personal effectiveness—*diversity, values, space, set point, fear, inclusion, passion* and *goals*— and how they affect their thinking, behaviors and ability to achieve, they can make a mental breakthrough and start to understand their own thinking. This breakthrough in thinking will lead to breakthroughs in their behaviors. Success starts with appreciating their own diversity and learning what their minds and hearts can do.

As a project manager, gaining an awareness of your human factors gives you three important advantages; it helps you to:

1. Understand and accept who you are—"being comfortable in your own skin."
2. Understand what motivates you to achieve your goals and do great things in your career.
3. Know what it takes (internal and external) to bring out the best in yourself and to realize genuine success.

By raising your consciousness of human factors, you can better understand how they drive your behaviors and affect your motivation. The objective is to optimize these eight human factors to enable greater performance, achievement and personal effectiveness.

SUMMARY

✓ Diversity is formed from one's culture, experiences and genetics. The key is to learn how to "operationalize" your diversity to make better decisions, solve problems and improve performance.

✓ Diversity is a "personal library" of continuous learnings, good and bad experiences, strengths and weaknesses, skills and deficiencies, and abilities and limitations. Each experience is an opportunity to learn more about yourself and those learnings are archived in your subconscious and utilized when you make decisions and judgments.

✓ Valuing diversity means recognizing and understanding those human factors that motivate you to perform at your best. Diversity has several important dimensions: (1) everyone has a unique blend of "stories" learned from culture, experiences and genetics; (2) the wide range of strengths and weaknesses and personal experiences builds character, humility, gratitude, restraint, elasticity and compassion; and (3) it's important to identify those diversity factors that you value and utilize the most.

✓ Everything you do, experience and learn is an inner drive to do something special or different, and this natural drive to *differentiate yourself* enables you to accomplish great things in life.

✓ You succeed when you express your *diversity*, live your true *values*, work in an inspiring *space*, achieve a high *set point*, manage your *fears*, ensure *inclusion*, find your real *passions*, and achieve your personal *goals* in life. These eight human factors are not the visible attributes of diversity but the invisible and hidden aspects of yourself.

✓ This chapter covered key concepts in why diversity is important in project management:

  ✓ *You are at your best when you are yourself* so it is essential to understand who you are, your strengths, weaknesses, beliefs and motivations.

  ✓ Taking inventory of your diversity factors is a vital step in "operationalizing" your diversity. Knowing who you are and utilizing and growing your breadth of knowledge and experiences increase your uniqueness. *It is your uniqueness that makes you successful.*

  ✓ Once you are able to *feel comfortable in your own skin*, you are relieved of pretension, self-consciousness, fear, stress and worry, enabling you to make good decisions and perform at your best.

3

Values
How to find your true beliefs

While diversity defines who you are, values define what you believe in, the principles you live by and the factors you use to gauge what is good and bad. Values are formed early in life and further developed by experiences that become preserved as a human factor. Values are one of the most powerful intrapersonal motivators of success because they define people's beliefs and constantly guide thinking, behaviors and decision-making.

It has been long established in cultural and social psychology that behaviors are guided by values and judgments, and that values emerge at different stages of human development (Kohlberg, 1981). Based on numerous theories, values are inner goals and serve as guiding principles in people's lives (Rokeach, 1973) and provide much motivational energy (Schwartz, 1996). No doubt, values are deep intrinsic motivators of human activity, and even though values are internally hidden, they are clearly expressed in people's thinking and behaviors. In project management, human behaviors are behind every task and activity. They determine whether people are motivated or de-motivated, whether activities are completed on time, how tools are used, what information is communicated and whether projects will succeed or fail. Most important, you can't competently manage behaviors without first understanding people's values, including your own.

HOW ARE VALUES AND DIVERSITY RELATED?

Your great diversity of knowledge, skills, genetics, experiences, strengths and weaknesses helps form your beliefs in life. Beliefs are things that you assume are true or will be true. Your beliefs are assumptions based on perceptions, judgments and observations. But if you step back and take inventory of all your beliefs and critically assess what proportion is in fact *true*, you'll find that the proportion is very small. Truths are perfections and absolutes (always, never) that are rarely known but constantly sought. In the absence of truth, people create assumptions, imaginations and perceived "truths" to guide and justify their thinking and behaviors. The perceived truth is only a translation and interpretation of personal observations.

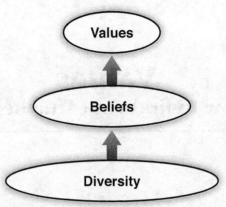

Figure 3.1 Values Are Formed from Beliefs and Diversity

Knowledge is not truth but a set of internal beliefs that are carried forward and reinforced. Over time, the strongest beliefs become "values" and they are a subset of one's beliefs that helps to distinguish good from bad, right from wrong, and true from false (Figure 3.1). People's regard of what's right and wrong is not grounded in truth but stems from personal beliefs and values. Next time you are engaged in a "right and wrong" argument, keep in mind that essentially everything you know has a degree of uncertainty and your decisions are based on values and assumptions. Your effectiveness in project management depends on your ability to manage uncertainty and assumptions.

Values develop from a broad set of beliefs and assumptions and as experiences and knowledge change (diversity) so do beliefs and values. More important, values are strengthened when beliefs are reinforced over many years and changing a person's values requires a significant change in beliefs, knowledge and experiences. That's why it's important in project management to create a culture of shared values that are continuously reinforced by institutional stories and positive leadership behaviors.

What Are Your Values?

How do you recognize a personal value? Your values are revealed when you become excited or upset over an issue or situation. When your values are disturbed, your behaviors dramatically change. Take for example people's behaviors when they drive their cars in heavy traffic. Let's say you are stuck in a traffic jam, waiting in a long line of cars to exit a freeway. As you patiently wait, it seems inevitable that at least one car will break out of the line, zoom alongside all of the other cars and attempt to squeeze into the head of the line. This is infuriating—you think, "How dare they do such a thing!" You silently watch this car trying to force its way into the front, while you root for the other cars to "don't let that cheater in!" But eventually someone lets the cheater in and you fume about it. You're not alone. Many people find this "line-jumping" behavior to be rude, unfair and disrespectful. It violates the values of honesty, justice and equality. Depending on how many of these values are violated, your reaction can range from mildly disturbed to outright road rage. You may even find yourself venting emotionally about it in your car, while angrily thinking, "Who does this person think he is?", or "What makes this person think he is better than us?" If values evoke such anger, should they be considered bad human factors? Not at all, such emotions from your values protect and help you cope with conflicts.

Not everyone sees this situation the same way. Some people are not fazed by line-jumpers; in fact, they do not see an unjust act but an *act of kindness*—a driver who came to their rescue and allowed them in. These "kind" observers are thinking, "That was so nice of that person to let him in." To them, *they did not see a bad behavior but a good behavior*! Isn't it interesting how two different observers can see the same scene in opposite ways? Who's right and who's wrong? What you see is not the "truth" but a belief that is perceived through your values. Values are the lenses through which people see right and wrong, and good and bad. Do you see a person who is cheating or do you see a person who is showing kindness? Also, both perceptions are personal judgments, that the person cutting in line has bad intentions and the accommodating driver has good intentions, when in fact, neither may be the case. Who knows, perhaps the "line jumper" was responding to a dire emergency and was justified in cutting to the front. How would your *judgment* change if you knew the line-jumper was a doctor rushing to save a child's life? How does that strike your values now? The interpretation is up to you. *There are no truths, just perceptions.* Each observer's reaction is perceived through his or her culture, experiences and personality types and their behaviors are based on those perceptions. In project teams, different perceptions and judgments due to differences in personal values are root causes for interpersonal conflicts. Project managers often think interpersonal conflicts are just "misunderstandings" when in fact they are conflicts in values and those conflicts will continue until it's recognized and reconciled. Values underpin all behaviors, good and bad.

The workplace is a common venue where values are expressed. How do you feel about:

- People who break their promises or betray you?
- Your boss who puts you down in front of others?
- People who whine and complain constantly?
- People who are dishonest or shade the truth?
- People who do not work as hard as you do?

People are usually disturbed by at least one or more of these situations. These bad behaviors tug at people's values and trigger intense emotions that are hard to control—they can't help themselves! Values are embedded in the subconscious but emerge when emotional situations occur or "triggers" are pulled. These triggers are called "hot buttons" because they initiate sudden, extreme emotions. Everyone has hot buttons. When pushed too often, hot buttons can hurt people's performance and create behavioral biases.

Values are derived from beliefs that are continuously shaped by one's diversity, via culture, life experiences and genetics (Figure 3.2). Diversity and values are derived from intrinsic biology along with what is learned and experienced in life; a true blend of biology and environment—a "nature and nurture" effect.

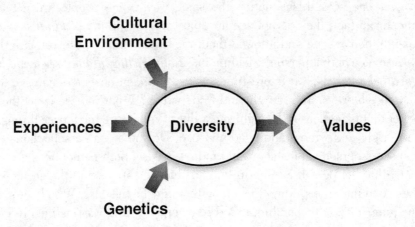

Figure 3.2 Values Model

No two people have the same set of values and react the same way to a given situation. Even when people share the same values, they may possess different meanings or priorities of those values based on personal experiences or cultural beliefs. For example, loyalty to family and friends may take priority over loyalty to the company. People may lie to strangers but not to their friends. Values are shaped based on people's motivation to satisfy their individual needs and reinforced based on their individual experiences and culture.

The secret to finding your values is to introspectively look back in time to discover the true origins of your values. For example, where do values such as tradition, hard work, honesty, freedom and education come from? The sense of tradition may be learned from parents through family stories, from experiences in school or church or through other cultural customs. Family values can also be learned through genealogy and ancestry. Family and cultural values give you a clearer picture of who you are relative to your place in time and what your ancestors experienced along the way. To discover your values, you need to look back to understand your present.

Each person interprets events and behaviors according to their own cultural values.

Values come from many different places yet many are unknown or unclear to most people.

Values drive behaviors and understanding how values shape people's thinking and actions is an important aspect of project management. The following sections will explore the role of culture, experiences and personality type in forming personal values and provide a mapping technique to identify your core values.

CULTURAL VALUES

Culture is the shared ways in which groups of people understand and interpret the world. Culture consists of ideas, values, attitudes, beliefs, morals and customs. Together, these act to drive personal behaviors and serve as filters to determine what types of behaviors are considered "normal," and each person interprets events and behaviors according to their own cultural values. For example, in many cultures, education is a strong value and how well you perform in school is considered a key determinant of your social status, rewards and success.

Cultural values for success are not limited to family beliefs and expectations. In fact, a great deal of success is dependent on the personalization of national, professional and social values. For example, in the United States, values of capitalism, commercialization, freedom of speech and religion, democracy, environmental protection and equality are embedded in the national culture. Each country or region will have different cultural values that shape and influence people's values. In professional trades, the beliefs in integrity, knowledge and mutual respect are common values. In project management, prominent values include teamwork, leadership, best practices and education. Social values have a substantial effect on what is considered right and wrong as well as success and failure.

Unfortunately, certain cultural values can sometimes lower expectations of success. In certain cultures, women are treated as inferior to men and are given fewer opportunities for education, professional advancement and political influence. Immigrants are historically discriminated against by native cultures. Also, countries vary widely in their regard of various professions; for example, educators are more highly valued in Asia and Europe while less valued in America. In the United States, top-tier professional athletes, entertainers, politicians and celebrities garner more prestige and wealth than top-tier educators and scientists. In any society, success is defined by cultural values.

What are your cultural values? Are you aware of the cultural values of your project team? What did you learn from your family, religion and social environment that helped form your beliefs? The faith that people have in each other on a project is directly related to the faith that they have learned from their culture. It is critical to understand your cultural values relative to the values of your project team.

EXPERIENTIAL VALUES

In addition to culture, life experiences affect personal values. The types of experiences that impact personal values are *individual* and *generational*. Both good and bad experiences that occur individually or shared with other people challenge and shape people's beliefs. Life events that have high emotional content have an especially long lasting effect on people's values. The more profound the event, the longer and deeper it sticks with people.

Good and bad experiences are opportunities to learn more about yourself and what you truly believe in. A bad experience can be a life-changing event, and it even happens to highly successful people such as Steve Jobs. After dropping out of college at age twenty-one, Steve Jobs, formed Apple Computer Company with Stephen Wozniak in 1976. After leading the company for over 10 years in developing and selling innovative personal computers, software and printers, Steve Jobs, was forced to resign from Apple due to poor sales and internal problems in 1988. It was a bitter fight and he was devastated and publicly disgraced. But years later he reflected that, "I didn't see it then, but it turned out that getting fired from Apple was the best thing that could have ever happened to me. It freed me to enter one of the most creative periods in my life." He created a new company called Pixar, which became wildly successful. In 1997, Jobs was hired back as CEO of Apple to reverse Apple's struggling business and restore profitability. Jobs stormed back and made Apple the most highly valued company in the world, with revolutionary products such as the stylish iMac personal computer, the legendary iPOD digital music player, the universal iPhone and the elegant iPad. It has been a stunning turn-around for Steve Jobs and Apple Computer.

But you don't have to be a Steve Jobs to convert losses and failures into successes. Bad experiences are opportunities because it forces people to choose a different path or to do things differently, which create new ideas and solutions. It's a choice—a bad experience can become either a mental barrier or a great opportunity to learn more about yourself and discover what you were meant to do in life. Also, the struggle of failure can bring forth new strengths and make you more resilient and resourceful. Although painful at times, losing can yield more benefits than winning—that's because *deep challenges and struggles strengthen your values and brings out the best in you.*

In project management, failures and disappointments are all part of the process. But failures are only temporary setbacks; the human spirit brings you back and helps you find new ways to satisfy your needs and go forward with greater resolve. Some of your greatest successes can result from your worst failures—that's why it's so important to *take some risks in your career.*

Both positive and negative experiences play a role in shaping your values and behaviors. It's the high and low experiences that give you motivation, introspection and clarity about your values. Successes reinforce values, while failures challenge values. Positive experiences validate your behaviors and lift your spirits; failure produces self-disappointments and negative emotions. When it comes to personal values, failures and not successes tend to speak louder because it violates the belief you have in yourself. If you want to find your true values, you need to look hard at your failures and disappointments as well as your achievements.

Shared Experiences: Generations

In addition to individual experiences, human factors are influenced by shared experiences and circumstances that affect large populations of people. The values that are formed from shared experiences are held in the collective memories of generations. Current generations are commonly categorized as traditionalists, baby boomers, generation X, and millennial generation (or generation Y). Traditionalists were born between 1900 and 1945, baby boomers 1946 and 1964, generation X'ers 1965 and 1980, and millennials 1981 and 1999 (Lancaster and Stillman, 2002).

These distinct sub-populations of people share a common set of beliefs that were derived from profound experiences of their day, including social movements, political events, music, books, fashion, wars, disasters, new inventions, technologies, tragedies, new medical discoveries, food, art, economics and many others. As generations live through these occurrences, they internalize their experiences as emotions, memories and learnings that re-shape their views and values about themselves and the world. After all, who wasn't changed by Pearl Harbor, World War II, the Vietnam War and 9/11? These types of events drive deep into people's memories and are not easily erased.

Many generations have been influenced by Martin Luther King, John F. Kennedy, Albert Einstein, the Beatles and Osama Bin Laden. How has your thinking and behaviors been influenced by the Great Recession, the Internet, social networking, climate change and smartphones? Going forward, your effectiveness as a project manager will likely hinge on your abilities to adapt to new generational values and behaviors.

Table 3.1 summarizes some key values that are widely shared within generations. Traditionalists are known for their loyalty to institutions, respect for authority and

Table 3.1 Generational Values

Generation (Birth Year)	Shared Value
Traditionalists (1900 – 1945)	<ul><li>Loyalty to the company, faithful to institutions</li><li>Respect authority and seniority</li><li>Take personal satisfaction in a job well done</li></ul>
Baby Boomer (1946 – 1964)	<ul><li>Achievement: Money, title, recognition</li><li>Challenge authority and status quo</li><li>Build a successful career</li></ul>
Generation X (1965 – 1980)	<ul><li>Work-life balance</li><li>Freedom</li><li>Must build a life résumé, a portable career</li><li>Mentoring and personal development</li></ul>
Millennial Generation (1981 – 1999)	<ul><li>Technology-based, multi-task lifestyle</li><li>Networking and collaborative mindset</li><li>Work must have personal meaning</li></ul>

hard work. Baby boomers are bent on changing the world, not accepting the status quo and achieving social status. The X generation is less tied to their careers and jobs than their parents, seek more freedom and want better work-life balance. The newest generation of workers is the millennial generation who seek more social networking, collaboration and mobility.

Good Values Are Carried Forward

Generational values are not kept within each generation; some values cross generations where they are modified or reaffirmed by new generations. When parents teach their sons and daughters the value of hard work and to "pay your dues," they are instilling their traditionalist values. Values that are accepted today are naturally carried forward. Those that do not withstand the test of time, like "command and control" values in the workplace, fall by the wayside when they no longer fit the work styles and success factors of subsequent generations. Although people try hard to preserve and hold onto their existing values, values are Darwinian in nature—only the strongest survive.

Values are not meant to be static but dynamic—they need to be tested, challenged, debated, stretched, poked and refreshed from time to time. Testing your values is a healthy process because it creates stronger, more robust values for yourself, your organization and society. Enlightened organizations and individuals are not afraid of change; in fact, they welcome change and renewal. When traditional in-house functions are outsourced and offshored to other countries, people's values are being tested; when qualified women and minorities are promoted to upper management positions, company values are being challenged; and when new generation of workers replace retiring generations, team values are being refreshed. Though painful and scary at times, this Darwinian process of renewing values is essential if people and organizations want to be successful. That's why new leadership and continuous improvement of human resources are crucial for renewing organizational values.

Values are Darwinian in nature—only the strongest survive.

Like evolution, personal and cultural values do not dramatically change but how they are expressed and their relative priorities may shift more suddenly. People carry different values and their perceptions of good and bad may not be the same. Also, people and society may have competing values that take different priorities depending on circumstances. At times, family may be more important than work; health care more important than education; national security more important than civil liberties; and war more important than peace. There is no right or wrong, only differences in the *priority of values*. In projects, different people and generations will value different behaviors. Some people value quality over quantity, integrity over loyalty, results over effort, and teamwork over individual achievement. It's doubtful that everybody is going to see things the same way; that's where leadership becomes important in project management.

As people grow older and wiser, values and behaviors seem to both soften and harden. Because people are more experienced, they tend to choose their battles more carefully, save their energy and become more tolerant or "thick-skinned." On the other hand, for certain issues that people used to let pass, they now become more emotional, active and speak their minds on such values as injustice, equality, environment and peace. Certain values awaken in people as they gain more life experiences. That's why generational values are important factors in team relationships, decision-making and project performance. The key is to talk more explicitly about generational values and recognize how generational values can affect team dynamics.

PERSONALITY-BASED VALUES

Diversity is valuing and appreciating differences and similarities in people. The genetic component of diversity accounts for many variations and similarities in people's psychological and behavioral patterns. It has been well-proven by researchers, such as Carl Jung (1923), Isabel Meyers and Katherine Briggs (1957), and David Keirsey (1984), that people are born with distinct patterns of behaviors that are consistent with a certain temperament, personality or psychological type (Table 3.2). People are born with certain preferences in how they interact with the world and how they internalize, process and communicate information. These prominent scientists have been able to characterize predictable patterns of behavior in people according to personality types, and these patterns are independent of a person's age, gender, culture, ethnicity, background and geography. Each personality type shares similar preferences and behaviors because *they also share similar values*. Personality type is in-born, so values are linked to your genetics and subsequently shaped by culture and experiences.

By knowing your personality type, you gain a tremendous insight into your inherent values, motivations and de-motivations and why you do the things you do. Also, knowing other people's personality types and values helps you understand and work more effectively with others. Nothing is fool-proof but understanding personality types is a valuable skill for personal effectiveness and people management.

In the technical field of personality types, there are a variety of different names, classifications and models, but David Keirsey's four temperament types—rational, idealist, guardian and artisan—is a popular, well-proven model in the study of personality types and will be the model used in this text. The values and motivations for the four personality types can be characterized as follows:

- **Rationals** are motivated by mental challenges, such as problem-solving or creating a new process or strategy, and they value competency, invention, independence and efficiency. They want to be right, never wrong, about everything they do and seek autonomy in doing it. Rationals want to feel *valued for their mind and ideas* and are driven by achievement, impact and a need for continuous learning.

- **Idealists** are motivated by compassion, purpose and social causes, and they value honesty, integrity and respect for others. They want to help others and work successfully together. Idealists want to feel *valued for their good character and authenticity* and judge themselves through the eyes and actions of others. They seek personal growth, romance, harmony and happy endings in life.
- **Guardians** are motivated by needs—they need to work, "need to feel needed" and need to be appreciated. They value hard work, teamwork, organization, compliance and traditions. They want things done right, by the book and according to plan and policy, and done on time. Also, they expect others to be responsible, follow the rules and do things the right way. Guardians want to feel *valued and appreciated for their work* and seek control, stability, safety and security.
- **Artisans** are motivated by action, new experiences and freedom. They value flexibility, adaptability and individuality and they live for the moment. They want to make a difference, be excited, to cause others to be excited and they want freedom to express themselves. Artisans want to feel *valued for their bold actions, uniqueness and feats*, and they yearn for new opportunities to grow and shine.

What's Your Personality Type?

There are three effective ways to determine your personality type:

1. Take a "personality" survey on the Internet—search for "Keirsey personality test." They're easy to do and take only a few minutes.
2. Using Table 3.2, determine which personality type comes closest to you. Then you can verify your type (along with the results of your survey) by asking people who know you well, such as your family.
3. Determine your core values and then match them to the right personality type in Table 3.2. You can verify your core values by following the self-assessment "mapping" method provided later in this chapter.

No one is one hundred percent a single personality type; it's likely that everyone carries some traits of all four types but in general people have one predominant personality. Being one personality type or another doesn't make you any more or less effective. However, understanding personality types enables you to understand your inherent values and motivations and how they affect your interactions with others.

Table 3.2 Personality Types

Personality	Characteristics	Values	Motivations
Rational	Objective, analytical, technical, logical, strategic	▪ Achievement ▪ Efficiency ▪ Competency ▪ Independence ▪ Learning	▪ Having goals, being challenged ▪ Feeling recognized ▪ Having autonomy
Idealist	Amiable, sensitive, caring, collaborative, sympathetic, hopeful	▪ Honesty ▪ Harmony ▪ Respect ▪ Compassion ▪ Empathy	▪ Having purpose, a greater good ▪ Feeling respected and trusted ▪ Collaborating
Guardian	Organized, diligent, loyal, reliable, compliant	▪ Hard work ▪ Security ▪ Reliability ▪ Responsibility ▪ Loyalty	▪ Getting the job done ▪ Feeling needed ▪ Feeling appreciated
Artisan	Fiercely independent, creative, fun-loving, open, self-expressive, uninhibited	▪ Adaptability ▪ Flexibility ▪ Freedom ▪ Justice ▪ Individuality	▪ Having the freedom to act and express who they are ▪ Feeling unique and potent ▪ Having admiration

LIFE MAPS

Determine your personal values by using a simple two-part, introspective-retrospective, "values mapping" process.

Part 1. Introspective Values Map

First, determine what *you think your cultural, experiential and personality values are* based on the questions presented next and then construct your *introspective* values map as shown in Figure 3.3.

- **Culture.** What things have you learned from your family and community that have greatly shaped your views and behaviors? What are your strongest family customs, behaviors and beliefs? What vivid family memories do you value the most?
- **Experiences.** What are your generational values? What negative or positive events have impacted you the most and why? Remember, your worst experiences may define your values better than your best moments.

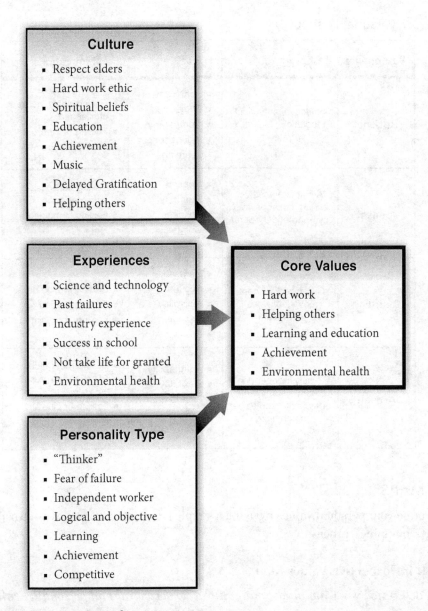

Figure 3.3 Introspective Values Map

- **Personality type.** What is your dominant personality type (rational, guardian, idealist or artisan)? What personality values do you strongly relate to?

Identify Your Top Core Values

To identify your core values, step back and try to recognize any common themes or beliefs that appear across your cultural, experiential and personality values. Are there certain recurring values in your life?

Part 2. Retrospective Life Map

How do you know for certain if your introspective core values are genuine? The secret to verifying your values is to take a retrospective assessment of your past experiences. A "life map" of your highest and lowest moments over your life (or past few years) will reveal what your true values are and what things have greatest meaning to you. Write down the most important moments in your life, both personally and professionally. Try to remember your highest moments—those successes and achievements that gave you the greatest joy, pride and elation. Also, list your lowest points or worst moments in your life—your biggest disappointments and emotional lows (Figure 3.4). Now ask yourself *why* these moments represented your best and worst experiences. Your "why" answers will reveal your genuine "core values." You might have to ask yourself "why" a few times to find your root reasons and feelings.

Your true core values are contained in your emotional memories, especially in the worst moments of your life. They represent your basic human needs and motives. It is also important to understand how your high and low moments differ. Which ones were planned and unplanned? If you look at all the steps and circumstances that ultimately led to your best and worst moments, how much of it was planned and predicted? Which ones were relatively out of your control and in your control? What does that tell you about *how* your high and low moments occur? It's likely that most of your bad moments were out of your control and unplanned, while your high moments were mostly planned actions, with some good fortune, that led to a happy outcome.

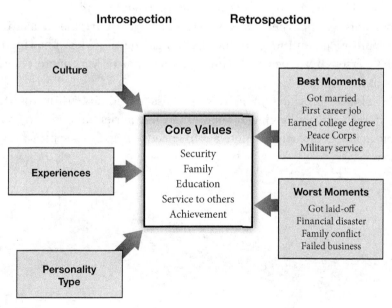

Figure 3.4 Life Map

In examining your introspective and retrospective life maps, do they match each other? Have you truly *lived your values*? Are your actions consistent with your personal beliefs? This retrospective process is a powerful "back-casting" technique for revealing your core values. If your introspective values match your retrospective values, you have identified your true values!

SUMMARY

✓ Values are personal beliefs that are revealed when you become excited or upset over a situation or issue.

✓ Your values are formed from three sources: culture, life experiences and in-born personality and they are your strongest beliefs and assumptions. As experiences and knowledge change so do your beliefs and values. Changing a person's values requires a significant change in beliefs, knowledge and experiences.

✓ Values are critical to personal effectiveness because they determine your thinking, perceptions, judgments and behaviors. Your success depends on how well you live your values and how well your job, career and achievements stay aligned to your beliefs.

✓ In project management, human behaviors are behind every task and activity. Managing projects means managing behaviors and you can't competently manage behaviors without first understanding people's values, including your own.

✓ In project teams, different perceptions and judgments due to differences in personal values are root causes for interpersonal conflicts.

✓ Your personality type is a key determinant of your values, motivations and de-motivations and why you do the things you do. Also, knowing other people's personality types and values enables you to work more effectively with others.

✓ This chapter provided an effective process to find and affirm your true values by introspectively looking at your cultural, experiential and personality-based beliefs and comparing them to a retrospective map of your life's best and worst moments.

4

How to Make Great Decisions

Decision-making is a critical skill in project management. Project managers are expected to make hundreds of decisions in a given project and decision-making is a key differentiator between good and bad managers. The process for making decisions is individualistic and circumstantial, and great decision-making requires the right frame of mind by being well-informed, unbiased, objective and open-minded. Project management is a decision-driven process and whether it's a small or large decision, the thinking process is the same—what needs to be decided, what are the facts and assumptions, and what is the best option? Because diversity and values affect thinking and behaviors, they also play a vital role in people's judgments, perceptions, internal dialogue and decision-making.

In project management, the secret in making great decisions is to have a great process. Great decision-making processes have three steps:

1. **Step 1: "Quiet the mind"** *before* the decision—quality decision-making requires clear internal dialogue that is free of mental conflicts (need-want conflicts, value biases, false beliefs, self-deceptions).
2. **Step 2: Listen to your "mind" and "gut"** *when making* a decision— a good decision requires both gut intuition (feelings) and rational discourse (logic). It's a balance of instincts and intellect.
3. **Step 3: Be confident** *after* the decision is made—a decision is worthless unless it leads to a positive action or progress in your project. Not trusting your decisions leads to inaction and delays, which are costly behaviors in project management.

STEP 1: "QUIET THE MIND" *BEFORE* THE DECISION, ESTABLISH CLEAR INTERNAL DIALOGUE

Internal dialogue is a mental self-conversation process that occurs when people make judgments and decisions. When people are confronted with problems or conflicts, they subconsciously call on their values, diversity, conscience, feelings and logic to make sound judgments. To make the right decisions and actions, judgment is formed through an internal debate or dialogue that occurs in the mind.

The mind is a remarkable thing. People can talk themselves into believing almost anything. They can rationalize why they shouldn't do things or talk themselves into doing something crazy or risky. Making the right decision requires a healthy mental debate that considers all sides of the issue and leads to greater confidence and understanding of the problem. Persistent negative internal dialogue or self-deprecation, such as "I'll never figure this out," "This is probably a trick," "I'm going to screw this up," or "This is going to turn out bad,," is detrimental to good decision-making. More important, it isn't *real*. Negative internal dialogue is like bad gossip—it's imaginary and false. Bad outcomes and personal defeats only exist in the mind. Exaggerations, fear and pessimism create misjudgments, false conflicts, poor decisions and wrong solutions.

Assessing Your Internal Dialogue

Here are some questions regarding some common workplace behaviors that will help reveal your internal thinking process. Read each behavior and choose the answer that most closely matches your **instinctive** thoughts and feelings. There are no right or wrong answers.

What are you thinking when. . .

1. Your project manager revises your work without telling you?
   (a) He is disappointed with my work and doesn't trust me to do it right.
   (b) I would never disrespect and disregard people like that.
   (c) I should try to be more transparent and open with others.
   (d) It was nice of my boss to take the time to improve my work—I'm glad he's looking after me.
2. Your office partner's desk is messy and cluttered?
   (a) He's disorganized, sloppy and doesn't care—he needs to clean up his desk.
   (b) This is unsightly, and it makes me and my team look bad.
   (c) I'm going to keep my desk nice and clean.
   (d) He's so busy; I hope his work is not too overwhelming.
3. One of your team members is regularly late to your meetings and says, "Sorry I'm late" each time?
   (a) She is disrespectful to others and needs to improve her time management.
   (b) How can she do this to us? How would she feel if I showed late for her meetings?
   (c) I support my team by arriving to meetings on time.
   (d) It's nice that she apologizes for being late.
4. Your co-worker brings in a bag lunch to work every day and eats at his desk?
   (a) He must be frugal or doesn't like to socialize with others during lunch.
   (b) How can he bring a bag lunch every day? I hate eating stale food out of a bag.
   (c) I should bring in lunch more often; it will save me some time and money.

5. He's so organized to find time to prepare a lunch every day. Your project manager speaks very softly in team meetings and social gatherings?
   (a) She is shy, reserved and lacks assertiveness.
   (b) I hope I never act like that—it would make me look insecure, unconfident and weak.
   (c) I should speak softly more often too.
   (d) She is so polite and respectful to others.
6. In your monthly project meetings, your co-worker distributes a colored handout of her latest accomplishments whenever the project sponsor is present?
   (a) She is trying to gain favor with the boss; what a selfish, conceited thing to do.
   (b) She's trying to look good while making me and my team look bad.
   (c) I'm going to bring handouts to our meetings too.
   (d) She is so smart and organized to bring handouts to share with everyone.

Did you answer the questions *instinctively* or did you answer the way you thought you *should* answer them? Please review your answers. Honest and instinctive answers are important in understanding your internal dialogue. In reviewing your answers, did you consistently pick (a), (b), (c) or (d) or were they scattered?

Let's examine what your answers may mean (Table 4.1):

Table 4.1 Internal Dialogue Matrix

	Negative	Positive
Externalize	(a)	(d)
Internalize	(b)	(c)

(a) Selecting (a) means you made a negative value judgment. The observation (Q2: "keeps a messy desk") was not favorable to your values and you made it into a judgment about the person ("he is disorganized, sloppy, doesn't care"). This is an example of *externalizing a negative judgment.*
(b) In cases where you selected (b), you have a tendency to negatively **personalize** another person's behavior (Q5: "I hope I never act like that") in the context of your own personal values (i.e., speaking softly is a social deficit). This is a case of *internalizing a negative judgment* or negative internal dialogue.
(c) If you chose (c), it indicates that people's behaviors can trigger a personal value and motivate a positive behavior in you (Q2: "I'm going to keep my desk nice and clean"). This is an example of *internalizing a positive judgment* or positive internal dialogue.

(d) The last choice, (d), is an example of a positive value judgment. You have a positive perspective on the person's behavior (Q1: "It was nice of my boss to take the time to improve my work"). This is a case of *externalizing a positive judgment.*

If you chose a lot of (a) answers, it doesn't mean you're a bad person. It implies that you externalize negative judgments from your values and it may hinder your effectiveness if used excessively.

If you chose (d) often, it indicates that you externalize positive value judgments. That's a wonderful mindset, but it's also possible that being overly judgmental on the positive side can affect your personal effectiveness too. For example, you may be gullible or prone to trust people too quickly and that may lead to disappointments if that person takes advantage of your trust. Looking on the bright side is great but it can also blind you to the facts of the situation. It's best to be both positive and realistic.

If you chose (b), you are engaging in negative internal dialogue by putting down others or their ideas. This is *toxic internal dialogue* because negative talk about others can easily lead to negative talk about yourself. It's a common observation that people who are hard on others are usually hard on themselves. This is a slippery slope because negative thoughts about others can quickly become a mental routine or an automatic response. Also, some people use negative internal dialogue to put down others in order to make themselves feel better. This is not self-motivation but a belittling attitude toward others.

If you chose answer (c), it suggests that people's behaviors help you to reinforce or adjust your own views and values in a positive way. You're not judging other people but engaging in positive internal dialogue to improve your own behaviors.

Did you find that your first thought is usually negative or positive? Is your internal dialogue more often negative or positive about yourself? Are you aware of your thinking patterns and how they affect your decision-making? Because of human factors, people make negative or positive judgments about themselves and other people. Being highly judgmental has negative consequences for you and your projects— it makes you closed-minded.

When people repeat judgments and thought patterns over an extended period of time, they develop mental habits. Bad mental habits are like wrinkles on the brain—they are paths of least resistance, where the brain is programmed to accept negative dialogue and bad assumptions. People are amazingly fast in judging others through their human factors—the secret is to resist the urge to make quick, negative judgments. *Successful project managers make good decisions by reserving judgment.*

Mental Conflicts Are Noisy

Poor decisions are made when the mind is over-active, making false assumptions, rash judgments and wrong perceptions that lead to a bad decision. Making good decisions in project management requires a good internal process, and

Bad mental habits are like wrinkles on the brain.

it starts by having a "clear and quiet" mental foundation. Solving problems and making clear decisions require an absence of internal conflicts. The most common mental conflicts that interfere with good decision-making are: *need-want conflicts, values biases, false beliefs and self-deceptions.*

Need-Want Conflicts

People are at their best when they decide to do things that are true to who they are and what they believe in. Together, diversity and values play a vital function in decision-making because they represent the genuine "needs" and "wants" of people. "Needs" and "wants" are the two types of motives for making decisions, and people have three basic *needs* and three basic *wants:*

Needs:

- **Well-being.** People need *health, security, control, stability and safety.* They need to feel safe and in control, and have financial security, health care, and a good work and living environment. Well-being entails both physiological and psychological health.
- **Social acceptance.** People need *physical and emotional acceptance* and connection to others. Having the sense of belonging to a family, community or a culture is a basic human necessity. Positive affective emotions of joy, happiness, and love come from relationships and mutual support of friends, family, colleagues and community.
- **Self-purpose.** Other than well-being and acceptance, people need to feel right, just and purposeful in their lives. They need to express themselves and do things that make them feel validated and good about who they area. Feeling "right"—correct, true, proper or good—is an in-born trait that is linked to one's personality type.

Wants:

- **Achievement.** People want *success, accomplishments and victories* in life. They want to be challenged, prove themselves and win—to have impact. They want self-distinction, self-sufficiency, empowerment and autonomy. Achievement goes well beyond the basic need for control, safety and security.

- **Recognition.** People want *affirmations* that what they do has value, that their organizations and people value them through praise, recognition and rewards. They want to be respected by their colleagues, family, friends and employers and feel that their contributions are valued and appreciated.
- **Fulfillment.** People want *fun, happiness, excitement, positive emotions and rich experiences* in life. People want to continually learn, grow and realize their full potential. It's fulfilling to do things that have great personal meaning and have opportunities to experience extraordinary things. They feel great because life "fills their bucket."

The three needs and wants are internal motivators for functionality and personal effectiveness. "Needs" are essential necessities of life, while "wants" are wishes and desires. Well-being, social acceptance and purpose are needed for functionality, while achievement, recognition and fulfillment are the ultimate "wants." Other theories and lists have been developed over the decades regarding basic human needs and motives (Maslow, 1954; McClelland et al., 1953; Harter, 1978; White, 1963; Baumeister and Leary, 1995; DeCharms, 1968; Deci, 1975; Chirkov, Ryan, Kim, and Kaplan, 2003).

Each need is related to each want (Table 4.2). People need well-being but want achievement; everyone needs social acceptance but wants recognition; and people need self-purpose but want self-fulfillment. Needs and wants are internal forces that never go away—the goal is to achieve a healthy balance between needs and wants.

Table 4.2 Needs and Wants

Needs	Wants
Well-Being ⟶	Achievement
Social Acceptance ⟶	Recognition
Self-Purpose ⟶	Fulfillment

Needs and wants are internal motives that are related to people's diversity and values. *Needs* are protective and defensive; *wants* are proactive and achieving. People are in *need* when they act to avoid a *negative* consequence (loss of security, peer rejection and being wrong), while people are in *want* when they seek a *positive* consequence (achievement, recognition and fulfillment). For example, people *need* to stay employed so they don't take any chances on the job, yet they *want* to get ahead and that requires taking some risks. Some people *need* to be accepted so they avoid dissent, yet they *want* to be free to express their opinions. *Needs motivate avoidance behaviors while wants motivate achievement behaviors.* Because "need" and "want" behaviors are different, they are often in conflict with one another. This is an important distinction when managing behaviors in projects. Some common "need-want" conflicts in project management include:

- "I *want* to take risks but I *need* to play it safe and avoid mistakes."
- "I *want* to speak up in meetings but I *need* to avoid conflicts."
- "I *want* to make process improvements but I *need* to avoid disrupting the project schedule."
- "I *want* more recognition from others but I *need* to avoid criticism."
- "I *want* a more challenging role but I *need* to avoid losing my current position."
- "I *want* to spend more time with my family but I *need* to work on this project and earn more money."

How Neediness Affects Decision-Making in Projects

In a project, people may have the same needs and wants, but because their human factors are different, each person seeks and expresses their "needs" and "wants" in different ways. Also, the satisfaction levels for each need and want may be different. A need to be accepted may be stronger in certain people, causing them to constantly avoid conflicts, defer tough decisions and wait to be told what to do.

Neediness makes people indecisive.

This is a low-performing, indecisive state due to "need." Neediness makes people indecisive.

Balancing "needs" and "wants" is a zero sum game. Time spent on pursuing basic needs takes away from the time and energy on achievement, recognition and fulfillment (wants). In projects, people who have a constant need to "look good in front of management" spend less time pursuing new opportunities and challenges; their mindset is subservient (neediness), and not focused on high project performance. Also when people are more concerned about peer rejection than project success, they will either make decisions that are always agreeable to their peers or let others make the decisions for them. Furthermore, project managers who have a strong need for control and compliance typically make autocratic, closed-minded and defensive decisions. Never challenging the boss, letting others make decisions for you or making defensive decisions is a loser's game because *you can't win by playing defense all the time.* Being needy is like going home; it's a place where you feel safe, secure, accepted and "right"—you "settle," which is a low performing state. Neediness is the quickest way to mediocrity.

Too much "need" reduces personal effectiveness and limits opportunities for success. When project leaders and teams are "needy," they are typically risk-averse, distrustful, stressed and fearful, and morale and team engagement are low. As a result, people spend more time on their needs than pursuing their wants. *When needs are unmet, internal tension mounts.* Thus needs are manifested as avoidance behaviors and stress, and when left unsatisfied that tension can be released in negative ways, such as frustration, anger, passive-aggressive behaviors and bad decision-making. Reduce stress and tension in projects by encouraging and recognizing desired behaviors and not punish people for *deciding* to take a chance, challenge the status quo, take personal initiative and make changes—when people feel supported, empowered and *motivated to make decisions*, project performance improves.

The key is to achieve a good need-want balance in a project. It's a balance because in certain situations, a safe, defensive decision is needed, however in the long run, *the probability of success increases when people spend more of their time in a "want" state, while their probability of failure increases when they are too "needy."* Need-want conflicts are normal and expected; the key is to stay aware of these internal conflicts and not let "needs" dominate "wants" and negatively affect decision-making.

Of the six needs and wants, which ones are strongest and weakest for you? Which needs are the toughest ones to keep satisfied? For example, feeling insecure (need for stability and control), seeking approval from others (need for social acceptance) and needing to be right (self-purpose) are the most common "needy" behaviors in project teams. Among "wants," achievement and recognition are short-term wants while personal fulfillment is a long-term goal for most people.

Value Biases

When values are overactive, value biases can appear. When people over-filter and over-judge situations, it results in bad decisions and judgments. Value bias is a mental conflict of being too critical or favorable—*a conflict of judgment.* For example, do you notice people who show up late for meetings more than those who arrive on time? Without a doubt people have a sharper eye for late-comers. Do you react to praise the same as you do to criticism? Criticism usually carries more weight than praise; people are more emotional when they are singled out for being wrong than right. Do you ever play favorites at work? It's very common to find that "people like people who are *like* themselves." Do you praise people doing things right as often as you catch people doing things wrong? People have more energy to correct and solve problems than stopping to praise others. It comes from a need to feel "right."

Right or wrong, people like to impose their values and biases on others, and they subconsciously seek to confirm or validate them. When people look for faults or merits, they usually find them. It's a self-fulfilling prophecy where they continuously feed their own beliefs and create prejudices and "mental grooves." It is important to recognize your subconscious biases and ensure that they do not obscure your judgment of people and situations. These inherent biases lead to misperceptions, bad choices and poor decision-making.

False Beliefs

Another factor that affects thinking and project decision-making is false beliefs, which is a mental conflict of accepting *external* beliefs that are contrary to one's own values. This happens when people treat beliefs as temporary values, and behave in a manner that is detrimental to themselves. False beliefs frequently occur during times of insecurity, vulnerability and stress. Peer pressure and work demands can cause people to lose focus on their values, such as family, honesty and integrity. Instead of looking within themselves and trusting their own values, they defer to the values of other people who say, "Trust me, it's the right thing to do," "The end justifies the means" or "Don't worry, everyone gets away with it." They betray themselves when they bend or break the rules in order to achieve greater profits or gain advantages over others. Under stress, it's convenient to take refuge in someone else's values and accept false beliefs. Somehow they justify it in their own minds. Unfortunately, when people carry false beliefs, they usually make bad decisions.

False beliefs can occur in projects when extrinsic motivators such as political correctness or peer pressure override inherent values. The need to feel secure and accepted by others is a strong, subconscious force. Also, it is not uncommon to find project managers adopting false beliefs when they lose themselves in their company loyalty, ego or "leadership" persona. Values are not a popularity contest; values should not be relinquished to others. Political correctness and peer opinions can change with the wind and should not be used as the criteria for judging what's right and wrong. It is certainly not a good basis for building your own values. Values are not about conforming to popular opinion; it's about ensuring that the decisions you make are *right for you*. When people adopt the beliefs of others that do not align with their own values, they are giving up their values for others. As a result, they struggle to find true happiness in their work and personal lives.

> *When people are uncertain about the intention of others, they naturally assume a worst case scenario.*

Self-Deception

In contrast to false beliefs, self-deception is a mental conflict of creating *internal* beliefs that are unfounded or contrary to reality. This happens when project managers are faced with possible bad outcomes and they overestimate the risks and underestimate their ability to succeed. Basically they falsely rationalize why they should or shouldn't do things and deceive themselves into making the wrong decision. Automatically looking on the bad side of things or putting yourself down is a poor mental behavior. This behavior especially occurs during conflicts when people feel uncertain, needy or fearful. For example, when a team member sends an electronic document to a colleague for their feedback and receive no response for days, people usually interpret a non-response as a negative one, such as "I guess he was too busy to reply," "He probably doesn't think it's important," "He doesn't care about me," when actually, the person was simply absent or had no access to his email.

Why do people deceive themselves? Most conflicts are more imagined than real and the mind exacerbates the problem. When people are uncertain about the intention of others, they naturally assume a worst-case scenario. It's a matter of protective psychology—they hedge themselves mentally for possible bad outcomes by imagining worst cases. People don't need to do this—to reduce negative thinking and self-deception, it's best to keep things factual, well-balanced and realistic. They need to "keep small things small" and don't let biases, false beliefs and self-deceptions override their common sense and good judgment. Self-deception, false beliefs and values biases are detrimental to good project decision-making.

How to Maintain a Healthy Internal Dialogue

When leading projects, it's important to keep a healthy perspective and a positive internal dialogue. Too often, people mentally punish themselves over a mistake or they can't let go of a bad thought and it continues to haunt them and brings down their performance. Poor internal dialogue leads to defensive thinking and negative judgments. Maintaining a healthy, positive internal dialogue leads to greater self-confidence and good judgments. Here are several good mental techniques for maintaining a healthy internal dialogue:

- **Keep it real.** Avoid overanalyzing the situation, imagining conflicts and bad outcomes, complicating the issue and blowing things out of proportion. Focus on the reality and facts of the situation. *Keep small things small in your mind.*
- **Keep your boat afloat.** When stressed and uncertain, you can be easily swayed, persuaded and steered by outside voices. It's critical to *"keep your boat afloat"*—stay level-headed, use commonsense, be practical, keep both feet on the deck and don't jump ship—trust your inner dialogue.
- **Maintain a "want" state of mind.** Great decisions come from your "wants," not "needs." Ask yourself, "Am I thinking and acting from a state of want or need?" and "What do I *want* to see happen?"
- **Stay open-minded.** A closed mind is the pathway to conflicts, value biases, false beliefs and self-deceptions. *Make observations, not judgments; focus on the process, not the outcome; create options, not predictions.*
- **Make your first thought positive.** When judging yourself and others, always *think of the positives first.* Think of "what I liked" or "what went right," instead of "what I hate" or "went wrong."
- **Lighten up.** Trying to make the right decision can be extremely stressful and taxing. A little fun and humor are great ways to de-pressurize the brain. *Enjoy your imperfections*—it's all part of being human.

STEP 2: LISTEN TO YOUR "GUT" AND "MIND" *WHEN MAKING* A DECISION

With a clear and healthy mind, a great decision is made by gathering information from your internal "diversity library" and rational consciousness. Great decision-making requires a blend of gut intuition and rational discourse—a combination of art and science. It is an instinctive and cognitive process that draws from both the subconscious and conscious minds. Learning to use both aspects of your mind will help you make more effective project decisions.

Gut Intuition

Gut intuition refers to one's ability to use their subconscious experience and knowledge—their "diversity library"—to make judgments and decisions. People make the mistake of assuming that intuition is too emotional and should be avoided in decision-making, when in fact, intuition helps to *de-emotionalize* decision-making by drawing on common sense, basic instincts and natural inclinations. Intuition is important in project management because: (1) gut intuition taps into your experiences, culture, conscience, strengths and weaknesses, feelings and personality type and gives you the wisdom and common sense to make great decisions; (2) you don't always have the time or information necessary to make a rational decision—gut intuition is all you have; and (3) information is never perfect, no decision is purely rational.

It is hard to hear your heart when your mind is racing.

There are six effective techniques to access the "library" in your subconscious:

- **Relax the mind.** It's difficult to listen to your subconscious if your mind is thinking too much. Your best ideas, solutions and decisions emerge when you are calm, relaxed and quiet. Sitting in a peaceful place, walking, meditation, prayer, showering, sleep and other calming retreats are excellent ways to relax the mind and allow your deeper feelings to flow to the surface. It's hard to hear your heart when your mind is racing.
- **Simplify the problem.** It's much easier to find the right answer when the question is clearer in your mind. Often times when you're faced with tough problems, you may needlessly overanalyze, worry over minor details and complicate matters when a simpler approach will do. Simplifying the question or breaking the problem down into smaller pieces will help clear your mind to reach the right decision. Try to find the bare essence of your problem or question.
- **Avoid pressured decisions.** You are at a disadvantage when you have to make decisions under emotional distress. Fear and anxiety reduce your ability to make not only a reasoned decision but also one based on your true values and diversity. Fear brings out your bad mental behaviors—value biases, false

Your first gut reaction is usually right and represents an accurate reflection of your values and diversity library.

beliefs, self-deceptions and neediness. When people are fearful, they become defensive, protective and risk-averse. This is not a state of mind to make a good decision. Rushing to a decision usually ends in regrets. "Flaming" emails are good examples of emotionally tainted decisions. If you want to send a disapproving email to someone, do it when you're calm and collected. Make sure your communications are as cool as your decisions.

- **Go with initial feeling.** Once you have relaxed your mind and simplified the problem, your first gut reaction is usually right and represents an accurate reflection of your values and diversity library. Your initial response is purer, unfiltered and untainted by any highly emotional or irrational internal dialogue.

- **Flip a coin.** Try to boil your decision down to two alternatives or choices, such as "yes" or "no." Take a coin and designate one side as "yes" and the other "no" (heads versus tails); flip the coin in the air, letting it fall to the ground and when it settles onto one side, look at what side came up and *immediately* "listen" to your feelings—are you pleased with the results or not? What is your "gut" telling you? Listen to your subconscious.

- **Seek early feedback.** Another good method for finding your gut intuition is to make a preliminary decision and take a small, first step in executing that decision. How do you feel after taking this initial step? Does it feel right? Oftentimes your gut will tell you whether you are heading in the right direction or not. In projects, a pilot test or "dry run" are more formal techniques for testing both your emotional and intellectual reactions.

Rational Discourse

The other facet of great decision-making is rational discourse, which requires logic, reasoning and objective thinking. It's a conscious, cognitive, methodical process for reaching a decision. There are a number of theories, analyses and processes for logical decision-making, but these are the best five mental behaviors for making *rational* decisions:

1. **Observe the problem.** Regardless of the problem, one of the most important tenets in great decision-making is to be clear and focused on what you're trying to solve. A common technique is to "focus on the problem, not the person," which works fine unless the problem *is* the person. Then the better technique is to "focus on the behavior and its consequences, not the intent," which makes it more factual but still too subjective. The best technique for framing a problem is to *make observations, not judgments.* This forces you to focus on the realities and facts of the problem, avoiding the pitfalls that come

from making quick judgments, false perceptions and drawing the wrong conclusions. It keeps your mind quiet, cool, open, objective and less emotional. Being observant puts you in the right frame of mind to solve the right problem.

2. **Make clear rational judgments.** After observing and framing the problem, you want to apply your best judgment in making a decision. But again, just as you want to be clear on the problem, you need to be clear on your judgments; you don't want to make random, uncontrolled judgments. Bad judgments occur when the mind is too active, biased, emotional, perceptive and imaginative. Pre-judging and personalizing the problem destroy great decision-making and they are the most common mistakes in problem-solving.

> *You increase the chances of making the right call when you use the right set of values.*

How can judgments be made without personalizing them? Isn't that what decision-making involves, making *personal* judgments? The answer is yes, but judgment is about having the right basis for doing the right thing. The right basis are your *values.*

The secret is knowing which values to use. In project management, decisions are based on strategies that are founded on company values. When you make decisions for yourself, you need to use your personal values; when you make decisions for your organization, you need to apply your organizational values. You increase the chances of making the right call when you use the *right set* and *priority* of values. For example, worker safety and profit are both important values when making company decisions, but safety should always trump profit.

3. **Balance the mind.** One important concept in the process of reaching a great decision is being "intellectually balanced," which means not having a strong rational bias in your thinking. You want to make fair and objective judgments of the information. There are four good techniques for keeping your mind balanced in decision-making:

- **Determine viable alternatives.** Every decision has alternatives or different options. Even "do nothing" and "wait" are possible options. Develop as many different alternatives as possible; this keeps you open-minded, unbiased and balanced. For a given decision, try to identify at least three alternatives.

- **List pros and cons.** Identify the positives (pros) and negatives (cons) for each alternative and write them down side-by-side. This gives you a more complete and balanced view of your choices.

- **Use statistical tools to keep your assessment fair and balanced.** Statistical analyses, such as decision and risk analyses, Monte Carlo simulations and probabilistic analyses, are sophisticated, rigorous, quantitative approaches for obtaining a balanced view of risk and the likelihood of different outcomes (McNamee and Celona, 2005).

- **Seek opinions from other people, especially different personality types.** As discussed in the last chapter, everyone has a predominant personality type that creates natural preferences and biases in thinking, and people can't repress their own biology. To counter that tendency, you should seek opinions from other people, especially other personality types. For example, if you are a Rational, seek input from Idealists, Artisans and Guardians (and even other Rationals).

*The goal is not to find **the** answer but make a good decision.*

4. **Don't over-think it.** Over-thinking and over-analyzing a problem do not improve decision-making; they only prolong it. Also, over-analyzing a problem feeds into one of the biggest problems in decision-making—fear. When fear creeps into a decision-making process, it becomes more emotional and less rational. Worries about making mistakes, not having the right data and disappointing other people can penetrate your thinking. Ironically, a mind worried about making mistakes is *more* prone to make errors, values biases, false beliefs and self-deceptions. There is no perfect answer and making a mistake is not the end of the world. It is futile and *irrational* to seek a 100% solution. Furthermore, the goal is not to find *the* answer but to make a good decision. You can't control the outcome, only the decision. Focus on the process, not the outcome.

5. **Develop a decision criteria.** A critical part of making cool and objective decisions is to develop a decision criteria. Decision criteria are the key factors that your decision will be based on. In most cases, decision criteria are used to choose among mutually exclusive alternatives. For example, if a company wanted to hire a new scientist for their research and development division, they would set up a hiring team and seek applicants who would have certain work and academic qualifications. They would set up a screening and interview process for the candidates. To decide on the best candidate for the job, the selection team would agree in advance on the decision criteria for choosing their "best" candidate (Table 4.3). The criteria would likely

Table 4.3 Decision Criteria Table

Candidate	Experience	Tech	Communications	Team	Desire	Total
A	★★	★★★★	★★	★★★	★★	13
B	★★★	★★★★	★★★★	★★★★	★★★★	19
C	★★★★	★★★	★★	★★	★	12
D	★★★	★★★	★★★★	★	★★★	14

Rating: Excellent ★ ★ ★ ★ to Poor ★

have factors such as industry experience, technical strength (credentials, awards, publications), communication skills, how well he or she would fit in with the team and their desire to work for the company. To ensure clarity among team members, each criterion or factor would have a brief description as well.

This criteria is used as the basis for judging the strength of each candidate for the job. For each factor, each team member would rate all the candidates (excellent to poor) and the results averaged (or the team can do it together). The candidate who has the highest overall score (in this case, candidate B) would be the best choice. If the totals are too close to declare a winner, the team can rate again but assign different percentages or multipliers to each factor, reflecting their relative importance in the criteria (e.g., industry experience = 3x; team compatibility = 2x). Also, a team may agree on a minimum acceptable score, in which case "don't hire" any of the candidates or "do nothing" may be the best decision. Keep in mind that "do nothing" is not the same as indecision—"do nothing" is an alternative; *indecision is a lack of a good decision criteria.* If you have a clear understanding of your problem and have identified several viable alternatives and still can't make a decision, it's probably due to a weak or unclear decision criteria. Make strong decisions by having a strong decision criteria.

Table 4.4 Techniques for Strengthening Decision-Making

Decision-Making	Techniques
Gut Intuition	■ **Relax the mind:** Listen to your subconscious "library" ■ **Simplify the problem:** Keep it simple, find the bare essence of the problem ■ **Avoid pressured decisions:** De-emotionalize the issue ■ **Go with initial feeling:** First feeling is usually right ■ **Flip a coin:** Test your gut feelings ■ **Seek early feedback:** Take initial steps and check feelings, do a pilot run
Rational Discourse	■ **Observe the problem:** Make observations, not judgments—be clear on the problem or question ■ **Make clear rational judgments:** Use the "right" set of values in making judgments ■ **Balance the mind:** Identify alternatives, list pros and cons, use statistical tools, seek opinions from different people ■ **Don't over-think it:** Avoid over-analysis due to fear; focus on the decision, not *the* answer ■ **Develop a decision criteria:** Have a rational basis for the decision

Since every decision and decision-maker are different, there are no standard decision-making techniques in project management. The intuitive and rational techniques that work well for you may not work for others and vice versa—the secret is to find what works best for you. Also, each decision is different, requiring a different balance of techniques; some require more intuitive thinking while others are more rational, but always use some degree of both. In general, the harder the decision, the softer the process—tough decisions require more gut than mind.

To be a great decision-maker, learn and use as many of these techniques as possible to increase your skills and experience. Being fluent in these techniques will help you make better decisions.

STEP 3: BE CONFIDENT *AFTER* THE DECISION

It seems like the hardest part of decision-making comes *after* the decision. It might be a case of post-decision anxiety, "buyer's remorse" or simply a lack of confidence in your decision. Making decisions is easy; the hard part is committing to your decisions and taking action. In project management, a critical mental behavior is having the self-confidence to *trust your instincts and decisions*. Self-confidence is believing in your abilities and trusting the process. You can't control the outcome but you can control the process. Without trust, people end up questioning their decisions, recycling the process and changing their minds. How often have you doubted or second-guessed your decisions?

The secret to feeling more assured about your decisions is to *"test"* it with the following three questions:

1. **Is this the *right* thing to do?** In other words, have you used the right set of values and priorities to derive your decision? The biggest mistake is applying the wrong values to a key decision.
2. **Is this a *good* decision?** The best decisions are made from your "good side." Everyone has a "good side" and a "bad side" to their personality. Your good side is positive, open-minded, transparent, caring, collaborative and forward-looking. Your bad side is fearful, "needy," selfish, exclusionary, pessimistic and backward-looking. Have you made a positive, want-based, open-minded, forward-looking decision? More will be covered in Chapter 6, *Set Point*.
3. **Does it cover the *big* picture?** The best decisions are broad-minded and inclusive. Have you considered the concerns and effects of your decision on others (all stakeholders)? Have you received input from the right people and sources? Does it have the support of your team and organizational spaces, such as sponsors and customers? Is your decision inclusionary? More details can be found in Chapter 5, *Space* and Chapter 9, *Inclusion*.

LEARNING TO MAKE GREAT DECISIONS

Bad mental processes always lead to bad mental behaviors. If you have a poor decision-making process, you will likely end up with a poor decision. Having a confident process is critical for making a great decision. However, no matter how good the process is, if you can't execute the process well, you can't make great decisions.

One common barrier that people have in making decisions is their fear of making a mistake or disappointing others. Fear causes inaction, anxiety, avoidance, procrastination and over-analysis. The tougher the decision, the more people worry, avoid and delay. What is the remedy? To be a good decision-maker, you have to *practice making decisions*—to be good at anything, you have to dedicate yourself to learning and practicing the process. Successful decision-makers learned their skill by making decisions and many of those decisions were awful. In fact, most good decision–makers will admit that their best decisions were bad ones. Their bad decisions helped them make better decisions later, and that the quality of their decisions would not have been nearly the same without those past mistakes. Making good decisions is easy, making *great* decisions takes practice.

SUMMARY

- ✓ In project management, the secret to great decision-making is having a great process. Great decision-making processes have three steps:
  - ✓ **Step 1. Quiet the mind *before* the decision:** Have a healthy internal dialogue free of mental wrinkles, imagined conflicts, value biases, false beliefs, self-deceptions, over-analysis, neediness and excessive negative judgments.
  - ✓ **Step 2. Listen to your gut and mind *when making* a decision:** Great decision-making requires gut intuition and rational discourse. Intuition is important in project management because: (1) it taps into your diversity and values, giving you the wisdom and common sense to make great decisions; (2) you don't always have the time or information necessary to make a rational decision; and (3) information is imperfect, no decision is purely rational. Rational discourse means making observations when framing problems, using the right values when making judgments, and using balanced thinking and a decision criteria to make cool decisions.
  - ✓ **Step 3. Be confident *after* the decision:** Ask yourself the three final "test" questions to reduce self-doubt and increase trust and confidence. Ensure that you have made the *right* decision, from a *good* perspective and with the *big* picture in mind.
- ✓ The final secret to great decision-making is to practice the process of making decisions. The more decisions you make, the better you become, so the secret is to have a great process and learn to execute that process with excellence. Great decision-makers are not born but are made through hard work, experience and practice.

Module II

Motivation

5

Space
What work environment brings out your best?

Although diversity and values are powerful intrinsic motivators of human behavior, people's thoughts and actions are often overridden by extrinsic factors, such as laws, policies, customs, incentives, rewards and other external elements. In fact, research has shown that external incentives and rewards consistently undermine intrinsic motivation (Deci, 1975; Ryan and Deci, 2000).

Human behaviors are motivated by a group of elements in the environment called "spaces," and there are three conceptual spaces in project management—organizational space, team space and personal space (Figure 5.1). These three spaces are both dynamic and interdependent, and people's motivations and behaviors are regulated by all three. To motivate high performance in projects, project managers must be effective in managing these three interactive spaces.

ORGANIZATIONAL SPACE

Organizational space is the largest space and it represents the authority, laws, regulations, policies, rules, resources and standards that guide the planning and implementation of projects. When a new business system is installed, it must comply with government regulations, industry standards, company policies and project management procedures. Project managers must ensure that the work meets the strict requirements of government, industry and their company and that the project has received the necessary approvals, permits and authorizations to operate. These rules, policies and functions are controlled by organizational space and because it's the largest space, it has the strongest influence on people's behaviors and perceptions.

In companies, organizational space is the management structure of the business. It contains all the corporate functions and procedures, such as legal, finance, human resources, planning, treasury, public affairs, benefits, safety and management. It sets the vision, mission, objectives, strategies, and business plans for the workforce. This space is owned by the company, and it expects all employees to abide by its rules and policies. Business cultures are private communities with their own

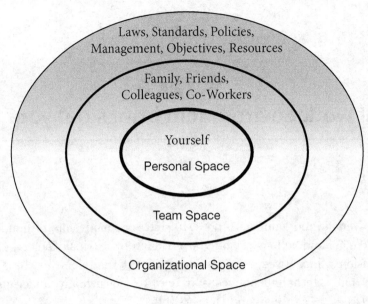

Figure 5.1 Three Space Model

procedures, reporting structures, and codes of conduct, such as dress codes, office etiquette, policy compliance, company values, business ethics and process controls. These company codes guide work behaviors and help to create a sustainable culture and behavioral norms.

Organizational space provides structure, governance and order that enable people to work together toward a common goal. To work successfully, people need resources, guidance and incentives that support their jobs, projects and personal desires. People expect compensation, fairness and leadership from their organizations; in return, organizations expect compliance, commitment, cooperation and performance. *Organizational space is objective, structured, unemotional and explicit.*

TEAM SPACE

Team space resides within organizational space and represents the interpersonal relationships and interactions among family, friends, colleagues, co-workers and other people. It is a space where people interact, socialize and work together as a group or community. Unlike organizational space, team space is co-owned by people and is a closely shared space with its own culture, dynamics, chemistry, processes and team behaviors. Because it is a shared space, people are mutually dependent and must modify their behaviors to conform to the norms and expectations of the group. People assume a different set of behaviors when they interact with their family, friends and colleagues than when they are alone. These team behaviors are motivated by a common need to be accepted and respected by others. Living and working together require teamwork, trust, cooperation, flexibility, interdependency and compromise. Therefore, *team space is more emotional, variable, interactive and less explicit* than organizational space.

PERSONAL SPACE

The third and inner-most space is personal space where human factors and intrapersonal elements operate. Unlike organizational space and team space where ownership resides with the company or team, personal space is owned by you. This is *your space*; it is not shared with other people or run by the company or other authorities. In personal space, your human factors motivate your behaviors and help you respond to environmental changes. This is your authentic self, and you are in full control.

Personal space is where your values, experiences, memories, feelings, conscience and motivations are stored and developed—it is a powerful space, containing the intellectual and emotional energy behind your behaviors. More important, this space determines your internal dialogue, self-confidence, accountability, mental strength, self-esteem and other intrapersonal competencies. Of the three spaces, *personal space is the most autonomous, discretionary, implicit and controllable environment.*

HOW SPACES IMPROVE PROJECT PERFORMANCE

Every project is dependent on these three spaces and they affect the thinking, feelings, behaviors and motivations of people. They shape the dynamics of the work and project team. Unfortunately, most project managers do not distinguish these three spaces but manage projects as "one big space" with no appreciation of how these spaces affect individual and team motivation. With better knowledge of the three-space model, managers can use this concept to improve project performance.

Below are two examples of how the three-space model is used to motivate desired behaviors and project performance.

Safety in Project Management

A high priority among all organizations and project managers is to ensure that the project is performed safely and that everyone returns home at the end of the day. Over the years, leading companies such as DuPont, Chevron, Dow Chemical, Alcoa and Motorola have successfully implemented long-term safety initiatives with a goal of driving down workplace injuries to zero. Today's programs are highly sophisticated, systems-based, and well-integrated into the company's daily business operations.

Many decades ago, safety programs existed but were ineffective in preventing a high rate of worker injuries. Safety was implemented as a company policy and employees were expected to be trained in following safety rules and standards. These traditional policies and procedures were "command and control" mandates from *organizational space*. Anyone not following company safety procedures was in violation of company policy and subject to disciplinary action, so safety in the early days was a *compliance* behavior. Over the years, companies and safety experts have found that *compliance behaviors* directed from *organizational space* do not drive down injury rates but motivate avoidance behaviors (avoid punishment and citations) instead of achieving desired safety goals.

If a project manager's goal is to achieve employee compliance and adherence to rules and policies, the process should be managed out of organizational space—it's authoritative, centralized, standardized and legalized. But if the goal requires a team effort, where people *want to work together* to keep each other safe and it's a team value ("nobody gets hurt"), the process needs to operate from *team space* and with a strong *safety culture*. If a process requires mutual trust, cooperation and accountability, it is best done from *team space*. When quality management principles and practices were installed in the 1980s and 1990s, it helped companies adopt a team-based approach to safety, which led to a significant drop in injury rates, but nowhere near zero.

In the ensuing years, a step change in safety occurred when improved technology, new regulations, better safety practices and stronger leadership led to a safer work environment. Moreover, industry adopted the belief that industrial accidents are preventable and zero incidents can be attained.

Safety practices were upgraded with behavioral-based safety principles where *individuals* accepted personal accountability for their own safety and every worker was given authorization to intervene in other people's work or even halt an operation to ensure worker safety. What made this a step change was the concept that safety was a *personal space* issue and that for safety to improve, it had to reach each and every employee on an *individual basis*—safety had to be personalized. Unlike the centralized, top-down, *organizational* directive and *team-based* initiatives, behavioral based safety took the responsibility, power and control to the individual level, *personal space*. When this occurred, along with other individual-based approaches to safety, safety rates improved dramatically in many companies and injury rates continue to decline today. It works because personal space is where the greatest motivation and will power reside; it's the space that produces the strongest emotional commitment and therefore creates the greatest *discretionary* effort. *Organizational space motivates compliance (have to) behaviors; personal space inspires discretionary (want to) performance*, a willingness to go the extra mile.

Organizational space motivates compliance behaviors; personal space inspires discretionary performance.

Spaces Also Apply to Personal Projects

Improving health and physical conditioning is another good example of how these three spaces affect behaviors. Individually, people use their three spaces as sources of motivation. For example, people have a desire to stay healthy and fit and will try a variety of means to stay in shape. Some people like to use *organizational space* to lose weight and stay trim—they join health clubs, spas, gyms and diet programs. Because they prefer structure and systems, they like belonging to an organization, having access to good equipment and classes, signing a long-term contract and paying dues. The commitment of a contract and the act of paying a monthly fee are as motivating as the service itself. They think, "Paying a monthly fee will force me to go the gym and stick with it" or "Joining a gym will motivate me to get in shape." People use organizational space to impose a sense of urgency and motivation in their lives. Each January, health clubs are jammed with people who have made urgent New Year's resolutions to get back in shape. However, even with these motivators in place, people still struggle to stick to their commitments and fail to lose weight. Because *organizational space is impersonal and unemotional*, it does not affect their human factors deep enough to motivate a genuine change in their eating and exercise habits.

Things that stir emotions, such as relationships, are more effective in changing behaviors than joining a health club. Thus, certain people are more compelled to use *team space* for motivation. To stay fit, they recruit their friends, neighbors and other people to help motivate them—they exercise with a companion, hire a personal trainer or take classes with other people. They make themselves dependent on others rather than a system. They think, "If I make a pact with someone to exercise, I will follow through on my commitment." Making a promise to a friend is a more powerful human factor than signing an agreement with a gym.

Social interaction is needed to establish human interdependencies. *Team space* has more emotional punch than organizational space and it stimulates a deeper commitment. Losing weight is a tough process but it feels easier when people diet or work out with friends who share the same goals and pains. Team space has good staying power when people have a shared commitment; but, when mutual support and relationships end, so do the motivations. Nevertheless, companionship remains a good motivator at the gym as well as the workplace. It's one of the reasons why people come to work and why project teams are effective in generating higher performance.

THE MORE SPACES THE BETTER

Whether it's safety, staying fit or other projects, it's important to use the right spaces to motivate people. In project management, "the more spaces the better" when it comes to motivating desired behaviors. In continuing the safety example, companies can inspire an even stronger commitment to safety by expanding team and personal spaces to include their families as a motivator. By connecting safety to an employee's family, the company is creating a bigger reason (space) for staying safe. The key is that the company is adopting a *value* that is held by all employees—their families. To reflect that value, companies such as Chevron have safety mottos such as "I stay safe for me and my family," and employees are encouraged to wear family photos on their company badges. This gives a person not only three spaces of motivation—company support, individual and work team, but it also expands their space by including family values. Personal space expands and motivation increases when people feel that they have more at stake. You can do the same for staying fit: join a gym, work out with a friend and *be healthier for your family*. In all examples, people are motivated by all three spaces: a structured system, strong team support and a greater individual commitment.

When project objectives, team roles and responsibilities and individual expectations are strategically aligned to each other (organization, work team, family and personal space), personal space, motivation, work performance and job satisfaction increase because their work is directly linked to the success of the team and organization. *Strategic alignment* is powerful when a person's personal values, goals and processes are consistent with those of the people and organization around them—when they succeed, the organization succeeds and vice versa. When people feel strongly connected to other spaces, they think more clearly, make better decisions and communicate more effectively, which make conflicts less probable. *Motivation and commitment increase when all three spaces are working together.*

Successful project managers draw energy from organizational and team spaces to help them achieve their personal goals. They know how to network, manage information and resources. They understand that their success is dependent on their initiative, self-motivation and enthusiasm to work with other people and garner resources from organizational space. They are good with both systems (organization) and people (teams)—they understand the power of organizational and team spaces in supporting their personal performance. They set goals, fix problems, facilitate change, help other people, learn new skills and think ahead.

Successful people are able to control and cope with the influential powers of organizational and team spaces. They do not let these spaces control and limit them. When people align their values and behaviors to organizational space, their actions have greater relevance and impact.

ULTIMATE SUCCESS DEPENDS ON PERSONAL SPACE

No doubt aligning your three spaces increases your motivation, and people's values are the critical human factors for strategic alignment. But whether you achieve your goals of safety, fitness or success is not ultimately dependent on your organization, family and friends, it's dependent on the strength of *your personal space*. When you are alone at home after a workout and no one else is watching, you can eat and do what you want. Similarly, you can take extensive safety training and wear family photos on your sleeve but what matters most is how you behave when no one is watching—the responsibility always starts and ends in personal space.

In personal space, values *determine* behaviors; external elements, such as money and people, *influence* behaviors. Even though organizational and team spaces have great influence on personal space, and these spaces offer tremendous support, the most powerful space is personal space because it contains the essence of human motivation. It contains the will power, passion and self-motivation. Aligning project goals to people's goals provides common direction but connecting project values to people's values offers the greatest leverage for performance because values drive behaviors.

Connecting project values to people's values offers the greatest leverage.

Success is not motivated by organizational systems or other people; personal success is motivated by you and how you interface with the other spaces. Use other spaces to support you but don't rely on extrinsic spaces to make your goals; your intrinsic motivation and values are more powerful and self-sustaining. Although all three spaces can work for or against you, *personal space is the only one that you can control.*

HOW SIZE AFFECTS BEHAVIORS

Personal space grows and shrinks depending on its interactions with organizational and team spaces. People are personally ineffective when they think and live in a "small space." *Having a small space means that their behaviors and actions are largely defined by others*—either by elements in organizational space, like rules and mandates, or by other people, like peer pressure—and it results in underperformance and personal dissatisfaction. A person's space shrinks when they are unmotivated, uninvolved and discouraged or when they feel minimized, marginalized or devalued. It's a state of low output and effort: they care more about what other people think of them than what they think of themselves; they have more self-doubt than self-confidence, and they would rather take directions from others than take personal initiative. They become subservient, subordinate and subsumed by team and organizational spaces. This "small space" mentality is usually a learned behavior honed from past experiences and consequences.

In a small space, people have little power and influence over team and organizational spaces. In fact, by default organizational and team spaces have great power over them. If they allow this state to persist, they become imprisoned and psychologically trapped. They become part of the background—silent, resigned and invisible to others. They avoid conflicts, responsibility and accountability. It is a state of neediness, which is common among low performers and unsuccessful people.

In project management, when people operate from a small space and have low influence, they make remarks such as:

- "Just tell me what you want me to do."
- "That's not my responsibility."

- "I did it because everyone else did it."
- "I don't have the energy to get into this."
- "It's not my fault."
- "I can't help you—my plate is full."
- "I would have done it if it was important."
- "Why are you picking on me, other people are worse than I am?"
- "What I say won't make a difference anyway."
- "Your instructions were unclear, so I couldn't complete the task."

In contrast, people operating from a large space or have high influence on organizational and team spaces make remarks such as:

- "What can I do to improve?"
- "What more can I do to help?"
- "What steps can I take to solve this problem?"
- "I appreciate the generous support from the people around me."
- "That was my mistake and I have taken steps to correct it."
- "I always welcome your input and feedback."
- "Thanks for correcting my mistake."
- "I don't know the answer, but I'll find out for you."
- "I owe my success to the team."
- "What more can I do to help the team?"
- "How can I further increase my value to you and our company?"

People with large spaces are "can do" people with great capacity to do more. People with small spaces are defensive and "can't do" more. "Can do" people make positive, constructive remarks because they possess a large space.

Space Producers

Personal space stays strong and stable when people are true to who they are and operate without hurting or invading other people's spaces. Although people expect mutual trust and respect, "small space" people seek space from others. Because they lack personal space, they "rob" (manipulate, impede, put down others) and "borrow" space from team members and others (they depend on others to feel good about themselves) (Figure 5.2).

Don't let small space players ruin your project. When people venture outside their space, they exhibit controlling, needy, small space behaviors. The most common behavior is to borrow space from others (i.e., letting other people make decisions for them or let others define their feelings and behaviors). The best project managers are *space producers*; they motivate, influence and inspire others to take positive actions, support others, produce high quality work and develop new ideas and processes.

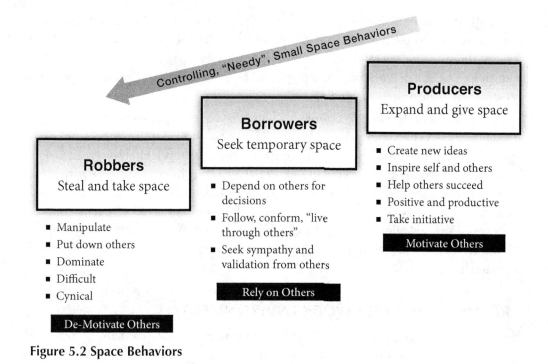

Figure 5.2 Space Behaviors

LOSING PERSONAL SPACE AND INTEGRITY

In the dynamics of team projects, people are vulnerable to losing space (giving up space) when they do not respect the integrity of their own personal space. This commonly happens when: (a) they give up their space and let other people define their behaviors and feelings; (b) when they modify what they say or do in fear of what others may think; and (c) when they give up their own beliefs, views and values in preference to the beliefs, views and values of others. When people are unsure of themselves, they may wait for permission to act, worry about what other people may think, or avoid taking action in fear of people's reactions. When people change their behaviors to satisfy others in contrary to their own *beliefs*, they are deceiving themselves, which is a form of *personal dishonesty*.

Another example of losing integrity and personal space is *personal abstention*. In project management, classic examples are groupthink and herd mentality where people "go along to get along" as a result of peer pressure, conflict avoidance or other inherent fears. They may have different *views* but they abstain and give up their own voice in preference to social acceptance. When they relinquish their *voice* to others, their space shrinks.

Sometimes, under pressure from organizational or team space, people can relinquish not only their voice but their most cherished *values*. At Enron Corporation, where illegal practices led to the collapse of the company in 1993, greed and power apparently caused people to lose sight of their beliefs in honesty, integrity and ethics, resulting in the downfall of all three spaces. It is easy to confuse their values with those of organizational and team spaces. Forsaking your own *values* is *personal betrayal* and it destroys personal space.

To be personally effective, project managers need to preserve their integrity, live up to their values and express themselves in productive ways. Successful managers are skilled communicators who speak honestly and effectively and don't avoid issues or blur spaces. They do not let their integrity and values drift. When personal space lacks strength, people tend to blur boundaries of personal, organizational and team spaces and falsely accept the opinions of other people instead of expressing what they honestly think, feel and want. When they falsely assume the values and beliefs of others, they lose their identity, integrity and the sense of who they are.

CREATING YOUR BEST WORK ENVIRONMENT

How well you manage your work environment is a key determinant of personal success. When your project values and goals are aligned to organizational and team spaces, it increases the chances for support, recognition and achievement. However, unless you're working in a motivating environment, personal satisfaction and project goals will not be accomplished. Who has the responsibility for creating a motivating work environment? Most people believe that management has that responsibility, that employees don't have the personal power or authority to modify their work situation, and they're expected to work within the system. This is a falsehood.

Personal power is about *influence*. The more influence that people have on organizational and team spaces, the greater power and control they create within their own space. Personal influence expands when people demonstrate:

- Self-confidence and initiative
- Leadership
- Teamwork
- High character and ethics
- Effective communications
- Strategic alignment
- High performance

People are better served when they step up and proactively create a work environment that fits their human factors. People crave for more job freedom; yet they let organizational and team spaces define what they do, when they do it and how they do it. They accept that they cannot do anything about it, allow extrinsic motivators to override their intrinsic motivators and suffer in silence. Why can't people make their work environment *work for them*? In other words, why can't they create the type of work environment that increases their motivation and maximizes their performance? Yes, there are many factors in the workplace that people cannot control, such as their boss's behaviors or the structure and resources of their company, but there are many things that people can control and influence, such as improving the way they do their jobs, what training they can take, career development, helping others, working with a mentor, networking, volunteering for new assignments, making new friends and many others. Too often people accept the status quo and leave their fate in the hands of others. When the work environment works for people, they gain tremendous personal power and effectiveness. When they force fit themselves into a system that conflicts with their values and diversity, it is a formula for failure.

How does a person make their work environment more motivating? It starts by understanding what enables them to perform at their best. Everyone has specific preferences in how they want to be treated and motivated. When people are treated in a manner that suits them, they will perform better on projects and feel good about their work.

IMPROVING YOUR WORK SPACE

In understanding your best work environment, there are certain factors in both organizational and team spaces that are critical for personal success. In these spaces, there are two types of environmental factors: "Base Performance Factors" and "Variable Performance Factors."

Base Performance Factors

These are *standardized* work elements commonly found in organizations and are *generically* applied to the workforce (Table 5.1). Workers expect these base factors to be in place and administered fairly and legally. When done well, people are satisfied; when base factors are administered poorly, they can be highly de-motivating to workers. Although it can be argued that salary may be an exception, base factors generally do not create high individual motivation; project performance and personal success require more than base factors.

Table 5.1 Examples of Base Performance Factors

▪ Title	▪ Equitable treatment of employees
▪ Work conditions	▪ Health and safety
▪ Salary and benefits	▪ Adequate resources
▪ Security	▪ Human resources
▪ Fair compensation	▪ Standard policies and procedures

Variable Performance Factors

Personal achievement requires individual- and team-based performance factors that fit people's interests and diversity. Unlike base factors, variable performance factors are discretionary and are utilized and regarded *differently* for each person. Personal success resides in variable performance factors, not base factors. Variable factors relate to individual preferences, work style, personality type and goals. Base factors keep people *satisfied* and *support* their values, but variable factors are the environmental elements that enable people to perform at a *higher level*. Thus base factors are essential and fill people's "needs," while variable factors support "wants" (Chapter 4).

Variable factors are work preferences that motivate discretionary effort and produce sustainable, superior results. There are six variable factors that are critical for high performance—three come from organizational space and three from team space. The variable performance factors from *organizational space* are:

- Job Responsibilities
- Career Development
- Supervision

For some people, formal career development and coaching programs may not exist in their organizations but they do exist in other venues, such as professional associations, external networks and informal mentoring programs. The absence of formal in-house programs should not preclude people from engaging in career development opportunities. The variable performance factors in *team space* are:

- Team Behaviors
- Team Relationships
- Team Projects and Processes

Assessing Your Variable Performance Factors

Since variable factors are essential to your success, it is important to determine how well your current work environment is *working for you*. Similar to the introspection-retrospection process with values in Chapter 3, you can assess the health of your work environment by comparing your *desired state* against your *current state*, i.e., "what I want" versus "what I get," respectively.

(1) In Table 5.2, review the six variable performance factors (in bold) and the numbered descriptors under each factor. For each of the six performance factors, give an overall rating on its "Motivation Value" to you (*what I want*), using a scoring scale from 1 to 5 (1=low to 5=high). In the next column ("Current Value"), rate how well that factor is working for you in your current job (*what I get*). For project teams, take the individual scores for each factor and calculate an average team score.

Table 5.2 Discretionary Factors in Organizational and Team Spaces

Variable Factors for Success	Motivation Value *What I want*	Current Value *What I get*
	Score (1–5) 1 = low, 5 = high	
Job Responsibilities		
(1) Clear roles, responsibilities and expectations		
(2) Clear work goals, alignment to team/company goals		
(3) Job freedom/control to express my talents & abilities		
(4) Decision-making authority		
(5) Feeling challenged and empowered in my job		
(6) Feeling trusted to perform my responsibilities		
(7) Able to take risks, invent and try new things		
(8) Feeling valued, recognized, appreciated for my work		
Career Development		
(9) Personal skills development and training		
(10) Mentoring and coaching		
(11) Continuous learning and growing opportunities		
(12) Career planning and counseling		
(13) Promotions and job advancements		
(14) Professional growth (industry or trade participation)		
(15) Job fulfills my ambition, passion, career expectations		
Supervision		
(16) Supervisor knows my motivators and de-motivators		
(17) Supervisor understands my strengths and weaknesses		
(18) Supervisor values my diversity and work style		
(19) Effective communications with my supervisor		

continued

Table 5.2 Discretionary Factors in Organizational and Team Spaces (*continued*)

Variable Factors for Success	Motivation Value *What I want*	Current Value *What I get*
	Score (1–5) 1 = low, 5 = high	
(20) Supervisor and management feedback		
(21) Work relationship with supervisor		
(22) Management leadership and engagement		
Team Behaviors		
(23) Trust and respect from my team		
(24) Team relies on and supports my work		
(25) Mutual transparency (open, honest, direct)		
(26) My individual diversity is valued		
(27) Mutual accountability and follow-through		
(28) Sharing information and learning together		
Team Relationships		
(29) My personal values match well with my team's values		
(30) Aware of each other's motivators/de-motivators		
(31) Camaraderie, fun, enjoy getting together		
(32) Interpersonal conflicts are infrequent/well managed		
(33) Feeling interdependent, meaningful contributor		
(34) Feel valued, recognized and rewarded by team		
Team Projects and Processes		
(35) Team structure and meetings support my job		
(36) Clear roles, responsibilities, expectations from team		
(37) Communications and alignment across my team		
(38) Understand/participate in team's decision-making		
(39) My work is integral to team's performance metrics		
(40) Team feedback on my performance		

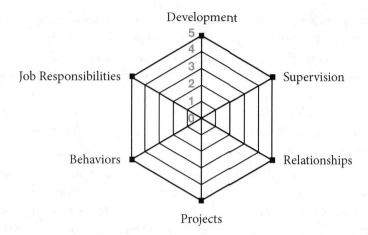

Figure 5.3 Space Map Template

(2) Using the space map template in Figure 5.3, plot your "Motivation Value" and "Current Value" scores for each of the six performance factors. The template has values ranging from 1 (lowest) to 5 (highest), increasing from inside to outside.

(3) Finally, looking across the entire table, select twelve descriptors (sub-factors) from the list of forty, labeled (1) to (40), that provide the greatest motivational value for you. As an option, you can rate and map those twelve sub-factors as well.

Space Map

Plot your "Motivation Value" and "Current Value" scores in Figure 5.3 and connect the points as illustrated in Figure 5.4.

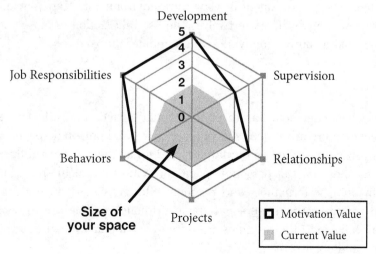

Figure 5.4 Sample Space Map for Workplace Performance Factors

In your space map, please note that the shaded area encompassing your six points represents the size of your space (inside plot: current values) relative to your desired work environment (outside plot: motivation values). Your opportunities to grow your space are the gaps between your motivation values (*what I want*) and current values (*what I get*). Factors having the largest gaps mean that you have personal preferences that aren't being met and you can perform better if these gaps were narrowed. These preferences may be due to poor team behaviors, lack of a good career development program or a bad boss.

In the specific example provided in Figure 5.4, personal development and job responsibilities are the widest gaps. If your two plots match well, it implies that your current work environment is *in sync* with your desires, needs and wants, and your current job fills your space and supports your personal effectiveness cycle. A tight fit usually indicates a strong probability for high job satisfaction and performance. It is also helpful to rank the six factors to determine your personal priorities. Which of the six variable performance factors were considered the most important to you?

If the six variable performance factors seem too broad, perhaps the forty sub-factors are more valuable to you. Review the twelve sub-factors that you have selected from the six broad categories. These sub-factors are your strongest work preferences. Which variable factors carry the highest value for you? Were most of your sub-factors from one or two categories or evenly balanced? Do you see any patterns in your space?

Because of the dynamics of organizational, team and personal spaces, the size of your space can change over time. This self-assessment is important to do on a regular basis, and it takes self-initiative and influence to ensure your spaces are in sync. As a project manager or team member, your happiness depends on your continuous re-assessment and improvement of your work environment. Map your current baseline and review it again in six to twelve months. Take action to close your gaps and you will gain more control, motivation and happiness in your job.

SUMMARY

✓ Project management has three conceptual spaces that affect motivation and behaviors: organizational space, team space and personal space.

✓ Organizational space is the largest, and it has the strongest influence on people's behaviors. But personal space is the most powerful space for motivating individual performance, and personal effectiveness is dependent on the size and strength of your personal space. Although people are in control of their own behaviors, their actions are often overridden by extrinsic motivators in team and organizational spaces.

✓ Five key reasons why the three space model is important in project management:
  ✓ Organizational space is effective in motivating *compliance* (have to) behaviors, while personal space inspires *discretionary* (want to) performance, a willingness to go the extra mile.
  ✓ The more spaces you have supporting your project, the greater the motivation and probability for success.
  ✓ The greatest leverage point for increasing motivation is connecting project values (from organizational and team spaces) to people's values (personal space).
  ✓ When project values, goals and processes are aligned across the three spaces, performance increases. Motivation and commitment increase when all three spaces are working together.
  ✓ The best project managers are *space producers*—they motivate, influence and inspire others. Small space players are "robbers" and "borrowers" of other people's spaces. Don't let small space players ruin your project.
✓ People are vulnerable to losing space when they do not express and respect the integrity of their personal space. Personal space shrinks when personal dishonesty, abstention and betrayal occur.
✓ Successful project managers understand their *variable performance factors* and how to maximize them to achieve personal, team and organizational success.
✓ This chapter enabled you to measure the size of your personal space by assessing the differences between "what I want" and "what I get" in your current work environment. This *space map* enables you to identify the biggest opportunities for improving your work environment and motivation.

6

Set Point
How to manage your motivational state

One of the most observable and controllable human factors in personal effectiveness is *set point*, which is your average daily disposition, mood or attitude. Set point is a state of mind that reflects your level of self-motivation and confidence. In contrast to space, which represents *extrinsic* motivation, set point reflects your *intrinsic* motivation.

Intrinsic motivation consists of a positive, higher state of mind (upper state) and a negative, lower state of mind (lower state) and people continuously cycle between these two conditions depending on their mood, attitude and perceptions. Although everyone is unique, people generally show the same types of behaviors in their upper and lower states (Figure 6.1). Upper state is a successful, confident state of mind, projecting a positive, winning attitude and being open-minded, secure, collaborative, transparent and optimistic. In contrast, the lower state is a self-limiting, defensive, closed-minded condition that is dominated by fear, insecurity, selfishness, neediness, uncertainty and low confidence. It is a low performing, negative state of mind. On balance, the higher your set point the greater your probability of success.

Upper and lower states of mind are internally motivated and self-determined. Although set point is always subject to extrinsic influences, people have the self-awareness and ability to self-regulate—to control their thinking and attitude. For example, external criticism, conflicts and disappointments may upset you and get you down, but you can still maintain a high set point by remaining optimistic, engaged and opportunistic. Your ability to self-regulate and stay in your upper state, especially under stressful situations, is a key intrapersonal skill in project management.

UPPER STATE

Upper state is the best psychological level for achievement and success. Everyone has an upper motivational state of mind. When people are motivated, they move their set point or equilibrium to a higher level of performance and influence; they work well with others, establish positive relationships and possess influence across

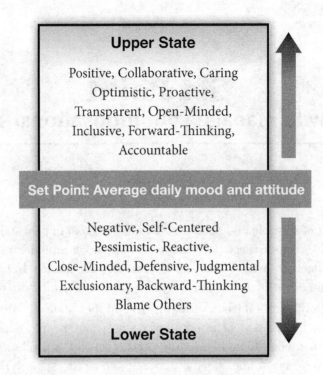

Figure 6.1 Set Point: Behaviors in Upper and Lower States

spaces. People do more and accomplish more when they are in a good state of mind, being relaxed, caring, patient, happy, transparent and secure.

In upper state, people are not afraid to show themselves, express how they feel and share their thoughts. It is a place of low stress and high achievement where there is no fear of conflict, rejection, embarrassment and failure. It's a state of freedom where you're not afraid to show your vulnerabilities. People like people who are positive, happy and "up" in life and when you show your good side, that's when people enjoy you the most. As a project manager, your positive relationships with people depend on your ability to assume an upper dynamic state. At a higher equilibrium, you have a better view of the world and the world has a better view of you, which means that your openness and transparency allow others to see who you are, and you are at your best when you are yourself. The upper state is your best side and *you feel best when you carry a high set point in life.*

Acts of Kindness

One of the best upper level behaviors is kindness. When people see others in need, they eagerly jump in to help, whether it's a local fund-raiser or a national campaign to help the disadvantaged. Even small acts of kindness can be just as meaningful, such as when a child brings flowers to their mother, when people help others who are lost, or when a bus passenger gives up their seat to a senior citizen. These acts of kindness come from your upper state. You have a nice thought that comes "over you" and you do it.

Opportunities for kindness are abundant and acts of generosity tend to be remembered for a long time. I'll never forget my first visit to company regional headquarters in New Orleans. I met my host at a local land base to catch a helicopter to an offshore drilling platform in the Gulf of Mexico. Her name was Peggy and she was an early career petroleum engineer assigned to the Gulf of Mexico business unit. Her job was to support the drilling and production operations at the platform. She was busy and had worked practically non-stop for ten days to complete a critical part of her project. Despite her busy schedule, Peggy took time to give me a tour of the worksite and thoroughly explained the facility operations to me. While on tour, I could see that although she was a woman working in a traditionally male-dominated business, she more than held her own. Right away, I could tell that the men and women on the platform highly respected her expertise and leadership. Also, I could tell that she trusted and appreciated the workers on the platform too. Peggy had a quiet, confident demeanor that mixed well with people. I enjoyed meeting her team and spending the day on the oil production platform.

When we returned to New Orleans, she went out of her way to show me around town and showed me all the preparations and traditions of Mardi Gras. It was October but I had always heard about Mardi Gras and the rich history behind it. We visited a bakery and she explained the "king cake," the symbolic "toy baby" inside the pastry and "throw beads," which greatly intrigued me. I told her that I looked forward to attending a Mardi Gras one of these days but I would probably not have a chance anytime soon. I left the next day.

About four months later, I received an unexpected FedEx package at home. I curiously opened it and the moment I saw the contents, I knew right away who had sent it. The package contained a neatly wrapped "king cake" with a batch of throw beads from the New Orleans bakery. What a nice surprise! I invited a few friends over and we had a fun Mardi Gras celebration that night with my family and friends. It was a small act of kindness but I will never forget how Peggy went out of her way to remember me four months after my one-day visit to New Orleans. Maybe it was southern hospitality but it made me feel good. These small acts of kindness helped raise my spirits, and I think it raised hers too when I expressed my gratitude to her the next day.

A higher motivational state gives people a more positive and broader outlook. In the upper state, people are growing, learning and proactively applying their knowledge and skills. They are unselfish in their thinking and open to new ideas and challenges, which create opportunities for change. This is exactly the mindset that is desired in project management. Upper level project managers are more productive, creative and motivating and in times of stress and conflict, they are able to stay "up" and positive.

The Big Softball Game

A wonderful example of people rising to their upper state at times of pressure occurred in a college softball game in Ellensburg, Washington in 2008. Central Washington and Western Oregon University were playing in an important conference game with a bid to the National Collegiate Athletic Association (NCAA) Division II playoffs. Central Washington was one game behind Western Oregon in the Great Northwest Athletic Conference and Central Washington desperately needed to win the game.

In the top of the second inning, Western's Sara Tucholsky came up to bat with two runners on base. She dug in at the plate and watched the first pitch go over for a strike. On the next pitch, the senior did something that she had never done before—she smashed the ball high and deep into center field for an apparent three-run home run. She excitedly raced to first base but as she was following the flight of the ball, she missed stepping on first base. As she was several feet past the bag, she stopped abruptly to return to touch it. But her right knee buckled and she collapsed on the base path. With urging from her first-base coach, she tried crawling back to the base but she was in great pain. To the concern of teammates and spectators, Tucholsky continued to crawl slowly through the dirt to the bag but couldn't go on to score the home run. Her first-base coach and teammates could not help her or she would be called out.

With an injury, Western's head coach had the option of leaving the injured player at first or replace Tucholsky with a substitute runner. Either option meant erasing the home run. Moreover, the coach had to get her injured player off the field for medical treatment. Under the rules, a player cannot be assisted by their team around the bases. In that moment of concern and disappointment for Tucholsky and the conference playoffs at stake, the star player on the other team, Mallory Holtman of Central Washington, stepped up and asked the umpires if the rules allowed the *opposing* players to help her. The umpires said nothing in the rulebook prohibited aid from the other team. So, in an extraordinary act of sportsmanship, Holtman along with her teammate, Liz Wallace, picked up Tucholsky on either shoulder and leg and carried her carefully around the bases, making sure she touched every bag with her good leg. It was an awkward scene but one that everyone will remember. "My whole team was crying," Tucholsky said. "Everybody in the stands was crying. My coach was crying. It touched a lot of people." Western Oregon went on and won the game 4-2 and extinguished Central Washington's playoff hopes. However, no one lost that day—that one act of kindness and unselfishness will forever carry a much *higher* meaning for Tucholsky, Holtman, Wallace, the colleges, and everyone who attended that game. It took great emotional strength from Holtman, Wallace and the Central Washington team to take the interest of others first. This was truly an unexpected moment of great kindness and success.

What enabled Mallory Holtman of Central Washington to take action was her inherent motivational state—as a successful all-star in the league, Holtman's focus was not on herself or to prove her skills in baseball but in responding to the immediate needs of others. It happened spontaneously and with great self-confidence and those are the hallmarks of highly successful, upper level people. Kindness is never genuine when it is extended from a "needy," lower level state. When personal "needs" and "wants" are satisfied, kindness comes from a positive space; *upper level players see opportunities that others can't see*, and they act quickly and confidently. Opportunities are recognized by those who have a "higher" view of things and it results in unexpected successes.

In project management, it's easy to maintain a bright attitude when everything is going well. Like the softball game, the true test of your ability as a manager is when problems, conflicts, disputes and incidents occur that impose stress, indecision and uncertainty. In these situations, lower level project managers become protective, defensive and fearful of doing the "wrong things," while upper level project managers see the big picture, recognize opportunities, demonstrate leadership and do the "right things." Having the wherewithal to do the right thing in a moment's notice only happens from the upper level.

LOWER STATE

Sometimes people can't help but fall into a bad state of mind and become short-tempered, impatient, controlling, judgmental and close-minded. When people don't meet their expectations, they have a tendency to put themselves "down" and take a lower state of mind. It's a psychological state where nothing seems to go right—a place of low self-confidence, low motivation and distrust. It can be a vicious downward spiral when people assume a negative equilibrium. This is a condition of low interaction and collaboration, where people are more self-absorbed and occupied by their own problems and ego. Being in the lower state darkens your perceptions and leaves you psychologically hidden.

Being in a lower equilibrium increases the chance for failure, not success. Due to low confidence, people hedge their behaviors and fear failure (not taking risks), responsibility or even working with other people. You cannot inspire from your lower state. The better course is to look upward. By being more transparent and open in your upper state, you become more visible and exert greater influence and power. Spend more time in your upper state by being more transparent and visible to others—that is the secret. Upper level players are winners; lower level players are losers. Examples of upper and lower level characteristics are listed in Table 6.1.

What are your most common upper and lower level behaviors? Under what circumstances do you find yourself falling into your lower state? Where do you want to spend your time? The choice is yours.

The Lower-Level Project Manager

Although the lower level is an undesirable state, many well-meaning, competent people prefer to operate there. This was the case of a project manager at a major chemical company named Jeff who was a Ph.D. chemist and an experienced new product

Table 6.1 Upper- and Lower-State Characteristics

Upper State	
■ Idea generator	■ Team player
■ Optimist	■ Problem-solver
■ Contributor	■ Help others
■ Learner	■ High productivity
■ Self-starter	■ High capacity
■ Organizer	■ "Can do"
■ Observer	
■ Defensive	■ Self-centered
■ Poor listener	■ Difficult
■ Impatient	■ Low productivity
■ Pessimist	■ Skeptical
■ Intolerant	■ Non-collaborative
■ Blame others	■ Cynical
■ Judgmental	■ "Can't do"
Lower State	

developer. He was well-spoken, smart and creative but had a critical side to his personality—he was skeptical of new programs, cynical of management, judgmental of other people and hated "working with idiots" as he would say. Because of his experience, he had excellent analytical skills and problem-solving abilities but he was impatient, conceited, defensive, dominating and self-centered. People generally ignored his arrogant behaviors and were thankful that he preferred to work alone most of the time. He had a low set point, but *he liked it there*. It was a safe, secluded place where he had control of his personal environment and didn't have to put up with any "idiots," but he was not a good project manager because he lacked leadership, collaboration and openness to other people and ideas. Nobody liked working with him, which further reinforced his lower level behavior. He enjoyed being the devil's advocate and management tolerated his behaviors because he was a highly experienced chemist. Jeff preferred to operate from his lower level because it gave him a sense of power, independence and control but in reality, he had little influence, trust and respect from others. Jeff lasted eight years at the firm and finally left for another job because he "didn't feel appreciated."

Personal space shrinks when people operate from their lower state. The lower level is a hideaway—a place to go when you feel threatened, devalued, excluded or fearful. That's why people are defensive, closed-minded and controlling in their lower state. They are self-centered, self-serving, protective, and not trusting or secure enough to show themselves. When people act this way, they don't build trust, respect and peer acceptance, instead they receive disdain and exclusion, which makes them feel "needy" and unappreciated.

The lower level is a hideaway—a place to go when you feel threatened, devalued, excluded and fearful.

If you believe in yourself, you will show yourself by being more accepting, positive and transparent with others (upper state). People who doubt themselves "loop" into their lower level, such as when people avoid difficult issues, avert responsibilities or ignore conflicts. They dip into their lower level as a defense mechanism due to fear, insecurity, stress and other intrinsic factors (Figure 6.2). They believe that hiding is a good coping mechanism to escape harm but it's *a mental trap*— going into your lower level is like "circling the wagons," closing yourself off and hunkering down.

What motivates people to stay in their lower level? In the lower level they are self-reinforcing their own behaviors and ego, and therefore they feel in control and safe and aren't dependent on others; people who play the "victim" game and wallow in self-pity are classic lower level actors. Also, it takes less energy to stay down.

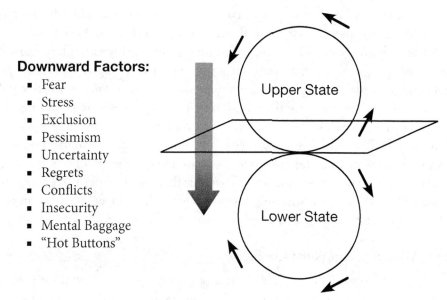

Downward Factors:
- Fear
- Stress
- Exclusion
- Pessimism
- Uncertainty
- Regrets
- Conflicts
- Insecurity
- Mental Baggage
- "Hot Buttons"

Upper State

Lower State

Figure 6.2 Upper and Lower Motivational States

Rising to the upper level takes more effort, vulnerability, dependency and risk. To be a high performing project manager, it takes self-initiative, transparency, visibility, risk-taking and collaboration, which only happens at the higher level. A great manager rises up; a mediocre one hunkers down.

Personal Forgiveness

When people experience repeated self-disappointments, regrets, fears, inner conflicts, anger, frustrations and transgressions, they can gradually recede into their lower level. These are powerful feelings that can weigh heavily on people's minds, preventing them from rising to a more successful motivational state. However, the longer people stay down, the tougher it is to get back up.

To reach a higher equilibrium, people need to unload their mental baggage and free their minds to think differently—to be more creative, take more risks and envision greater possibilities. This requires a behavioral shift and a mental renewal because *a change in behaviors requires a change in thinking*. It begins by *forgiving your past mistakes, disappointments and failures and moving forward*. It's a mental choice that everyone has each day—indulge in self-misery and do the same old thing or courageously step up and take the initiative to pursue a productive course. The lower state is a dominating force that can imprison people. Don't let past mistakes and disappointments ruin your self-confidence and self-esteem.

Throw Your Old Baggage Away

Other than personal forgiveness, a second action that you can take to raise your set point is to unload old mental baggage. Here's a good technique: identify one piece of old baggage (a negative memory, bad thought or worry) that you have kept for a long time, write it down on a piece of paper and then symbolically shred it or burn it and throw it out of your life. After destroying your negative thought, *replace it quickly with a stronger positive thought, image or action that you can do **right away***. Don't allow any room for the negative thought to return—re-program your thinking. It may take several days or weeks to install this new positive image and internal dialogue but stay with it. It may be helpful to write a positive reminder to yourself on a slip of paper and keep it in your wallet or purse so you'll see it repeatedly. Better yet, post a reminder on your bathroom mirror, refrigerator door or phone. *If you can see it, you can do it*. This small action will help relieve some of the unnecessary weight on your mind. Change your thinking and it will change your behaviors.

Tips for Managing Emotional Conflicts

Discarding old baggage may be a good strategy for old wounds and disappointments but what about more acute situations when you're faced with emotional conflicts, rejections, put downs and other stressful situations? Most people tend to immediately fall into their lower state when they feel threatened by other people. When people are in conflict, they become defensive, self-centered and emotional, leading to feelings of resentment, frustration, anger, hate and animosity. By understanding your lower level behaviors and "hot buttons" (situations that trigger an intense, negative, emotional response), you can consciously avoid your lower state. Project managers are expected to stay cool and demonstrate self-control. But in the heat of the battle, it's tough to just talk yourself into a better mood. Conflicts and arguments may be intellectual but it's the negative emotions that drive people deeper into their lower level. People need something more tangible and visible. To remedy the situation, you

> *To change feelings, change your behaviors.*

need to re-set yourself emotionally. You can change your behaviors by changing your thinking but how do you change your feelings and emotions? *To change feelings, change your behaviors.* There are several simple behavioral changes that you can do to change your feelings at any time:

- **Take a time out.** When things are too emotional, simply excuse yourself and take a break. If you can't excuse yourself, take a couple of long, deep breaths, focus on your breathing and release any tension. Moving and stretching your body will relax your mind.
- **Externalize.** When you're in an emotional conflict, you are likely focused on your own feelings and state of mind. Relieve that self-centered tension and reset your attention on something extrinsic and calming. Talk about the weather, your kids, a funny story or some other relaxing subject to help externalize and relieve your thinking.
- **Polarize.** Change your behaviors to change your mood. You can calm your anger, frustration or any other negative emotions by doing something completely the opposite (polarize)—smile, relax your body, say a kind word, do something positive, or give a compliment to someone.
- **Be mindless.** Do something "mindless" for a few minutes to calm your nerves and refresh your mind. Have a cup of tea or coffee, eat a snack, watch something on your computer or television, go outside for some fresh air, listen to music or meditate for a few minutes. Just put your mind on hold for a while and it'll quiet your feelings.

INTRINSIC MOTIVATORS AND DE-MOTIVATORS

Set point is a net effect of your *intrinsic* motivators and de-motivators that stem from your diversity, values and other human factors. When more de-motivators are in play, you can't help but be down but when motivators prevail, your attitude is up. An effective way to achieve a higher set point is to reduce your de-motivators and/or increase your motivators. Examples of common intrinsic motivators and de-motivators are listed in Table 6.2. What are your greatest internal motivators and de-motivators?

Table 6.2 Examples of Intrinsic Motivators and De-Motivators

Motivators	De-Motivators
• Feeling appreciated, valued	• Insecurity
• Feeling trusted	• Feeling micromanaged
• Feeling respected	• Feeling under-utilized
• Feeling empowered	• Uncertainty
• Meaningful goals/purpose	• Stress
• Having responsibilities	• Pessimism
• Having knowledge/experience	• Lack of energy
• Well-informed, "in the loop"	• Regrets
• Feeling "I make a difference"	• Low confidence
• Learning and growing	• Feeling irrelevant
• Feeling healthy	• Over-worked
• Feeling relevant	• Feeling unappreciated
• Feeling accepted	• Feeling excluded
• Freedom and control	• Work-life imbalance
• Feeling challenged	• Internal conflicts
• Feeling needed	• Self-doubt

Motivators give you energy and urgency to perform, while de-motivators feed your fears, insecurities and inadequacies. When you are able to express and utilize your individual talents and strengths, you are likely to have positive results; but when your diversity is suppressed and your values are dismissed or violated, you are apt to drop to your lower level. How long you spend in your lower level is going to depend on your intrinsic motivators to raise yourself "up." It is important to know which intrinsic motivators are most effective in regaining your motivation. Also, it's not uncommon to find that your short-term motivators (e.g., feeling valued) are not the same as your long-term motivators (e.g., learning and growing).

How to Measure Your Set Point

A quick method to determine your set point is to do a side-by-side comparison of your top motivators against your top de-motivators. Using the examples in Table 6.2, make two lists—pick your top five or more motivators and an equal number of your top de-motivators. For each list, rank order their relative effect on you; then do a pair-wise comparison of your #1 motivator against your #1 de-motivator and put a check against the one that is more dominant in your life at this time. Dominance is defined as the strength of one feeling over the other. If they feel about equal, call it a tie and don't give a check. You repeat this comparison for #2, #3, #4 and so forth. Table 6.3 illustrates how the comparisons are done using five motivators and de-motivators. This method works best when at least five or more pairings are used.

Table 6.3 Pair-Wise Comparison of Motivators Versus De-Motivators

Rank	Motivator	Rank	De-Motivator
1	✓ Freedom in my job	1	Work-life imbalance
2	Feeling valued	2	✓ Stress
3	Knowledge and skills	3	Over-worked
4	✓ Learning	4	Internal conflicts
5	✓ Optimism	5	Lack of energy

Which side dominates? The more checks you have for motivators, the higher your set point. In Table 6.3, we have three motivators that are prevailing over three similarly ranked de-motivators (#1 freedom in my job, #4 learning and #5 optimism), one tie (#3 knowledge and skills, and over-worked) and one dominant de-motivator (#2 stress). A two-to-one ratio of motivators winning over de-motivators is a healthy set point. Conversely, a two-to-one ratio of de-motivators over motivators indicates a low set point. In this example, the ratio is three to one motivators over de-motivators, which indicate a high set point. Although the two feelings that are being compared side-by-side may not be directly related, the overall picture is valuable for assessing your motivational state. Also, your list helps identify where you can improve and reach a higher performance level.

SUMMARY

✓ Set point is your daily disposition, mood or psychological state. You have a positive, higher state of mind (upper state) and a negative, lower state of mind (lower state) and you continuously cycle between these two states.

✓ When you carry a high set point in life, you are more open-minded, patient, caring, optimistic, self-confident, responsible and happy. More important, it enables you to see and pursue more opportunities, ideas and solutions. Your ability to self-regulate and stay in your upper state is a key intrapersonal skill in project management.

✓ The lower level is a "dark" place where you become defensive, resistant, self-centered, hidden, insecure and fearful. It is an emotional hideaway that makes you uninvolved, inaccessible, needy and pessimistic.

✓ The true test of a good project manager is when problems, conflicts and disputes occur that impose stress, indecision and uncertainty. Lower level project managers respond by being protective, defensive and do the "wrong things," while upper level project managers see the big picture, demonstrate leadership and do the "right things."

✓ Two important secrets for regulating your feelings and behaviors are: *to change behaviors, change thinking*; *to change feelings, change behaviors*.

✓ This chapter enabled you to measure your set point by assessing your personal motivators and de-motivators. Elevate your set point and improve your behaviors by recognizing which conditions and situations take you "up" and which ones take you "down."

7

How to Increase Motivation and Self-Confidence

Just as diversity and values are interrelated in helping individuals make quality decisions, space and set point work together in producing motivation. Motivation comes from two dimensions: a high *set point* (intrinsic motivation) and expanded *space* (extrinsic motivation). Since one can override the other, both extrinsic and intrinsic motivations are needed for high performance. Attaining and maintaining these two desired states require *self-confidence*. Motivation is a "want to" attitude to accomplish something; self-confidence is a "can do" belief that one can accomplish it. For project managers, self-confidence is the key enabler for increasing set point and space.

A high set point means possessing a positive, open-minded, optimistic, "upper level" attitude. An expanded space is a state of broad influence, autonomy, personal empowerment and proactive outreach to organizational and team spaces in facilitating change, improving processes, creating ideas and helping others succeed.

Also, space and set point improve personal performance by producing two additional benefits: expanding space *creates opportunities* and a high set point enables a person to *see and act on those opportunities*. Space represents extrinsic motivation and influence that can be depicted as horizontal expansion (Figure 7.1), while set point reflects internal attitude that moves vertically (upper and lower states). When you have a good attitude coupled with support from other spaces, you are a "top" performer and operating with great efficiency, focus, energy and mental balance. Successful project managers possess high motivation and self-confidence.

RAISING YOUR SET POINT

In executing a project, it's the project manager that sets the right tone and pace of the work; good quality managers lead by example and must role model the behaviors and attitude that he or she wants in the project team. Motivation and self-confidence create a "want to," "can do" attitude. The benefits of having a high set point and positive attitude are not only feeling good but also gaining more energy and capacity to do more, think clearer and work better with other people. Your relationships and

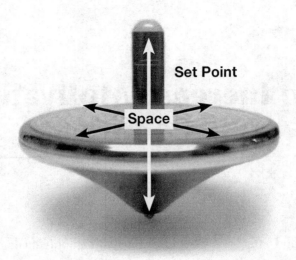

Figure 7.1 Self-Motivation

work are less stressful; you feel relieved, lighter, transparent and everything seems smoother and easier—you're literally "riding high."

Setting a higher set point means shifting personal consciousness to a more positive and optimistic level where you feel free to speak up, take chances and not fear making mistakes. Because of that positive mindset, you are able to see and do more (motivation) and worry less (confidence). In fact, you enjoy the challenge of exploring new ideas, learning new skills, doing things differently and working with other people. Maintaining a high equilibrium provides many advantages:

- **See new opportunities.** When you operate from your upper state, you are more open to new approaches, ideas, and opinions, which generates new opportunities for innovation and success. Not only do you see more opportunities but also you are more excited, energetic and motivated to go after them.
- **Build self-confidence, self-initiative and self-trust.** You're more transparent, accountable, less fearful, forward-thinking, collaborative, optimistic and open to taking risks. You believe and trust in what you're doing. Self-confidence breeds initiative, action and resolve.
- **Win friends and supporters.** You can't be successful and win friends and supporters if you're down in your lower level. Upper level people attract great people, sponsors and mentors. Who wants to hang out with people who are downers? People like to work with people who are "up," positive, open-minded, flexible and caring. It's a lot easier to do great things when you have great people supporting you.

It takes training and constant practice to carry a high set point. Here are eight tools, tips and strategies for improving your set point:

1. **Identify things that lift your mood and mental outlook.** What activities, people and things do you enjoy the most and give you a mental lift? Write them down and do those things more often—*have more fun!*

2. **Set personal goals that stretch your thinking and skills.** Set goals and strive to be better each day. This can be improving your knowledge, skills, reputation, health and relationships. Setting goals *broadens your outlook and brightens your future.*

3. **Establish a mental sanctuary.** Meditate for ten to fifteen minutes each day. Mentally reset your perspective by thinking of the positive and uplifting things in your life. *Count your blessings.* Establish a mental sanctuary where you can quiet your mind and renew the belief in yourself.

4. **Practice acts of kindness.** As discussed in Chapter 6, nothing moves you higher and faster than doing acts of human kindness. It's a *double win—it makes both you and the other party happy.* Giving to others is a pure upper level behavior: positive, caring and selfless. You'll be surprised; just one act of kindness each day will make a difference.

5. **Spin forward.** Don't dwell on past mistakes and disappointments; shift your thinking to identify *positive* (spin), *future* (forward) *actions.* Learn from your mistakes and move forward in time (e.g., "How can I do better next time?" "How can I improve myself?" "What can I do to solve this problem?").

6. **Have a pivot point.** Always have a positive thought ("point") that can *quickly move you upward* (pivot) when you're feeling down about yourself. It may be a picture of your children, your spouse's smile, a happy memory, an achievement, a song, a poem or a piece of artwork.

7. **Surround yourself with positive, upper level people.** Work and socialize with *happy, positive people.* It's fun and you'll learn what keeps them happy and motivated. Their successful habits are bound to rub off on you.

8. **Forgive yourself and shed emotional baggage.** Don't let past problems, self-disappointments, regrets and failures weigh you down. You can't pursue future opportunities if your mind is restrained by past mistakes. Self-forgiveness occurs when bad thoughts are replaced with good thoughts, which lightens the mind.

SELF-CONFIDENCE

The most critical factor in achieving and maintaining a high set point and expanding space is self-confidence. Self-confidence is the willingness to take action in the face of an uncertain outcome. As a project manager, it is a pivotal part of your personal effectiveness cycle. When your actions result in favorable outcomes, it builds your self-confidence, turns your cycle and you are less afraid to take the same action again. This repeated self-initiative takes competence, experience, positive internal

Self-confidence is a mental tug-of-war between the belief in yourself and belief in a bad outcome.

dialogue, inner strength and accountability. Self-confidence is built through continuous learning, skills development, knowledge, experience and trust. The secret is to know who you are, know what you have (in terms of abilities, knowledge and experience), know what you want and go for it. However, your fear of a negative outcome—such as conflict, failure, ridicule, embarrassment and criticism—is an opposing force that hinders your ability to "go for it." If you believe in your abilities and trust what you're doing, you can counter your fear of failure. Hence, self-confidence is a mental tug-of-war between the *belief in yourself* and *belief in a bad outcome.*

The Internal Paradox

Self-confidence is an internal paradox. When people have low confidence, they give *more trust and certainty* on negative outcomes ("This is going to be really hard." "I'll be lucky just to survive." "I know I'm going to mess up."), which are actually *uncertain* and out of their control, and give *less trust and certainty* on the things that they have *high certainty* and control over, which are their abilities and behaviors ("How am I going to do this?" "I don't believe I'm ready." "Where will I find the time?").

Self-confidence is having the self-assurance, trust and certainty in one's ability to perform. Self-doubt creeps in when people are unsure of their abilities and the consequences that may occur. To perform well as a project manager, one needs to feel comfortable about what they want to do, their ability to do it and what may happen. Dealing with uncertainty is a tough challenge in project management because people tend to fill uncertainty with anxiety and fear. Because of fear, people give greater certainty to bad outcomes even though it is purely imagined. To avoid this psychological trap, consciously fill uncertainty with facts, reason, ability and optimism. Fears and negative thinking are diminished when people are more certain, realistic and self-motivated—certainty improves with greater knowledge, experience, competencies and preparation. In projects, counterbalance the uncertainties of risks and consequences with the certainties of knowledge, competency and process.

Self-confidence takes time and effort. Confident project managers put their energy toward self-preparation and self-assurance and not on fearing bad outcomes. Winners believe in themselves more than negative outcomes; losers believe in bad outcomes more than themselves. The best state of mind is to focus your energies on what you can control and not fear what you can't control:

(a) Focus on "what is" (facts), not "what if" (imagined)
(b) Focus on the process, not the outcome
(c) Focus on what you can control and what you can improve in yourself—knowledge, experience, ability and proficiency

"Can't Lose" Tip for Building Confidence

When project managers doubt themselves, their mind is vulnerable to anxiety, worry and failure. When they fear failure and losing control, they can't commit and move forward. The best tip is to remember that failure only exists if you mentally *expect* or *accept it* as an outcome. It's hard to escape the feeling of fear because people have nothing else to mentally compete with it. However, you can mitigate this feeling and regain control by replacing your fear of failure with a "certain" mindset that "you can't lose."

Take the perspective that regardless of what happens, only three possible things can occur: (1) you do good, (2) you do great or (3) you have a fantastic learning experience. That's it! You either do good, great or fantastic—you can't lose! This technique gives you certainty and control of your future. If you want more *certainty*, remember that whatever happens, your family will still love you, your friends will support you and the sun will come up tomorrow. *Fill uncertainty with certainty instead of fear and anxiety and your confidence will go up.* Don't see tough tasks and difficult projects as hard and final but consider them as a continuous preparation and learning experience. Even when things don't turn out as planned, confidence gives you the strength to try again. Remember, when you have certainty and control on your side, *you can't lose!*

When you learn to trust yourself, you build confidence to take action and have the strength to accept whatever happens. Internal dialogue is the thinking process; self-confidence is the commitment that you feel that reinforces your internal dialogue, compels you to act and fuels your inner strength. Confidence is generated when you know who you are, know what you want and have the abilities to execute your decisions and work plans. When that happens, you reduce your doubts and fears. Doubts and fears are silent killers in project management, causing one to pause, wait and quit. "Can't lose" thinking is a great technique for suppressing those inhibitions.

Best Stress Breaker

One simple technique for boosting your self-confidence is fun. Fun is a stress breaker, an "ace in the hole" that eases your fear because it's a lot easier to face fear when you have a smile in your heart. *Fun always defeats fear* and adding a sense of fun to a challenging task lightens the weight and pressure of the moment. It relaxes you mentally, physically and spiritually. For example, when making a presentation, try to include something humorous—a funny cartoon, a happy quote or a joke that makes people smile. Fun de-stresses and de-pressurizes the task. When you're having fun, your confidence level goes way up. You are at your best when you are yourself and when you're having fun, you're showing your authentic self. Fun is another "can't lose" bet for raising your set point and expanding your personal space.

> *It is a lot easier to face fear when you have a smile in your heart.*

HOW TO EXPAND PERSONAL SPACE

Project management has a political side, which means you need influence and support from organizational and team spaces to run a successful project. The purpose of growing personal space is to gain influence and it's a personal commitment for positive, proactive change. Instead of sitting back and waiting for change to happen, you initiate and produce change. To do that, seek to understand the problems and opportunities that exist in your organization and apply your project skills and knowledge accordingly. The secret is to know yourself, understand what you're good at, and find new opportunities to grow and apply your talents in a way that is meaningful to all three spaces. To achieve that level of influence, it starts by understanding and expanding your personal space.

Expanding space is a positive, "I can make a difference" mentality that puts thinking into action. It requires self-confidence, a high set point, self-initiative and a positive outlook. Barbara Fredrickson (2003) demonstrated that positive emotions create increased levels of creativity, inventiveness and a "big picture" perceptual focus. Expanding space is supported by the "broaden-and-build" theory and positive thinking in psychology where positive emotions can widen thinking and build greater interest, exploration, skills, resources and influence (Compton, 2005). Positive emotions expand cognition and behavioral options and can contribute significantly to personal growth and development. Without positive mental outreach in life, organizational and team spaces can squeeze you and inhibit you from realizing your full potential. In the absence of being proactive, your personal space will naturally retract and limit your opportunities.

Personal space is supported and squeezed by numerous elements that exist in team and organizational spaces (Table 7.1). How well you manage these positive and negative factors determines the size of your space.

Organizational and Team Elements that Expand Personal Space

A successful project management system helps to expand personal space by meeting people's expectations. Given the diversity of the workforce today, it's a huge task to meet the ever-changing needs of people. It requires a good management system that supports its employees, provides a motivating work environment, uses high quality processes and recognizes employees for their performance. Successful organizations foster high performing teams and have a culture that believes in team-based management, collaboration, learning and development, participative decision-making and information sharing.

Today, organizations are challenged by increased employee job dissatisfaction and work-related stress that reduce personal space. Good project management relieves this squeezing effect by communicating, reducing pressures on personal space and meeting the needs of their workforce. When organizations excel in people management, employees feel challenged, valued and fulfilled—they are motivated to do more, create more and work together as a team.

Companies are recognizing that high employee performance is requiring more career management resources. With rapid rates of job turnover, employees want

Table 7.1 Effects of Organizational and Team Spaces

	Expands Personal Space	Squeezes Personal Space
Organizational Space	■ Excellent resources ■ Supportive management ■ World-class processes ■ High corporate integrity ■ Fair work practices ■ Leadership ■ Clear strategic direction ■ Promotions and merits	■ Work life imbalance ■ Bad management ■ Poor work conditions ■ Poor pay and benefits ■ Autocratic culture ■ Dishonesty ■ Micromanagement ■ Discrimination
Team Space	■ Mutual care and concern ■ Team recognition ■ Shared purpose ■ Clear responsibilities ■ Employee learning and development ■ Team training ■ Social networking ■ Coaching and mentoring	■ Interpersonal conflicts ■ Excessive competition among co-workers ■ Bullying, criticism ■ Peer pressure ■ Difficult people (bullies, whiners, control freaks, power mongers, cynics)

more career development, faster advancement, higher decision-making authority and greater freedom in their jobs. Companies are investing more in mentoring and training people and in accelerating their development. This fits well with the pace and expectations of new generations of workers who are more technologically skilled, resourceful, connected and opportunistic, forcing organizations to create a new work environment that supports these new expectations. Older generations wanted security and money; new generations want to change the world.

With new generational expectations, personal space is gaining influence on the future strategies of project management systems. Companies are providing more collaborative organizational structures, flexible work hours, coaching, mentoring, telecommuting, career mapping, social networking, work-life effectiveness, and health and fitness. Successful companies move with the times to meet the needs of future generations. The needs are becoming more demanding as the workforce and projects become more sophisticated. Personal space is a powerful force that continues to induce new changes in project management. Make sure your work environment is keeping pace with your rate of change. Does the trajectory of your organization, in terms of providing increased resources and opportunities, match the trajectory of your career? Your personal space can't expand if organizational and team spaces are static.

Project Management Elements that Squeeze Personal Space

When people feel "needy" in terms of better work conditions, job growth, supervision and career development, they feel unappreciated, under-valued and mentally squeezed.

In projects, lack of adequate resources and work overload are common sources of stress and dissatisfaction. When people feel squeezed, they mentally retract, hunker down and "circle the wagons" to protect themselves. They become more defensive than creative, show less initiative and involvement and become smaller in scope and attitude.

Team space has a greater emotional effect on personal space than organizational space. It stems from the strong human need to feel secure, accepted and relevant. Elements in project management that squeeze personal space include interpersonal conflicts, micromanagement, excessive competition, bullying, peer pressure and working with difficult people. Interpersonal conflict is probably the most destructive element to team and individual project performance. When people don't get along, work is mediocre at best since people "just want to get it done." Quality suffers and work is not a fun place when there are constant squabbles among co-workers. It is one of the most stressful situations for people—resulting in low productivity, errors and sabotage. Other than conflicts, the most common interpersonal factors in project management that squeeze personal space are *peer pressure, difficult people and harsh criticism.*

Peer Pressure

In addition to conflicts, peer pressure from team space can hinder project performance. Because social acceptance is a strong intrinsic need, people are motivated to conform to cultural norms and support each other. But when people compromise their values for peer acceptance, it lowers their personal effectiveness and reduces personal space. When people act in contrary to their beliefs by withdrawing, accommodating and letting others command them (e.g., "just tell me what you want me to do"), they lose accountability. When you allow other people to define your behaviors, you lose personal space, confidence, control, influence and self-respect.

Difficult People

Another project management element that can squeeze personal space is difficult people, who by definition are those who *impede the progress of others.* Difficult people lower team productivity, morale and project performance by behaving badly, creating problems and conflicts, and de-motivating other people. Who are these difficult people? Difficult people are whiners, bullies, control freaks, know-it-alls, power mongers, gripers, victims, downers, doubters, cynics, slackers and deadbeats. These people are found in your workplace, neighborhood, restaurants, bars and even right where **you** sit! Yes, everyone can be difficult at times and impede progress.

Difficult people are those who impede the progress of others.

Difficult people reside in team space and they are potential threats to project performance. Difficult people wreck teamwork and productivity by complaining incessantly (whiners and gripers), dominating others (bullies), controlling other people (control freaks), proving others wrong (know-it-alls), showing people up (power mongers), looking for sympathy (victims), putting others down (downers), criticizing new ideas (cynics) or not contributing (slackers and deadbeats). Difficult people are easy to spot; they share the same bad traits of being self-centered, controlling, negative, backward-looking, low accountability and bad attitudes. In effect, they hurt other people; they're *emotional vampires*, attacking and sucking energy and confidence from others.

Protection from difficult people requires an understanding of their intent and mode of operation. Difficult people are "small space" players who lack personal space and they want to take space from others. They suffer from insecurities, lack of confidence and failure in meeting their "needs" and "wants." These deficiencies leave voids in their personal space and they strike out to fill them. Difficult people are *space robbers*—they want to steal your space to restore themselves by trying to control your behaviors, putting you down, showing you up and bringing you down to their level. Little do they realize that personal space cannot be transferred from other people. What they are missing is inside of them—positive internal dialogue, self-confidence, self-trust, inner strength and accountability—which can only be self-generated.

To be an effective project manager, it is important to resist difficult people and not relinquish personal or team space to them. People treat you the way you *let* them treat you. If you lose space to difficult people, it's because you allowed it to happen. When you let people dominate you, use you or bring you down, you lose space. It would be fine if difficult people kept to themselves but they have a void to fill and they're constantly looking for victims. Chase them away by *not* accepting their behaviors and never give up your space to them. If you do, like vampires, they will come back for more!

To be successful, you need to stand your ground and protect your space from difficult people. Use your energy to bring positive people into your lives and leave the losers outside. Positive people bring energy and joy to your space by supporting your values and thereby enhancing your success.

As a project manager, when you continually take actions to build positive relationships and influence with your team and organization, you have informal power to prevent conflicts, resist peer pressure and ward off difficult people. Having expanded space gives you the mental capacity, power and influence to lead, adapt and overcome difficult people.

Harsh Criticism

No one likes to be verbally attacked and harshly criticized and when those instances occur it seems almost impossible to stay cool and not react defensively. You feel tense, angry and squeezed and such feelings usually lead to conflict and poor behaviors.

How do you stay cool and not let these situations affect you? There are three secrets for managing these situations: *(1) externalize, don't personalize, (2) deflect back and (3) take it upward and forward.*

- **Externalize, don't personalize.** When you hear harsh criticism, externalize it by mentally "sky writing" it in the air between you and the speaker. In other words, don't try to judge or internalize what you hear, regardless of how bad it may be. Grab those harsh words and send them into the air space above you. Don't let those words touch your mind or heart—leave them outside where they belong. There's a good saying, "Don't bring that trash into my house." Leave those negative remarks in a neutral, innocuous space. What makes this technique work is that you literally expel that bad remark into an endless, open space, and it keeps your emotional state intact.

  > *Externalize harsh criticism by mentally "sky writing" it.*

- **Deflect back.** Another good technique for handling harsh criticism is to "deflect back" the negative remark to the speaker (return to sender). For example, if someone is putting you down, instead of reacting, stay calm and deflect it back to them, such as, "What compels you to say such hurtful things?", "What do you want me to say?", or "How is this related to the project?" Don't ignore the comment but "de-emotionalize" it and keep things constructive by *asking* for purpose and relevance. Be sure to start with "what" or "how," and avoid using "why," which triggers defensiveness. Another option is to deflect to others, "What do other people think about that comment?" or take it out of the discussion, "Let's take this issue offline." Don't let bad comments "get to you"—deflect back and ask for relevance.

- **Take it upward and forward.** A good technique for staying cool and in control when you feel attacked is to stay in your upper level—be positive, optimistic and solution-oriented (remember difficult people want to take you down)—and be *forward-looking*. Respond to harsh criticism by asking, "What can we do to improve the situation?" "What ideas do you have for solving this problem?" "What do you think the next steps should be?" Or, "What would you like to see happen?" These are positive, forward-looking questions that prompt the other party to look ahead and adopt a *broader and higher motivational level.*

IS YOUR PERSONAL SPACE EXPANDING?

Expanding personal space is an ongoing activity that requires a personal commitment to be proactive, increase influence and get involved. How active and successful are you in expanding personal space and influence? Table 7.2 lists ten questions to determine your level of influence.

Table 7.2 Self-Assessment on Personal Influence

Score yourself on a scale of 1 to 5 (1 = low and 5 = high)

_____ How would you rate your level of self-initiative, being proactive and seeking change?

_____ How active are you in leading, developing and participating in team and organizational projects?

_____ How often do you contribute ideas and process improvements to your team and organization?

_____ How often do you help and support others? (How would your colleagues rate your support?)

_____ How visible are you in the organization; i.e., being involved in team activities, participation in meetings, sharing your opinions and expertise?

_____ How would you rate your level of activity in mentoring, coaching and sharing knowledge with others?

_____ How active are you in seeking and developing new opportunities for your team and organization?

_____ How active are you in helping others to achieve their goals?

_____ How often do you volunteer to do things for your team or organization?

_____ How would you rate your ability to collaborate and work with others?

Total Score: [   ]

Check your total score in Table 7.4 at the end of the chapter.

ACTIONS TO EXPAND PERSONAL SPACE

Based on your self-assessment, you may see some opportunities to improve your space and influence. The secret to expanding personal space is to go "BIG" and Table 7.3 provides tips and strategies for improving your space and influence.

- **B**e Proactive
- **I**ncrease Influence
- **G**et Involved

Table 7.3 "BIG" Tips and Strategies for Expanding Space

Be Proactive	
Propose new ideas and process improvements	Don't be satisfied with the status quo; always look for better ways to do things for your team and organization, and work to improve team interactions. Be a creative, innovative force in your work environment.
Welcome change	Be a change agent—support and lead change by taking action, engaging others and being a forward-thinker.
Maintain a positive internal dialogue	Thinking positive increases self-initiative; fight the urge to take the negative view. Don't let negative thoughts hold you back and reduce your confidence. Errors and mistakes are learning opportunities. Positive thinking produces positive results because it gives you the inner strength to keep trying.
Be a future thinker	Learn from the past but act on the future. Be a person that thinks ahead and solves problems. Blame, regrets and complaints are negative past events. Losers dwell on the past, winners look to the future.
Increase Influence	
Maintain positive account balances with people	Relationships are like bank accounts. You earn "interest" (influence) when you make more deposits (give to others) than withdraws (take from others). Your personal account balance grows when you help others. Build goodwill. Give more than you receive and your space will expand.
Invest in relationships	Influential relationships require long-term investments. Build a lasting, diverse network of friends and resources, inside and outside your organization.
Recognize and reward others	Actively praise others for exceptional performance and express sincere gratitude and appreciation for their help. To ensure sincerity, be *timely* and *specific* with your feedback. Support others and they will support you.
Lead by example	Model desired behaviors and stay true to your words. Be enthusiastic, optimistic and positive even under stressful situations. Be hopeful when others are discouraged. Trust and hope create influence.
Establish a positive brand image	When you build a positive reputation with people, you gain trust, respect, influence and understanding. Build a positive, "can do" brand image.

Table 7.3 "BIG" Tips and Strategies for Expanding Space *(Continued)*

Get Involved	
Be visible: "you must be present to win"	Get involved in as many different activities and projects within your organization. Active participation shows your interest, support and loyalty. When you are involved, people take notice.
Volunteer	Be known as a generous volunteer. Whether it's helping to organize the company's annual picnic or stepping up to fill in for someone, volunteering implies that you care about your team and organization; it will pay dividends for you down the road.
Foster collaboration	Successful people are good facilitators, communicators, negotiators and consensus builders. When you are able to lead, facilitate and foster teamwork, your value and influence increase immensely.
Mentor and coach others	Be willing to share knowledge and coach others. Help others succeed. Ensure others have access to your knowledge and skills, providing advice and mentoring.

Successful project managers do *not* let other spaces define, control and shrink their personal space. Instead, team and organizational spaces work for them and they grow their space through positive, proactive actions. They think "BIG"—propose new ideas, lead change, build positive relationships, collaborate, mentor and maintain strong work relationships. Expanding space is not a personal conquest; it's about working with others to achieve a win-win-win outcome in all three spaces.

SUMMARY

✓ Self-motivation requires two dimensions—a high set point and an expanded personal space. Attaining and maintaining these two desired states require *self-confidence.*

✓ Expanding space generates more opportunities because of increased involvement and influence across team and organizational spaces. To expand space, think beyond yourself, contribute new ideas, lead change and make process improvements.

✓ In project management, the most common interpersonal factors that squeeze personal space are team conflicts, peer pressure, difficult people and harsh criticism. This chapter provided sixteen tools, tips and strategies to expand personal space, including managing difficult people, peer pressure and criticism.

✓ By raising your set point and achieving a positive, optimistic, "can do" attitude, you are able to see and act on new opportunities. Eight tools, tips and strategies were presented to raise your set point.

✓ For project managers, self-confidence is the key enabler for increasing set point and space. Self-confidence is the ability to take action in the face of an uncertain outcome—it requires self-assurance, control and certainty in your abilities to perform. Fear and self-doubt diminish when you are more certain, realistic and motivated; you gain more certainty and control when you improve your knowledge, experience, competencies and preparation.

✓ It takes self-initiative and energy to expand your space, enabling you to "go BIG" (**B**e proactive, **I**ncrease influence and **G**et involved) and avoid living in a small mental space. You lose space when you stand still, so your goal is to continuously expand your space.

Table 7.4 Influence Score

Total Score	Level of Influence
>44	High
39-44	Moderate
32-38	Good
26-31	Some
<26	Low

Module III

Achievement

8

Fear

What are you worried about?

Fear is both a curse and a blessing. Fear can distort thinking, inhibit action and delay projects. It causes people to fight, flee, hesitate and freeze and in its most destructive form, it invokes self-doubt and failure. Many people dislike fear and perceive it as a personal weakness or vulnerability. But fear is *not* an undesirable human factor. In fact, it is essential for survival and motivation.

Project managers can be better motivators by understanding the types of fears and how they affect the behavior of individuals and teams. Fear is a constant force and *managing fear is a key job responsibility for project managers.* The secret to managing fear is not to avoid or eliminate it but to recognize and use fear as an advantage. How can fear help project managers? When managed properly, fear is motivational and a vital human factor in project planning, implementation and success. It provides energy, focus, and urgency to meet project expectations. Fear instills caution and prudence in times of potential harm and generates human energy to initiate action and complete difficult tasks. Unfortunately, fears are hidden and when people are frightened and worried, they hide their fears in different ways, which negatively affects project performance. Covering up fears only clouds people's judgments. If fears can be managed more openly and honestly, individual and team effectiveness can greatly improve.

Fear of failure as well as the drive for success are strong motivators for achievement. In his achievement motivation theory, McClelland (1953) proposed two kinds of achievement motivation, one oriented around avoiding failure and the other on attaining success. The drive to succeed and the drive to avoid failure are both important determinants in achievement behaviors (Elliot and Harackiewicz, 1996).

The notion that a bit of fear and anxiety promotes performance is rooted in the classical Yerkes-Dodson's law (1908), predicting that the relationship between anxiety and performance is an inverted U-shaped curve; in other words, a certain amount of anxiety or arousal is effective in motivating change but too much will adversely affect performance. Janis (1967) further expanded the arousal-performance matrix to fear and attitude change (Figure 8.1).

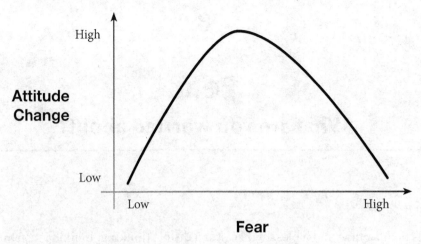

Figure 8.1 Inverted U Theory of Fear

The U-shape theory implies that fear can heighten performance. Indeed, some believe that the best work is done when people's "backs are against the wall." People work harder and more intensely when they perceive a threat. They even describe things in more dramatic and fearful ways in order to increase motivation, such as using deadlines, fatal flaws, drop-dead dates or sudden death. Many well-known coaches and managers use fear and intimidation to motivate people, and it works well because people respond to fear. Using interventions or harsh consequences can scare people "straight" and force people to change behaviors.

When used effectively, fear can immediately start or stop a behavior, or keep people within certain limits, such as driving within the speed limit for fear of getting a traffic ticket or being killed in an accident. Students are motivated to study hard and cram for exams due to their fear of failure and disappointing their parents. However, fear can also be antagonistic when it induces too much stress, becoming a "pressure cooker" and causing poor performance and bad decision-making. Also, constant fear feeds a vicious cycle of negative internal dialogue, inhibition and risk-aversion.

It is difficult to attribute the inverted "U" solely to fear since attitude and motivation are modulated by so many human factors. Also, attitude change or performance is a matter of definition. If a positive attitude change is defined purely by results or to enact change, a compulsion to take action is indeed created with optimal fear; however, if performance is defined as "getting results *and feeling good about it*," one can argue that the top of the curve only illustrates maximum attitude change and not the personal cost that was consumed. A "stick" approach may work but the hidden psychological cost may offset the benefit. Moreover, any positive effects may be short-lived and unsustainable—win the battle but lose the war. Alternatively, one can argue that the optimal point of performance is reached when fear evokes self-motivation *and* personal satisfaction. A low level of fear can evoke positive action and productivity; how much depends on the circumstances and the individual involved. Suffice it to say that a low level of fear is good but too much is bad. Later in this chapter, another model is offered to explain the effects of fear on performance.

With a bit of knowledge and practice, people can improve how they manage their fears and anxieties. Fear resides in personal space and therefore people can control their own fears. They can manage their fears by understanding where they come from, how they affect their behaviors, and how to minimize its negative effects while maximizing its positive effects.

There are many benefits for using fear as a motivator:

- **Generates focus and urgency**. Fear motivates and compels people to take prompt action, especially to avoid a negative consequence: "I need to solve this problem and meet the manager's deadline!"
- **Stimulates creativity**. When people are scared or worried, it forces them to push beyond conventional thinking. When people's backs are against the wall, they often come up with great ideas and creative options. Fear makes people think broader: "How can we take this threat and make it an opportunity for us?"
- **Rallies support and morale and brings people together.** Fear has a way of drawing people together to face a common threat. "We're in this together!" "It's us against the world!" and "We can't let our project fail!"
- **Ensures thorough thinking**. Fear also makes people more cautious: "Let's make sure we have a clear understanding of the problem before we jump to a solution"—fear causes people to think before they act.

WHERE DO PERSONAL FEARS COME FROM?

Like values, personal fears come from culture, life experiences and personality types. Culture produces fears through family superstitions, misfortunes, tragedies, religion, stories and other legacies, and these fearful beliefs can cut across many generations and communities. These shared beliefs affect behaviors, self-image and perceptions in life. For example, when a friend of mine was pregnant, her family forbade her from eating seafood because they feared it would give her baby webbed feet—a sort of "you are what you eat" superstition. During her pregnancy she accidentally ate some shellfish and she was worried about it for months. The family was relieved when she gave birth to a healthy baby girl with normal toes. Even in sports, like baseball, players adopt peculiar behaviors and superstitions to overcome the fear of losing or to help explain failures such as the "curse of the bambino" on the Boston Red Sox baseball team for trading away Babe Ruth, the bambino, to the New York Yankees in 1919; and the loser's curse on the Chicago Cubs for never winning a World Series. For most cultures, people create superstitions as a means to cope with fear.

Fears lie dormant in your personal space until you feel threatened. When people are frightened, they are prone to inflate risks and overreact to possible dangers based on rumors and speculations while ignoring available facts, logic and common sense. This effect was observed with such issues as UFOs, Y2K, gun control, immigration, health care reform and chemophobia. Fear mongering has been used to frighten and sway public opinions for political gains, such as McCarthyism, which fueled the fear of communism in the 1940s and 1950s and the massive fear of nuclear power plants after the Three Mile Island incident in 1979. These types of fears affect people by slowing their progress or causing them to make bad decisions. Dubious fears are ubiquitous and can cause self-doubt and poor thinking.

> *Doubt has killed more splendid projects. . . than any other enemy of the human race.*

As with culture, personal experiences also build fears. When people experience failure, tragedies and self-disappointments, deep fears can develop and stay with people for a long time. But having a bit of fear in your personal space is not a bad thing. In fact, the CEOs of some of the best run companies in the world, such as Costco, GE, Intel and Wal-Mart, attribute their success to a fearful mindset—staying fearful of competitors or new competitors entering the market—which keeps them on their toes, forcing them to constantly change to stave off organizational complacency. As Andy Grove, former CEO of Intel, once said, "Only the paranoid survive."

Some fear may keep people alert but too much fear can paralyze people. British writer, James Allen states that "He who has conquered doubt and fear has conquered failure. Doubt has killed more splendid projects, shattered more ambitious schemes, strangled more effective geniuses, neutralized more superb efforts, blasted more fine intellects, and thwarted more splendid ambitions than any other enemy of the human race."

Fear Lurks in Managers' Meeting

Subtle fears can emerge at unexpected times especially when people are suddenly called upon to speak, do a job for the boss or make a group decision. For example, during a Computer Expo last year in San Francisco, a group of information technology (IT) managers from different companies assembled for a meeting at a local hotel. They had met all day and finally took a break at six p.m. for dinner. Tired from the day's meeting, the group did not want to travel too far to eat. They decided to walk around Union Square, find a nice restaurant and enjoy a nice meal together since they were in a city with great chefs and wonderful food.

They stopped at a popular seafood restaurant but discovered that the wait was too long for a table, so they marched on. They came upon a small hotel restaurant that had a Michelin star rating. It was an elegant setting with an attractive menu. Unfortunately, the restaurant took only advanced reservations, and they found themselves on the street once again. Undaunted, they continued their search. They tried a large hotel but it only offered a buffet dinner, which they were not interested in. As they moved to the last part of the Square, one of the senior members in the group, Brian, spotted a restaurant that he recognized and said, "Oh, let's go there. I used to go to this place all the time, way back when I went to school in this area, and it has really good food." With that enthusiastic endorsement, everyone walked right up to the restaurant with great hope and appetite. It was a well-established, historic eatery that was well known for its lively entertainment and libations. They walked straight in and had no problems finding a table that was large enough for everyone to sit together. However, the seating was on old wooden chairs around an old wooden table surrounded by sports memorabilia, which appeared fresher than the corned beef and cabbage that was being served at the next table.

Based on everyone's body language, nobody wanted to be there but they sat obediently together, scanning the room that was filled with noisy service, smelly floors and a small but cantankerous clientele. Just when someone was about to say, "We can surely do better than this," Brian spoke up and asked, "Is this okay with everyone?" After a brief pause, one of the managers said, "Sure, no problem." Another person then said, "It looks like they have good beers here." Before they knew it, everyone was nodding in agreement even though their posture said the exact opposite. They ended up ordering meals that left much to be desired—it was certainly not the San Francisco treat that they wanted.

What went wrong? How could so many smart people make such a bad decision? Why didn't people speak their mind? What was holding people back from telling the truth? Why did they choose to eat at a restaurant that nobody liked? Each made a personal decision to stay despite their strong internal drive to leave. They made a decision that was contrary to their own beliefs and good judgment. There was a human factor in play that drove them to stay in that restaurant—fear. They were afraid to speak up. Although there were eight company IT managers, their passive-avoidance behaviors were motivated by different intrinsic fears. It was groupthink in action. Some of the fears that were operating in this story were:

- **Fear of conflict.** Afraid of confrontation, disagreement, "rocking the boat."
- **Fear of rejection.** Afraid of not being accepted, ostracized.
- **Fear of failure and criticism.** Afraid of making a wrong comment.
- **Fear of embarrassment and ridicule.** Afraid of not being valued and respected, feeling minimized.
- **Fear of disappointing others.** Afraid of displeasing others or hurting their feelings.

- **Fear of accountability.** Afraid of taking responsibility for a bad decision.
- **Fear of weakness.** Afraid of being vulnerable and incapable, looking like a "wimp."
- **Fear of insecurity and losing control.** Afraid of losing order and stability; afraid that people will not stay together and go their own way.
- **Fear of authority.** Afraid of challenging the leader or senior member of the group.

Now that's a roomful of fears! This is not unusual; these fears operate frequently in project teams and social settings. Anyone can succumb to worry, anxiety and "bad fears." Bad fears are those that provoke negative behaviors and consequences for you and/or others. These fears are triggered by the environment but they exist in personal space. Bad fear is a "need" response, not a "want" response (Chapter 4), which means that *people are acting to avoid a negative consequence*, such as failure or rejection, instead of seeking to fulfill a positive goal. That's why fear has an inverted U response—fear only fulfills a temporary need and therefore has limited motivational value. Motivation by fear is not sustainable for long-term success. Fears and worries distort reality, disrupt internal dialogue and diminish judgment.

Everyone, including successful project managers, possesses fear factors. Success is not achieved through the elimination of fear but rather through the ability to make sound judgments and decisions in the face of fears. Fear is bad when it adversely affects thinking and holds people back from performing at their best. Bad fears can paralyze thinking, erode self-confidence, lower self-esteem and reduce productivity. For example, many people are frightened to make presentations, and it's a killer to their self-confidence and careers. Loss of confidence is a telltale sign of bad fear. When people are fearful, they flee to their lower level where they are defensive, close-minded and stressed. Fear of negative consequences freezes the personal effectiveness cycle between motivation and achievement. They can't meet their goals if they're constrained by fear.

> *Success is not achieved through the elimination of fear but rather through the ability to make sound judgments and decisions in the face of fears.*

FEARS IN PROJECT MANAGEMENT

Passive-avoidance, fear-based behaviors are common in the workplace and projects. People stand back, withdraw and *accept inaction as the best choice for managing fear*, hoping that it will either go away or resolve itself somehow. These fears are so common that people have assigned "pet" names to them.

- **Elephant in the room.** When people are afraid to address a subject that weighs heavily on everyone's minds, they call these issues "600-pound gorillas" or "elephants in the room." They don't know what to do with it and no one wants to talk about it, yet the problem is clearly standing in the way. They're afraid to tackle the beast—it's like "If we arouse it, it'll get riled up and cause a bigger problem, so let's not go there." In projects, typical "gorillas" and "elephants" include legal and regulatory issues, personnel issues, quality assurance, self-reporting, policy deployment, management behaviors and compensation.

- **Sacred cow.** When people are afraid to challenge a project or belief that's highly favored by management, they treat these topics as "sacred cows." These are issues that should never be questioned or challenged. It would be sacrilegious to bash a sacred cow, and it could be a career killer. Management's "pet projects" are often sacred cows.

- **Ostrich head in the sand.** Sometimes when people feel uncertain or have a problem that they don't want to face, they hide from it, "like an ostrich with its head in the sand"—hoping the problem will go away. For example, people tend to "bury their heads" and hide when project audits occur or unpleasant tasks are required. But there is no escape because you still have the responsibility and your backside remains exposed to the consequences.

- **Chicken in the road.** When people are risk-averse or fearful of making a decision, they tend to sit on the fence or take a "middle-of-the-road" position. It's not uncommon for project teams to overly compromise on issues and agree on a "middle-of-the-road" solution to please everyone; but this team behavior usually leads to mediocre performance. Fear can dilute your effectiveness. When people sit in the middle of the road, they are eventually run over like a "chicken in the road." You can't be "chicken" too long—inaction will turn you into a "sitting duck."

- **Leaping lemmings.** People feel safer running in a pack, like lemmings. This herd mentality is so strong that they'll blindly follow their teammates without knowing the destination, until it's too late (leaping over the cliff). Following the crowd avoids the fear of conflict and weakness. This is classical groupthink behavior in project management. By sticking together, project teams think they're less vulnerable to failure; when in fact they're *more vulnerable* when they ignore critical thinking and outside input.

- **Worry monkeys.** Fear is sometimes like a monkey on people's backs; it clings to you like a weight of worry and demands to be fed. This commonly occurs in project management when people incessantly worry about their jobs, deadlines and their boss. It stays on their minds and they keep feeding it with their fear and anxiety. It won't go away until you stop feeding it.

These animals represent symbols of fear that prey on people. They're so truthfully humorous that people accept and perpetuate them in project teams and organizations. Avoidance and inaction are conscious fear behaviors that reduce project success. It's true what they say, "The workplace can be a real zoo."

HABITUAL FEARS

Bad fears are costly. It makes people inefficient and it consumes an enormous amount of human energy and reduces project performance. Many of the worst behaviors in project management are rooted in fear, such as jealousy, resentment, control, defensiveness, procrastination, anger and perfectionism. Because of fear, people spend needless time and resources fretting over meaningless details or stressed over what other people may think or do. They lose sleep and spend countless hours worrying about what may happen. They expend great time and energy in trying to please others or play office politics. How many times have you overcommitted yourself because you were afraid to say "No"? For some, the fear of criticism is so strong that they avoid any type of feedback. Because of your fear of making a mistake, how many pointless hours have you spent trying to write the "perfect" email? Reducing bad behaviors due to fear can benefit a project team enormously in terms of time and energy.

When bad fears are practiced repeatedly, they become "habitual fears," such as giving in to dominant personalities or avoiding conflicts and confrontations. What's interesting is that most of these fear behaviors seem tame and inconsequential, but habitual fears can slowly undermine confidence and motivation and lead to diminished performance.

Small but frequent negative fear behaviors are more dangerous than big fears because people don't pay great attention to them. Fears don't have to be big to hinder success. People worry and stress because they *choose* to worry and stress, and they program their minds to accept it like a bad habit. Having a fear of failure that causes people to triple check their work is not a terrible habit but doing it excessively on everything can drain your energy. Isn't it time to drop these habits and use that energy more productively?

EFFECTS OF HABITUAL FEARS ON PROJECT TEAMS

Everyone exhibits fear in one form or another. Habitual fears are linked to personal values and "needs," and they affect work performance and personal effectiveness. Habitual fears are serious threats to project success. Project managers can improve their motivational effectiveness by understanding the types of fears and how they affect the behavior of individuals and teams. The most common habitual fears and their effects on work performance are:

- **Fear of conflict** causes avoidance, procrastination and delays in making decisions and taking action. For example, fear of conflict can prevent project managers from confronting low performers, challenging project changes or stopping a worker who makes culturally insensitive remarks.
- **Fear of rejection** reduces individual effectiveness and participation. People are afraid to propose different ideas for fear of rejection by others. They conform to team norms rather than risk being an outcast.

- **Fear of failure** motivates risk-adverse behaviors, such as excessive data analyses, conservative decision-making, hedging positions (like inflating project budgets) and defensiveness. Fear of failure causes people to over-prepare, over-respond and over-worry, which can increase personal expectations and add stress and cost to a project.

- **Fear of embarrassment or criticism** reduces self-confidence, transparency and honesty. In projects, people deny problems, cover up mistakes and avoid issues. Also, a significant amount of energy is spent on rationalizing mistakes. Covering up a fear is like telling a lie—*lying leads to more lying*. People do strange things to avoid looking bad.

> *Covering up a fear is like telling a lie—lying leads to more lying.*

- **Fear of disappointing others** causes people to enslave their feelings to others. In project teams, these are called "yes" people. They agree with everything that the project manager or team member says or wants. To stay in favor, they say things that other people want to hear and they "go along to get along." It's a form of emotional dependency and enslavement because they feel better only when the other party feels better. It's nice to think of others but not to the point where your fear of disappointing others makes you subservient and ineffective.

- **Fear of accountability** makes people afraid to make decisions and take action. They avoid responsibility, hide mistakes and make excuses for their indecision. Worse yet, fear of accountability is contagious in a project team, causing people to avoid responsibility and decision-making. They wait for management or other parties to make decisions for them. Accountability is taking responsibility and personal leadership and it should be welcomed, not feared.

- **Fear of appearing weak** or inferior causes people to refuse help, follow the crowd, not admit defeat and hide their weaknesses. People with this fear believe that success is *"survival of the fittest"* and any demonstration of weakness will cause them to lose status and respect. Because they fear looking weaker than their peers, they are reluctant to recognize and praise others. As a result, *the project becomes a competition and not a team effort*. This is a common behavior in large project teams.

- **Fear of insecurity and losing control** compels people to put more processes and controls in place. Control behaviors include hoarding information, grabbing work from others, protecting turf and discouraging debate. When people refuse to delegate work, they rationalize it by saying things like, "If you want it done right, you have to do it yourself." It's not a matter of competency; it's a matter of fear and trust.

- **Fear of authority** prevents people from challenging the boss, experts and upper management. Also, fearing authority may include "staying in the box," not offering any new or risky ideas that may be contrary to existing rules, policies, processes and beliefs. *You can't do great things by doing things that people tell you to do.*

From this list, which ones are your strongest fears? Your fears may be situation-dependent but most people have one or two dominant fears.

PERSONALITY-BASED FEARS

Your dominant fears are likely linked to your personality type (Chapter 2). Rationals are analytical thinkers who fear failure and being wrong; idealists are sensitive to others and fear conflict and confrontation; guardians are hard workers who fear insecurity and instability; and artisans are freedom seekers who fear criticism and being inhibited (Table 8.1). For project managers and teams, knowing personality types helps to understand what people fear the most and how to manage those fears. This reduces team conflicts and increases mutual trust and respect.

In the discussion of habitual and "pet" fears, it's clear that fear is pervasive in the workplace and *people manage their fears by avoiding, hiding and covering them up.* People also use euphemisms to mask their fears. When rationals are afraid of making mistakes, they call themselves "perfectionists" to hide their compulsion to over-analyze. When artisans fear being ordinary or controlled, they call themselves "mavericks" or "risk takers" to make them feel unique. For idealist, they fear conflict and disharmony and see themselves as "peacemakers" to excuse their passive-avoidance behaviors; and when guardians fear losing acceptance and appreciation, they consider themselves

Table 8.1 Fear Factors by Personality Types

Personality	Characteristics	Fear Factors
Rational	Analytical, logical, independent, strategic	Fear of failure, being wrong *Fear of not being "right," making mistakes*
Idealist	Amiable, sensitive, collaborative, empathetic	Fear of conflict and confrontation *Fear of not being "righteous," not a good person" in the eyes of others*
Guardian	Hard-worker, reliable, organized, diligent, compliant	Fear of instability and insecurity *Fear of not doing things the "right way," improper conduct*
Artisan	Spontaneous, bold, freedom seeker, uninhibited	Fear of criticism, being inhibited *Fear of not being "rightful," unable to express who they are and operate freely*

"workaholics" to justify their fussy attitude. Hiding behind pet names and euphemisms does not excuse bad behaviors. Instead of hiding fears, *why can't people be honest and share their fears openly and constructively?* By revealing their fears, people can increase their transparency, honesty, trust and personal effectiveness. People are afraid to disclose their fears, yet *those who disclose their fears become less afraid.*

REVEALING YOUR FEARS: FEAR TORNADOS

Revealing fears enables people to see and appreciate their own strengths and weaknesses and improve their behaviors. When dominant fears are not recognized and are allowed to persist, they can become bad fears. Bad fears are repeated behaviors that yield adverse consequences for you and/or others. Achieving success requires awareness and management of your dominant fears. To keep it clear and simple, fears can be grouped into four major types in project management:

- Fear of failure, criticism, making a mistake, being wrong
- Fear of rejection, inferiority, being excluded
- Fear of insecurity, authority, loss of control
- Fear of conflict, confrontation, hostility, bad relationships

People may have one or two dominant fears or perhaps a bit of all four, but not all fears are bad. As mentioned before, fear is both a motivator of good and bad behaviors and each type of fear can motivate a broad range of emotions. Fear is not an on-off feeling but a broad continuum of emotions, ranging from highly constructive to highly destructive. *Fear is like a tornado* where a low level of fear stirs emotions and motivates people to perform harder, longer, faster and better, while a high level of fear puts people into a negative state of anxiety, stress, conflict and unhappiness. They're called tornados because fears can generate a tremendous amount of energy, power and influence, but at the same time, they can also be disruptive, unpredictable and uncontrollable.

Each type of fear can be depicted as a tornado with its own set of behaviors and different levels of intensity. Tornados are scaled from one to five, ranging from Category I for highly motivating tornados to Category V for highly de-motivating ones (Table 8.2). Category I and II tornados have positive effects on performance, while IVs and Vs are non-productive and have negative effects on projects.

What distinguishes Category I from II and Category IV from V is whether your fears are affecting yourself only or other people as well. Fears that motivate positive behaviors in *yourself* are Category I, while fears that promote positive behaviors in *both yourself and other people* are Category II. At higher levels, fears that motivate negative behaviors in *yourself* are Category IV, and fears that promote negative behaviors in *both yourself and other people* are Category V. Category III fears are in between—they can be mildly positive or negative, affecting yourself and/or other people depending on circumstances.

For each of the four major types of fears, rate your behavioral level (Category I to V) using the self-assessment in the next section.

Table 8.2 Category Descriptions for Fear Tornados

Category	Characteristics
V	Very negative behaviors that decrease *personal* and *team* performance
IV	Negative behaviors that reduce *personal* motivation and performance
III	Personal fears cause mild and variable effects with both positive and negative consequences for yourself and/or other people
II	Very positive behaviors that increase *personal* and *team* performance
I	Positive behaviors that raise *personal* motivation and performance

Classifying Your Fear Tornados

In this section (Figure 8.2), find your level of fear (Categories I to V) for each of the four types of fear "tornados."

Performance suffers when people allow their fears and worries to overwhelm them. Just like values, fears also shape and drive the best and worst behaviors and unfortunately they can push people subconsciously to their bad side. To show your good side more often, recognize your higher level fears (Category IV and V), consciously work to lower their intensity levels, and recognize those circumstances that trigger a bad tornado. The goal is to keep fears at Category I and II. Revealing your fears is the first step toward transforming your bad fears into good fears—make fear work for you, not against you.

IMPOSING YOUR FEARS ON OTHERS

When fears reach Categories III and IV, people are avoiding, hiding and covering their fears. But when people cross into Category V, they are now imposing their fears on others, attempting to control other people's behavior and hurting their performance. They steal space from others and insist that things be done their way. These fear behaviors are often autocratic, aggressive, dominating and costly. For example, when people are afraid of failure and can't tolerate mistakes, they make *others* analyze things to death, double and triple check work for minor errors and

FEAR OF REJECTION

V — I hate feeling "out-of-the-loop" and excluded; I worry about whether people like me or not; I try too hard to please others which leads to regrets, disappointments and conflicts

IV — I struggle with feeling inferior and insecure at times and don't feel confident about myself; I "go along to get along" a bit too often

III — I work extra hard to meet other people's expectations; I'm concerned when my contributions are not noticed or valued by others

II — I'm motivated to "fit in," help others and prove myself; my need for "acceptance" promotes mutual respect, trust and reciprocity

I — I feel confident that my skills, contribution and behaviors are accepted and valued by my team

FEAR OF FAILURE

V — I can't stand to be wrong, criticized or corrected by others too often; I get defensive, argumentative, angry over mistakes which adversely affect others

IV — I tend to over-analyze, over-worry, and over-plan my work; I have problems letting go of problems and mistakes; I get too competitive

III — My need to succeed both motivates and de-motivates people; I show more good than bad behaviors but occasionally get defensive and competitive

II — My drive to analyze and get everything right has a positive, motivating effect on others, resulting in higher team performance

I — I'm motivated to get things right; work hard to ensure accuracy and quality; I don't get defensive and I readily admit mistakes

Figure 8.2 Fear Tornados (*continued*)

FEAR OF INSECURITY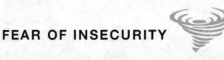

V   I dread uncertainty; I have anxiety when I have to face new challenges or make tough decisions; my lack of self-assurance adversely affects others

IV   I second guess myself and feel risk-averse too often; I worry about my job and whether I'm meeting expectations; my low confidence reduces my effectiveness

I   My need to feel secure about my work and that things are under control helps and hurts my performance; I should challenge authority, take risks and express contrary opinions more often

II   My need to feel self-assured and confident about my work makes me work harder and in close cooperation with my boss and team; my behaviors foster good teamwork and communications

I   My need for self-assurance and feeling in control makes me work diligently, accurately and carefully. I check-in frequently with my boss and others to ensure my work is acceptable.

FEAR OF CONFLICT

V   I hate conflicts and confrontations; they emotionally drain me and I avoid them as much as possible; I get highly stressed when conflicts occur; I dislike the process of trying to resolve conflicts with others

IV   Conflicts are not good—they reduce my morale, energy and motivation; I don't run away from conflicts but I prefer not to participate

I   I believe conflicts are both good and bad—debate and dissent yield better solutions but they also cause bad feelings; I don't like conflicts but I will cooperate and participate in resolving conflicts

II   My fear of conflict motivates me to get involved—to help facilitate "win-win" solutions for the team; collaborate with others to resolve conflicts

I   My fear of conflict improves my attitude and behavior—forces me to learn how to effectively prevent and manage conflicts

Figure 8.2 Fear Tornados (*continued*)

Table 8.3 Imposing Your Fear Behaviors on Others

Type of Fear	Imposing Your Fears
Fear of Failure	• You are overly critical of others and their work; demanding more analyses and perfection from others. • You bully and push people to do things your way. • You take over or redo people's work without their permission.
Fear of Rejection	• You want to be liked so much that you over-commit yourself to others, which leads to conflicts and regrets. • Because you're afraid to disappoint others, you procrastinate or defer decisions that negatively affects everyone.
Fear of Insecurity	• You micromanage others and install rigid structures and review processes in order to feel in control. • Your fear of change and uncertainty makes you risk-averse, causing you to reject new ideas, innovative solutions and contrary opinions. • Your fear of the boss makes other people fearful too—as a result, new thinking and leadership are suppressed.
Fear of Conflict	• Your inactions due to fear of conflict and confrontation allow problems to go unresolved, causing team conflicts and frustrations. • You convince others to compromise, withdraw and quit in order to avoid conflicts.

force people to work excessive hours. Also, when people fear conflict, they tell *others* to ignore disagreements, "don't rock the boat" and give in to others.

When people are afraid and worried, they can't help but impose their fears on others—"I'm afraid, so I want others to be afraid too." Maybe it's true what they say, "misery loves company." Table 8.3 lists some common fears that people impose on others.

FEAR MANAGEMENT IS A VALUABLE SKILL

Fear is a permanent resident in your personal space so the best approach is to learn to live with it and make it a positive asset and not a liability. *Fear management is a skill that should be treated in the same manner as any skill in project management— it requires training, development and practice.* Bad fears can be effectively managed using these ten strategies:

1. **Confront your fears**. Know your bad fear behaviors and avoid escalating them to the point of affecting your well-being (needless worry, stress, self-exclusion, lying, cheating or quitting), or hurting others (imposing your

fears on others, fighting, creating conflicts, jealousy, manipulation, sabotage and betrayal). *Control your fears; don't let fears control you.* Fear can quickly get away from you and become destructive.

Bad fears do not get better with time, so *confront it.* Avoiding, hiding and covering your fears do not lower your fear level. Try to face your fears periodically to loosen its grip on you. For example, if you're afraid to give talks, practice giving talks to small supportive groups of your friends and colleagues. Confronting your fears is an effective way of keeping your fears under control. In fact, *you gain courage and strength each time you confront your fears.*

2. **Externalize your fears.** If you continue to internalize your high level fears, it can become a "toxic" tornado. You need a way to release and relieve that negative tension from your space; otherwise it will weigh you down and drive you into your lower level (Chapter 6). But don't release your fears on others—imposing fears only reinforces your fears. A better way to relieve your fears is to: (1) honestly disclose your fears to people you trust, (2) discuss your bad fear behaviors and why you need to change, and (3) ask for help and feedback on how to improve. When you discuss your fears openly, tension is released and your fear is taken forward with positive action. *You can't improve your fears unless you externalize them first.* The best time to control and reduce your fears is before it happens, not when fear strikes you. Create hope, not fear in your future.

3. **Verify your fears.** Often your fears are not based on reality but on rumors, gossip, misperceptions and miscommunications. When you externalize your fears and get feedback, find out if your fears are well-founded and how they *really* affect others. Find out the real facts, *verify your fears* and then identify your options. Facts help mitigate fears, so verify before you act.

4. **Don't amplify your fears.** Fear brings out naysayers, cynics, defeatists and pessimists who *amplify* your fears. If you fear a disaster, it doesn't help to listen to stories about bad disasters. When the stock market is diving, it doesn't help to listen to pessimists and "I told you so" naysayers. Bad news only feeds your bad thinking. *Break fearful thinking by avoiding fear mongering.* Keep a balanced perspective—offset your fears with factual information, objective guidance and positive perspectives.

5. **Simplify.** Don't amplify, simplify. Turn down your fears by keeping things simple. The simpler, the better. *Complexity creates more uncertainty and fear.* Do not overwork, over-analyze or over-react to problems—give it a rest. Stepping away can sometimes help you see things simpler and clearer. The most successful solutions are the simplest ones. They are usually easier to explain and implement.

6. **Stay above the fray.** Fear of making mistakes and criticism creates undue stress and pressure. Keep a high perspective—the world will not come to an end if you fail, lose or disappoint other people. People will not hate you or

label you a loser over an honest mistake or misstep. Experiencing failure is part of winning. By keeping a high perspective on the outcome of your actions, your fear will subside. *Don't make it more than it is.* Even if the outcome is bad, the sun will come up tomorrow and you'll have many more opportunities to win next time.

Don't let possible bad outcomes dominate your thinking; consider all good outcomes too. It's okay to play devil's advocate but don't let it drive your decision. Don't let fear destroy your confidence. You can choose your own motivational state—so why not take a positive approach?

7. **Control the process.** You can't eliminate fear but you can control the process. When fear strikes, don't panic; stay level-headed by thinking process. Process the problem or situation at your own pace and comfort. Don't let fear rush you into a decision; take a few deep breaths and relax. Pick a time when you feel well-informed and ready. The worst time to make decisions is when you're most fearful. *Don't let fear control the process.*

8. **De-trigger your fears.** Understand what types of circumstances and issues trigger your worst fears. Once you are able to recognize those situations, take action to mitigate and reduce those fears. For example, if you're worried about meeting a customer's expectations on a project plan, turn in a rough draft or outline early and get some feedback; that action will mitigate and *"de-trigger" your fears.* Be open and honest with your customer: "I'm excited to do this plan and want to do it right and your feedback will help ensure I meet your expectations." When faced with fearful circumstances, always externalize, be open about your fear and control the process.

9. **Accept your in-born fears.** Based on your personality type, recognize and accept your innate fears (Tables 8.1 and Figure 8.2), and keep them on your good side, Categories I and II. You can't eliminate your in-born fears but you can consciously control them. Play away from your fears by asking yourself, *"What would I do if I were not afraid?"*

10. **Trust your instincts.** Don't let people or outside elements frighten you to make a decision that is contrary to your instincts. Consulting with people you trust and gathering different opinions are good practices but make your own decisions. Be logical but *trust your gut feelings* too.

SUMMARY

✓ Personal effectiveness is not achieved through the elimination of fear but rather through the ability to make sound judgments and decisions in the face of fears.

✓ Fear is both a barrier and a catalyst in project management. Fear can hold people back by squeezing their space, making one "small," protective, defensive, risk averse and by driving a person to a lower motivational state (set point). Yet, a low level of fear can give people great energy, focus, urgency, productivity and creativity.

✓ Habitual fears affect personal effectiveness by distorting people's judgment, causing them to act in contrary to their own beliefs and keeping them from pursuing and reaching their goals. Many of the worst behaviors are rooted in fear, such as jealousy, resentment, control, defensiveness, procrastination, anger and perfectionism.

✓ "Pet" fears are pervasive in the workplace and people manage their fears by avoiding, hiding and covering them up, which can be very costly to projects. The four most common fears in project management are fear of failure, rejection, insecurity and conflict.

✓ Fear is like a tornado where a low level of fear stirs emotions and motivates people to perform harder, longer, faster and better, while a high level of fear puts people into a destructive mode of anger, stress, conflict and unhappiness.

✓ Although excessive fear is damaging, people can use fear to their advantage by: (1) being open and honest about their fears; (2) confronting, externalizing and simplifying their fears; (3) not avoiding, hiding, covering and amplifying their fears; and (4) learning to control the process, trusting their instincts and expressing their fears in positive ways (Category I and II behaviors). This chapter provided ten effective strategies for managing fears.

✓ Fear management is a skill that should be treated in the same manner as any skill in project management—it requires training, development and practice. Project managers can improve their motivational effectiveness by understanding the types of fears and how they affect the behavior of individuals and teams.

9

Inclusion
How to stay in the game and win

Project management requires a team effort with a key goal of creating an inclusive work environment where everyone's ideas and contributions are welcomed, respected and valued. No one wants to feel left out, unwanted or excluded, yet at times people may unintentionally ignore others, avoid action, compete against other people, isolate themselves or withdraw socially. It's not uncommon to judge people based on looks and first impressions and not take the time to learn and appreciate the inner qualities of others. Worse yet, people can settle into a comfort zone and resist trying new things, preferring to stick with things that they know, thereby limiting their own potential. In projects, individuals and teams can become complacent, risk-averse and unwilling to change. Being successful requires taking some risks, welcoming new ideas, adapting to change, working with different people and thinking beyond oneself. Having an inclusive work environment is imperative for project success.

It's not uncommon for people to routinely exhibit both inclusionary and exclusionary behaviors, such as choosing whether to participate in activities, engage other people or to accept a new idea or opportunity. Non-engagement or exclusionary behaviors can be defined as the act of omitting or rejecting others and they exist in many different forms. The most common are *competitive* exclusion: a natural tendency to compete over limited resources (Hardin, 1960); *social* exclusion: a lack of societal participation that can result from marginalization or discrimination against others (Hills, Le Grand, and Piachaud, 2002); *workplace* exclusion: ostracism, rejection, retaliation and ignoring others at work (Leary, 2001; Hitlan, Cliffton, and DeSoto, 2006); and *gender* exclusion where women are treated unfairly and given less opportunities than men and vice versa (Hitlan et al., 2006; Mor Barak, Cherin, and Berkman, 1998). Exclusionary behaviors have an adverse effect on not only work performance but also personal health, self-esteem and psychological well-being (Schneider, Hitlan, and Radhakrishnan, 2000). The motivators of inclusion and exclusion come from all three spaces and probably stem from an individual's diversity and need for acceptance, collaboration, control, power and achievement. For project managers, teams and participants, being able to maintain positive, inclusive relationships with others is a constant challenge and a critical behavior for project success.

Inclusion means acceptance, engagement and collaboration, and it entails a commitment to embrace change, new ideas and other people. It's a personal outreach for new experiences and relationships in order to learn, understand and accept others. Inclusion is a desire to learn more about the world, other people and yourself. It's hard to accept others without first accepting yourself, which is who you are, what you believe in and what you truly want in life. As you feel more confident about yourself, you increase self-motivation, personal engagement and inclusive behaviors. In project management, being inclusive means *interacting effectively with others and possessing the interpersonal skills to bring ideas and people together to achieve common goals.*

INCLUSIONARY BEHAVIORS

Having a positive, inclusive interactive style is a key determinant in establishing a positive work relationship with other people. To be an effective project manager, it takes more than planning and technical skills; the true attribute of a leader is being able to motivate superior performance in both themselves *and other people*. The most important personal behaviors for improving leadership and team motivation are:

- **Seek diverse ideas and thinking.** Seek out different ideas, opinions and insights from diverse sources and individuals. Join people together who have different backgrounds, skills and knowledge to solve problems. Encourage people to challenge the status quo and think beyond current boundaries. Welcome creative options in problem-solving and decision-making. Support intelligent risk-taking and debate.
- **Listen, listen and listen.** Give people what they crave for—to be heard, acknowledged and accepted. Improve listening by putting your mind on mute, focusing on the present moment and resisting the urge to talk or judge too quickly. Listening is probably the most effective inclusive behavior in building trust, cooperation and concern for others.
- **Flex work styles to accommodate others.** Consider how others prefer to be treated and modify your behaviors accordingly—live the "platinum rule": treat others as *they* want to be treated; not the "golden rule": treat others how *you* want to be treated. Be proactive by anticipating the interests, concerns and feelings of others.
- **Facilitate agreement.** Work hard to build consensus and involve others in the decision-making process to ensure ownership. Listen with great interest and curiosity, and respect all sides of the issue. Recognize the value of dissenting opinions. Reaching agreement takes a willingness to compromise, take risks and trust others.
- **Be a good role model.** Demonstrate the behaviors that you would like to see in others. "Do what you say you're going to do" and others will take notice.

Not all behaviors are valued equally in an organization so determine priorities and *"model what matters most."*

- **Recognize others.** Praise, reward and reinforce desired behaviors. Give credit when credit is due. Provide timely rewards that are meaningful for the recipient. Reward performance and teamwork, not personalities.
- **Share knowledge.** Knowledge has more power and influence when you generously share it with others by communicating, coaching and mentoring. When you share knowledge, you gain valuable trust in return.

Being inclusive and accepting of others is easier said than done because it requires a mental shift from "me" to "we." It's hard for people to think outside of themselves when they are busy and overloaded with work. They may want to be inclusive but all too often because of people's competitive and fearful nature, they demonstrate the opposite—*exclusion.*

> *Being inclusive. . . requires a mental shift from "me" to "we."*

Exclusionary tendencies cannot be solely attributed to innate selfishness ("me first"). Behaviors are a product of the environment too. By living and working in a highly demanding culture, it's human nature to want to exclude ("fight or flight" response) when the situation is stressful and contentious. When threatened, people become defensive and want to separate. But that's when inclusionary behaviors are needed most and successful project managers have the ability to keep teams together during divisive times. To appreciate this valuable skill, it's important to first understand the underlying motivators of exclusion and inclusion.

EXCLUSION IN PROJECT MANAGEMENT

Exclusion is both a detrimental *intra*personal behavior as well as a harmful *inter*personal behavior within project teams. The ability to engage or disengage is controlled by an individual's human factors and his or her perception of the situation. He or she can choose to speak up, take action and get involved or check out, stay quiet and avoid. Inclusionary and exclusionary behaviors are conscious choices. But what motivates people to speak up, engage and take action in a project? Usually people will engage when they feel compelled enough to act; that is when the situation or subject is sufficiently important to them. For example, if your boss was discussing your team's project schedule and expectations, you would probably be heavily engaged and responsive. The point at which people engage or take action is their "threshold to act" (Figure 9.1). If a person has a low threshold, he or she is more reactive and aggressive in their interactions; if they have a high threshold, they wait longer to act and are more withdrawn and passive. Interpersonally, people are *least effective* when they are too aggressive (low threshold) or too passive (high threshold). This dynamic is captured in the "exclusionary model."

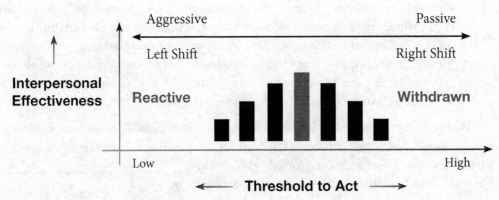

Figure 9.1 Passive and Aggressive Exclusion

Depending on the issue, most people show a range of thresholds—people can be overly competitive, demanding and even dominant at times, and at other times they are more passive, apathetic and withdrawn. But on average everyone carries a baseline threshold: some people are inclined to be more reactive and have a low threshold for action, appearing to the left of the range, while others are more "laid back," tending to be more inactive (high threshold) and behaving to the right. When these far left and right behaviors are practiced in a team setting, such as in meetings, people become *polarized*, creating a conflict of aggressive and passive participants where some people dominate the discussion while others passively listen.

Polarization is a *behavioral paradox*: people on both sides—aggressives (heavy talkers) and passives (heavy listeners)—believe they are accommodating the other party and behaving as a "good team player" when in fact the opposite is occurring: people on the left (aggressives) disdain people who are passive, disengaged and "wimps," and likewise, people on the right (passives) dislike people who are aggressive, dominating and "bullies." Of course, these are the perceptions of each party. Also, what they don't realize is that their own behaviors are encouraging the unwanted behavior in the other party—passivity fosters aggression and vice versa. This dynamic process leads to polarization, exclusion, poor decision-making and hard feelings. As a project manager, *your interpersonal effectiveness in leading and participating in project teams depends on how well you can avoid this behavioral paradox.*

Passive: Right Shift

When people work together in project meetings and teams, they have a choice in how they wish to participate. They can shift left and speak up or shift right and check out. As they shift to the right, they become more passive, indifferent and withdrawn. Why do people go passive at times? What is their thinking? What is holding them back? When people refrain from speaking or taking action, their internal voice may say:

- "What I say (or do) won't matter."
- "I'll wait and see what others say (or do) first."
- "I don't want to speak (or act) out of turn."
- "I'm not sure if I fully understood it."
- "I'm not sure if it's my place to say (or do) anything."
- "I don't want to stick my neck out."
- "I don't want to say something wrong."
- "I need to think about it some more."
- "I don't want to speak up and hold things up."

Passives talk themselves into being non-participants and they move to the right. This is an act of *self-exclusion*. They let others go first; wait for permission to speak; don't want to get involved; don't want to take any chances and say, "It's not worth my energy" and they take the safe way out. No one likes conflict or confrontation and shifting to the right is a common passive-avoidance behavior in project teams.

Aggressive: Left Shift

Team behaviors can also shift to the left. This happens when people are over-excited, anxious, arrogant and competitive. When they are overly aggressive, they talk over people, opine about everything and dominate the conversation. These are acts of *interpersonal exclusion*. When people talk more and listen less, cut off others and refuse to compromise, they are shifting their behaviors to the left. When they move too far left, they are overly critical, demanding and intimidating, which cause people to flee—they are excluding, annoying and scaring people away. This behavior is often driven by impatience, intolerance and ego.

Impatience

One common cause for exclusionary behavior is impatience, which is an inability to endure delays and waiting. Impatience is a left shift behavior that is accompanied by feelings of frustration, irritation, discomfort, stress, anxiety and anger.

Impatience is an external conflict of *process* and *efficiency* and an internal need for *certainty* and *control*. For example, Charlie is a project manager waiting in line at the county offices for a permit to start a new construction project. Charlie has his hands full of blueprints, maps and work plans to show to the county officials but he expects to get through the process quickly. To his disappointment, he finds only one county clerk at the counter and

> *Impatience is an external conflict of process and efficiency and an internal need for certainty and control.*

about six people ahead of him. After waiting fifteen minutes, he grows impatient as the one clerk is chatting with contractors and appears oblivious to the line of people waiting. His legs are getting tired from standing and there are no seats in the waiting area. Each minute passes like eternity. He grows increasingly tense. While other contractors seem unfazed, Charlie is starting to act impatient, giving evil stares at the clerk and even venting some sarcastic remarks. He looks for the office manager or another clerk to open more stations but he sees no one else. After another minute, he sees no progress; gives a big sigh and walks out in a huff. Of course, no one else seems affected by all this, and in fact, right after he leaves, two more clerks show up and the other people waiting are happily served. Why do people like Charlie have such lack of patience?

Impatience is a *learned behavior* that is shaped by extrinsic and intrinsic factors. Culture is a key extrinsic factor that contributes to impatience. The human attention span gets shorter and shorter each year, which may be related to the faster pace of life, need for instant gratification, increasing speed of communications, fast food and many other extrinsic factors. This drives people to expect faster turnaround and become dissatisfied when the rate of progress is not meeting their expectations.

Other than efficiency, patience is also a dissatisfaction of process. People don't like waiting in line, waiting to connect with friends, waiting for service and so forth. They hate it because they have *no control* over the process (the process of waiting in line is controlled by the clerk and county office) and they have *no certainty* over the wait time. So they are left feeling hapless, helpless and out of control.

By understanding the motivations behind impatience, people can regain patience by simply gaining more certainty and control over the process. How is this done? It's simple—*change the process*. If you hate standing in line, change the process by bringing your smartphone or tablet and do some reading or emailing while you're waiting in line. That way, you have full control and certainty of the process. That's why stores put candy bars, magazines and various sundries alongside checkout aisles to *change the process*—you are not standing in line, you're still shopping! Also, hotels change processes by putting mirrors by elevators so that people can patiently primp themselves instead of getting angry over a slow elevator. In congested freeway areas, electronic billboards show drive times to common destinations to give people a sense of control and certainty in their journey, thus avoiding impatient behaviors, such as road rage. *Having a sense of control and certainty is a psychological remedy for impatience.*

Changing the process is a good temporary fix but for sustained results, the change must occur internally. Patience is a learned behavior and if practiced often, can lead to a permanent improvement in the level of patience. Start by learning to wait with more patience in low stress situations, like driving in the slow lane when traffic is light, letting another person go ahead of you in line, taking a longer route to the store, or listening longer before speaking in meetings; then slowly move up to more challenging processes, such as standing in a long line, attending a long meeting, shopping at the mall during weekends or going to a crowded social event.

Each person has their individual tolerance for impatience and each must find their own recipe for improvement, but frequent practice is the secret.

When people's "need" for progress (self-purpose) and control (well-being) is not satisfied, internal tension builds unless they are in good mental shape to be patient. Such mental fitness can only be developed through frequent practice and self-control. Instead of relying on hotel mirrors and other mental gimmicks, learn to use your own processes (e.g., smartphones, tablets, music, e-books, and so forth) to break the feelings of impatience. Try to practice feeling in control and relaxed even when things are not moving as fast as you like. Despite what you may feel at the time, time is relative and you are always in control of your own feelings and actions.

With the heavy stress and processes in projects, project managers and teams are always at risk for impatient behaviors. An effective project manager uses efficient processes, empowers people with responsibilities and control, and has a robust work plan that builds confidence, order and certainty.

EFFECTS OF RIGHT AND LEFT SHIFTS

Large shifts to the right or left are *exclusionary behaviors.* When people are aggressive, reactive and overly competitive, they *exclude other people;* when people are passive, apathetic and indifferent, they *exclude themselves.* These are self-centered, self-serving, non-collaborative behaviors, a shift from "we" to "me." "Passives" invite other people to lead, speak and act for them; they're just along for the ride—risk-free, trouble-free and efficient. A move to the left is also controlling because "aggressives" want to control the decisions, get attention and have things go their way. Both of these exclusionary behaviors are rooted in fear. For passives, the fear is conflict and criticism; for aggressives, it's the fear of failure and criticism. Fear drives people to the "outside"—left and right—which causes polarization and selfishness. The role of the project manager is to prevent these "shifty" behaviors and maintain a well-balanced team dynamic.

Why Aren't You Listening?

Another by-product of moving to the extreme left and right is *poor listening.* The aggressive personality type is so hyper-reactive and self-absorbed that their listening shuts down. The minds of competitive personality types are so preoccupied with *winning* ("I'm right and you're wrong") that they have no room for listening. Their minds are so busy formulating the next remark that any incoming information is lost. On the other side, passives are pre-occupied with *not losing* and they shut down when they feel overloaded, bullied or threatened. It's like a circuit breaker going off, "This is too much, I'm going to shut down to protect my mind." In either case, poor listening by either types leads to poor teamwork, ineffective communications, misunderstandings and exclusion of others.

Fear drives people to the "outside" which causes polarization.

At times everyone exhibits exclusionary behaviors to the left (exclude others) or to the right (exclude yourself). They are not limited to strong dominating or avoidance type of behaviors. In fact, most exclusionary behaviors are subtle and occur more frequently than people think. People are usually accepting of "quiet" exclusionary behaviors, but they can have profound effects on project teams. Table 9.1 lists some popular left and right exclusionary behaviors.

Shifting either right or left is a withdrawing behavior, an unwillingness to show oneself, hiding behind passivity or aggression. Are you more right- or left-oriented in your interactive behaviors? On average, is your "threshold to act" relatively low (reactive) or high (passive)? The secret is to recognize the circumstances that drive you to the right or left and to understand how these shifts in your behaviors affect your personal effectiveness and influence. Try to stay involved, collaborative and centered and avoid escaping within yourself.

Aggressive-Passive and Passive-Aggressive Behaviors

Two related exclusionary behaviors, aggressive-passive and passive-aggressive, are frequent behaviors in project teams. These left-right and right-left shifts are negative behaviors that are *double exclusionary*—you are *excluding both yourself and other people;* the only difference is in the order of the behavior.

Table 9.1 Left and Right Exclusionary Behaviors

Left Behaviors (Excluding Others)	Right Behaviors (Excluding Yourself)
• Interrupting others	• Avoiding conflict and confrontation
• Losing your temper/patience	• No eye contact/withdrawing
• Not returning emails	• Resisting change
• Not praising, recognizing others	• Absenteeism/presenteeism
• Intolerance	• Reluctant to try something new
• Criticizing others	• Procrastination
• Defensiveness	• Not volunteering
• Doing things alone	• Not speaking up, backing off
• Not sharing info with others	• Saying what others want to hear
• Not listening to others	• Avoid making decisions
• Favoritism, cronyism	• Close-minded to new ideas
• Correcting other people	• Not networking
• Bragging	• Not accepting responsibility
• Sarcasm	• Being too self-critical
• Overly competitive	• Waiting for permission
• Over-analyzing	• Excessive self-doubt and regret
• Autocratic	• Martyrdom
• Stubborn—won't acknowledge defeat	• Self-deprecation: "I'm no good"
• False praise—insincerity	

Aggressive-passive behaviors occur when people use aggressive, controlling behaviors first and then use self-exclusion as a means of punishing the other party. Aggressive-passive behaviors are often used in attempt to persuade, threaten or manipulate others, e.g., "Take it or leave it— if you don't take this offer now, I won't be making another one"; "If you say that again, I'm leaving this meeting" or "If you don't play right, I'm going to take my ball and go home." When things aren't going their way, aggressive-passive people issue ultimatums in an attempt to get immediate cooperation. But rarely does extreme aggression lead to positive collaboration and most ultimatums are false threats. Far left or aggressive behaviors don't cause people to support you; it annoys and scares people away and you're left (passively) alone. For example, a colleague at work shared a painful experience that she had with her project team:

"Last week, an incident happened at a team conference call that triggered both extreme aggressive and passive behaviors in me. One team member disdainfully pointed out that I had corrupted the team's scheduling tool and it was causing problems for the other team members. I felt angry that I had been singled out publicly when the team member could have handled it privately with me. As I became more defensive, another person attacked and criticized me even more. I became overly reactive and sarcastic, and dumped all my emotional baggage on the team. The discussion soon spiraled out of control and I recognized my inability to regain control. I knew it, and I froze. At this point, I completely withdrew, stopped discussing and put my phone on mute. This caused the meeting to completely derail. However, it was my way of manipulating others, though I did not see it at the time. If I had just understood the exclusionary model before this, I would have been able to shift myself right and left to get closer to the middle. Instead, I made big swings to the left and right and ruined the meeting."

This example illustrates that aggressive-passive behaviors polarize people and destroy good teamwork, decision-making and team dynamics. Initially, people act in anger or frustration and then grieve or shut down after the battle. In contrast, when people are unable to express their emotions openly, they may resort to classical "passive-aggressive" behaviors where they self-exclude first (e.g., avoid, falsely agree, abstain) and then covertly express their displeasure later (aggressively exclude others); e.g., "I took the action item to get her to stop talking, but I'm not going to follow through"; "I told her that I would support her idea, but I'm going to veto it later." Insecure, fearful managers are prone to display these behaviors. Perhaps when it comes to conflict, it's a "pay me now" (aggressive-passive) or "pay me later" (passive-aggressive) scenario, but "pay me later" behaviors (passive-aggressive) are usually more hurtful.

Aggressive-passive and passive-aggressive behaviors are triggered when people feel criticized, stressed or fearful, which are "lower level" states of mind. Both sets of behaviors are *emotional vents* that are deployed to de-pressurize personal threats and fears. Dramatic aggressive and passive behaviors occur when people are pushed down and compressed into their lower dynamic state (Chapter 6). Aggressive-passives and passive-aggressives are double-losers—they exclude themselves and other people. In conflict situations, stay centered and seek a "win-win" rather than a "lose-lose."

EFFECTS OF EXCLUSION ON PROJECT TEAMS

Exclusionary behaviors have other undesirable side effects on project teams—they limit creativity, flexibility and new ideas. When people withdraw from the discussion or aggressively impose their views on others, they are not only repressing discussion but also hurting teamwork and learning. Failing to raise legitimate concerns diminishes the quality of decisions because teams are not made aware of other alternatives. Passivity or aggression results in narrowed thinking and biased decision-making. The longer exclusionary behaviors are tolerated, the more momentum builds behind the status quo (no change). The rationale to "pick your battles," "stay loyal to your superiors" or "wait for a better time to speak up" are excuses for not having the courage to break groupthink (Janis, 1972).

Like fear and a low set point, exclusionary behaviors can reduce inner strength, motivation (increasing "need" over "want"), accountability and self-confidence. Escaping, self-excluding and avoiding other people are self-destructive behaviors. When project teams ignore each other, don't take chances, resist changes or limit ideas, they are denying themselves new opportunities to learn, grow and expand influence.

Behavioral Creep

Repeatedly accepting exclusionary behaviors in yourself or other people can result in *behavioral creep* where a person's "threshold to act" gradually drifts to the left or right over time. This is analogous to *project scope creep* when repeated uncontrolled changes of work are added to the project. For people who creep to the left ("left-creepers"), the threshold to speak up or take action is quicker, more impatient; they interrupt and correct others, rush late to appointments, excessively criticize people, and are more demanding, autocratic and short-tempered. As a result, left-creepers are never satisfied, always pushing, always controlling, unwilling to compromise and leaving people twisting in their wake. What may seem like a harmless, infrequent, aggressive behavior can shift over time into a behavioral norm. Since they are so critical and demanding of others and themselves, their threshold for achievement goes higher and higher, and it becomes harder to have fun and enjoy themselves. Left-creepers can become more "centered" by taking things less seriously, seeking to experience life rather than control it, and rediscovering the fun and joy in the world.

On the "right" side, passives can suffer the same effects by moving too far right and setting low internal expectations. When they keep letting things go, avoiding conflicts, and allowing others to take all the risks and credits, they can find themselves creeping to the far right and becoming mere spectators at work. These "right-creepers" become mentally apathetic and remote. It's a shame when people start off involved and engaged in a project, and for some reason over time, they become progressively inactive, uncaring, routine and "creepy"—they have lost their motivation. People *settle into a comfort zone* where they resist change, don't take any risks and prefer the status quo. Their attitude is: "Don't rock the boat"; "If it ain't broke, don't fix it" and "That's the way we've always done it." Settling into a comfort zone robs people of the opportunity to do great things.

Behavioral shifts to the left and right are normal reactions. It's okay to have occasional passive and aggressive moments, but when these moments become days and these days turn into weeks, people can suddenly find themselves isolated and disengaged from others and subsequently lose sight of success. When people set overly high internal expectations or overly low expectations, they are setting themselves up for self-disappointment and when they fall short, they end up beating themselves up.

BEHAVIORAL CREEP INCREASES PERSONAL AND PROJECT RISKS

This gradual creep in exclusionary behaviors is easily rationalized and accepted because comfort zones feel safe and are self-reinforcing. People can settle into a comfort zone and stay stuck for years.

The risk in creeping too far left or right is that it takes much more time and energy to get centered again. The further and longer people stay to the right or left, the longer it will take to return to center. It's like when a person routinely drives in the faster left lane on the freeway for years and then suddenly is required to drive in the slower right lane. The person is so psychologically accustomed to driving in the left lane that driving in the right lane (or vice versa) becomes a torture chamber— they go nuts trying to adapt. Driving in the far left or right lanes has become a need (Chapter 4). People are more "needy" when their behaviors creep too far right or left and that's why it's so difficult for people to accept change sometimes.

Another example of "creepy" behaviors is in people's seating habits at meetings. Many people are psychologically accustomed to sitting in the back of the room, on the aisle or near a door. They need to have a sense of control and avoid feeling trapped. When behaviors creep to one side, thinking becomes rigid and complacent. Project managers are known to get too rigid on reporting formats, work plans, processes and tools—they don't want to change or take any risks. When mental flexibility is limited, personal and project effectiveness are drastically reduced. Thinking becomes defensive, controlling, self-centered and skeptical of new ideas and other people. Successful project managers are flexible, open-minded and never "creepy."

Behavioral Creep Befalls the Challenger Project

It appears that a form of behavioral creep led to a tragic accident for the National Aeronautics and Space Administration (NASA) on January 28, 1986 when the Space Shuttle Challenger disintegrated seventy-three seconds into its flight, killing all seven crew members after an O-ring seal in its solid rocket booster failed. NASA's culture and decision-making processes were key contributing factors to the accident. In the Report of the Presidential Commission on the Space Shuttle Challenger Accident (1986), NASA and Thiokol accepted escalating risk apparently because they "got away with it last time." According to Commissioner Feynman, the decision making was: "a kind of Russian roulette...(the Shuttle) flies (with O-ring erosion) and nothing happens. Then it is suggested, therefore, that the risk is no longer so high for the next flights. We can lower our standards a little bit because we got away with it last time. You got away with it, but it shouldn't be done over and over again like that." People silently accepted an intolerable operating condition; they chose to creep to the right and allowed the safety problem to persist.

In project management, people learn to live with certain risks and abnormalities in their projects and tolerate them even though they know it's wrong. They *slowly tolerate an unacceptable condition (creep)*, ignoring it in their minds and raising their threshold to act. It's like driving your car above the speed limit a bit more each day and nothing happens—until one day, you experience a near fatal speeding accident. Too often, organizations and people accept these types of exclusionary behaviors in their projects with heart-breaking consequences.

MENTAL FLEXIBILITY

Under pressure, rational and artisan personality types shift to the left, while guardians and idealists lean to the right—aggressives go dominant while passives withdraw. The secret is to stay centered, feel comfortable driving in "all lanes of traffic" and stay mentally flexible. People creep to the right or left because they don't have the ability to *flex* their behaviors. "Flexing" means having the ability to act passively and aggressively with others to achieve mutual agreement and satisfaction—they're able to give and take, ask and tell, and lead and follow. The center zone is a collaborative space where people are willing to work together to find a win-win solution. Moving one's threshold to the center (your *"sweet spot"*) enables people to achieve more mutual victories and respect (Figure 9.2).

Improving Your Mental Gears

People who are stuck in the far right or left are operating on one mental gear, while people who are centered are using multiple gears. It's like riding a ten-speed bike versus a one-speed bike. Having a flexible range of passive to aggressive behaviors provides extra mental gears, enabling people to conquer those uphill challenges.

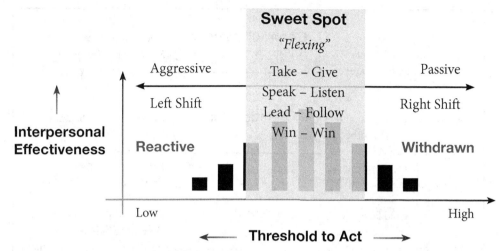

Figure 9.2 Inclusionary Behavioral Model

Just as people need multiple spaces to help them stay physically fit (Chapter 5), people need multiple inclusionary "gears" to stay mentally fit.

Managing inclusionary and exclusionary behaviors is vital to personal and team success. To be an effective project manager, one needs to have the ability to show compassion and sensitivity as well as assertiveness and competitiveness. Not having mental flexibility limits personal effectiveness. People stuck to the far left (always pushing, acting aggressively toward others) who are suddenly called upon to show patience and sensitivity will likely appear disingenuous, tight and uncomfortable. Conversely, habitually passive people who try to act aggressive and assertive will probably appear over-reactive, rude and over-bearing. Effective project managers are mentally-centered, sincere and flexible in their interactive behaviors, inspiring teamwork and collaboration. Being centered and flexible takes continual practice and behavioral change. Practice is what greases your mental gears.

ASSESSING YOUR INCLUSIONARY BEHAVIORS

Complete the assessment in Figure 9.3 to determine your current level of inclusionary and exclusionary behaviors under five main categories:

- Communications: How you share, listen and convey information.
- Relationship: How you regard and relate to others.
- Equity: How you view your impartiality and fairness.
- Control: How you prefer to work.
- Collaboration: How you view your interactions with others.

For each category, inclusionary and exclusionary behaviors are listed at either end of the scale. For each one, rate your personal behaviors from a scale of 1 to 5. A "1" or "2"

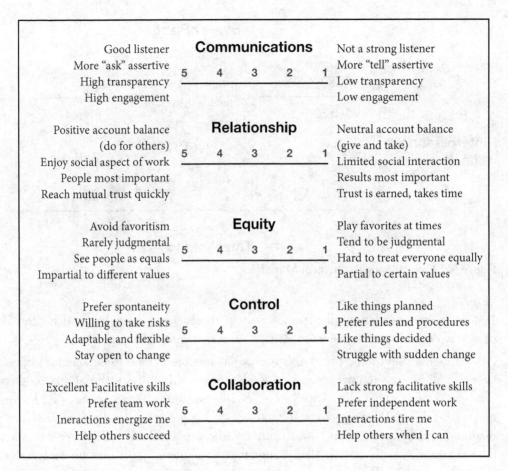

Figure 9.3 Inclusion-Exclusion Assessment

score implies that you exhibit *exclusionary behaviors more often* than inclusionary behaviors for that category, and a "4" or "5" score suggests you show *inclusionary behaviors more often*. A "3" score indicates that you show both behaviors equally for that category.

Which categories do you show the strongest and weakest inclusionary behaviors? No one is perfectly inclusionary or exclusionary—it's a range. Everyone has tendencies to exclude themselves or others given the right circumstances. The challenge is to avoid excessive exclusionary behaviors and avoid those circumstances that induce those behaviors.

HOW TO BE MORE INCLUSIVE

Here are six good strategies for strengthening your inclusionary behaviors:

1. **Broaden your thinking.** Be open to new ideas and opinions, and seek to understand other points of view. Challenge yourself to new experiences, continue to learn and be willing to try new things. Break out of your comfort

zone and do something different. Expanding your experiences broadens your values and diversity.

2. **Set realistic internal expectations.** When your internal expectations are too high or too low, you are creating unreasonable pressure to over- or under-perform, respectively. This tendency to push yourself harder and harder (to the left) or avoid and relinquish your personal desires (and move to the right) will likely lead to unhappiness and dissatisfaction over time. Setting realistic expectations will free you from this self-imposed pressure.

3. **Build more mental gears.** Expand your "sweet spot" by gaining more variety and flexibility in your behaviors. Practice being accommodative and assertive under different circumstances and find a balance within yourself (Table 9.2). Balance means having control of your passive and aggressive behaviors.

4. **Avoid polarizing.** Do not allow your behaviors to shift too quickly to the left or right. Achieve a good balance in your behaviors. Seek common ground and win-win solutions during disagreements and use a communication style that appeals to all parties. Be sensitive to others, have a strong self-awareness, seek feedback on your interactive style and make corrections as needed.

5. **Diversify your environment.** Creating new surroundings can help you adapt and embrace new ideas and people. A change of scenery is always good for the soul. Buy new clothes, redecorate your home or office, find a new way to work, join a club, try a new sport or hobby, meet new people or buy a comic book. Break out of your comfort zone at work by power-walking during lunch time, taking yoga or joining an employee club or network.

6. **Build social and professional networks.** Build a community of friends and colleagues for mutual support, learning and fun. Constantly seek to expand knowledge and influence with other people.

Table 9.2 Tips for Building Mental Gears

Actions for Aggressives	Actions for Passives
■ Solicit help and opinions from others	■ You have good opinions, express them more often
■ Listen and understand first	■ Volunteer to lead assignments
■ Respond, don't react	■ Ask more questions
■ "Let it go!"— Is being right that important?	■ Make eye contact in conversations
■ Be more sensitive and compassionate to others	■ State clearly what you want
■ Invite others to speak first	■ Be transparent—share your thoughts and feelings behind your words
■ Resist correcting every mistake, "suffer fools gladly"	■ Be visible—sit in front, get involved, show yourself
■ Be more "ask" assertive	■ Take more risks—stretch yourself, use your many talents
■ Praise and encourage others	

Thinking inclusively occurs when you take on a project that you have never done before, listen to new types of music, go to new places, experience different cultures, meet new people and take that trip that you were afraid to take. *If you're always practical, do something impractical; if you're always a planner, do something spontaneous, and if you're always serious, do something hilarious.* Embrace, engage and enjoy new experiences and avoid settling into an exclusionary lifestyle. It doesn't take much—the world is full of endless opportunities and fun.

SUMMARY

✓ Inclusion means acceptance, engagement and collaboration, and it entails a commitment to embrace change, new ideas and other people.

✓ In the absence of inclusionary behavior, people are prone to be exclusionary by default. Based on the exclusionary model, overly aggressive people exclude others (left shift), while overly passive individuals are self-excluding (right shift). When left and right behaviors are practiced in a team setting, people become *polarized*.

✓ Two important skills in project management are patience and listening. Impatience is a left shift behavior motivated by an external conflict of *process* and *efficiency* and an internal need for *certainty* and *control*. Poor listening results from shifting too far left or right, which leads to poor communications, misunderstandings and exclusion.

✓ In conflict situations, it's better to pursue a win-win and not a win-lose outcome with other people. Avoid the use of aggressive-passive and passive-aggressive behaviors, which are lose-lose behaviors.

✓ Behavioral creep occurs when a person's "threshold to act" gradually drifts to the left or right over time and settles into a comfort zone. When behaviors creep to one side, thinking becomes rigid and complacent. When mental flexibility is limited, personal and project effectiveness are reduced, sometimes with tragic results.

✓ People who demonstrate passive or aggressive exclusion are stuck in one gear. People who are centered and inclusionary are using multiple gears and are able to *flex* their behaviors to work collaboratively with others.

✓ Strive to maintain an inclusive mindset: flex your thinking to include other points of view, expand your breadth of knowledge, learn more about other people and invite new things into your life. It's about shifting from "me" to "we" and hitting your "sweet spot" (being centered in your behaviors).

✓ This chapter provided a self-assessment for measuring your inclusionary-exclusionary balance and provided six effective strategies for improving your inclusionary behaviors.

10

How to "Turn the Corner" for Achievement

Personal effectiveness is making the right decisions and taking the right actions that lead to positive consequences and achievements. In project management, achievement is meeting the goals and expectations of the project and it requires the ability to plan, initiate and complete challenging tasks. *Personal achievement* involves three mental behaviors—self-confidence, inner strength and accountability:

- Self-confidence is the belief in oneself and ability to take action (and occurs *before* the action).
- Inner strength is mental toughness and determination (and occurs *during* the action).
- Accountability is taking responsibility for the action, outcome, judgment and consequence (and occurs *after* the action).

In the personal effectiveness cycle, converting motivation to achievement is the hardest and most critical part of the cycle because it represents the ability to take action, even in the face of many mental barriers, such as self-doubt, fear, negative internal dialogue, exclusion and personal distrust. Mustering the courage and confidence to "turn the corner," which means *achieving* project tasks and goals, produces tremendous personal power (Figure 10.1). In fact, this is the "turning point" in the cycle where winners are separated from losers, doers from talkers, and players from spectators. *This is what enables ordinary people to do extraordinary things.* The difference between low and high performing project managers is in their ability to consistently make this turn—to complete their work with excellence and attain achievement.

People who cannot make this turn and struggle with the motivation-achievement part of the cycle are your "woulda, coulda, shoulda" crowd. These are people who say things like: "I *woulda* done it if I knew it was important"; "With more training, I *coulda* done a better job"; or "I messed up, I *shoulda* spoken up earlier." These are people who can't keep promises, are low performers, and can't finish what they start—they "want to" achieve but somehow can't. To make matters worse, these "woulda, coulda, shoulda" people are also *but* people: "I *coulda* finished the

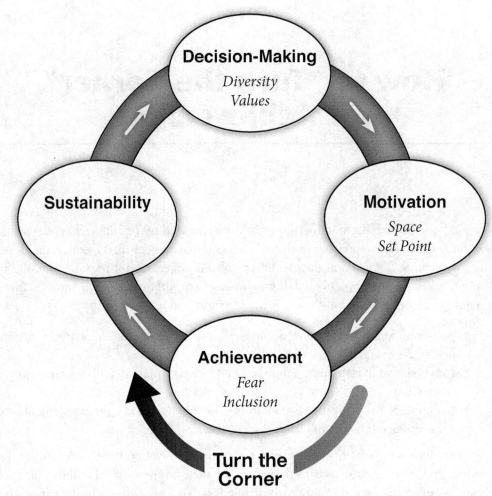

Figure 10.1 Achievement Requires "Turning the Corner"

project *but* I didn't know what the deadline was." "I *woulda* been a manager *but* they wouldn't give me a chance." "But" people can't make the turn and fall by the wayside. The bottom of the cycle is filled with unsuccessful people who can't make this turn. However, at one time or another everyone fails to make this turn.

WHY IS "TURNING THE CORNER" SO HARD?

"Turning the corner" in project management is performing with excellence, which takes skills, knowledge, motivation, confidence, courage and faith. Unfortunately, for many project tasks and goals, "turning the corner" is inhibited by five mental barriers: *fear, unwanted consequences, lack of ownership, backward thinking and downward pressures.*

   1. **Fear.** As discussed in Chapters 8 and 9, fear can distort thinking, lower motivation, reduce self-confidence and keep you from turning the corner.

Fear is like entering a dark room—you're feeling uncertain, not in control and cautious. You want to go in but you're a bit wary, suspicious and worried about what may happen, causing you to hesitate, wait, exclude or retreat within yourself. Self-confidence gets you into the door but what does it take to get through it and conquer the darkness?

2. **Unwanted consequences.** Turning the corner in project management requires courage, strength and the right set of behaviors. Motivation to achieve is determined by the consequences that follow behaviors and there are four possible consequences:

- No consequences, nothing happens (N)
- Behavior is punished (P)
- Behavior is negatively reinforced (R−)
- Behavior is positively reinforced (R+)

Turning the corner is tough because three of the four consequences are things that people don't want: N, P and R−. Only one of the four is favorable—positive reinforcement (R+)—so quantitatively the deck is stacked against you. You can't beat the "house" with those "odds"—it's a loser's game. Don't rely on external consequences for motivation. Turn the table and bet in your favor by finding ways to self-consequent, self-recognize and take pride in your behaviors and achievements. It's your choice: you can internalize and take control, or externalize and play the "house" game and suffer with R−'s, N's and P's. You can't control the outcome or other people's behaviors but you can control your own consequences. You need to *act as your own champion* and achieve a good balance between internal and external consequences.

3. **Lack of ownership.** Turning the corner is a challenge because people usually don't own their goals. Most of their goals are defined by organizational and team spaces. If you choose your own goals then the chances of making the turn are higher. However, most people don't have that luxury and must work on things they dislike or "have to" do. For example, typical work goals are "satisfy your customers," "meet the expectations of your sponsor," and "support your project team and organization." These are important goals but *do you really own them?*

Your motivations and behaviors are shaped by people, processes and consequences outside your personal space. Without strong personal ownership, the task or goal is driven by your "need" to avoid negative consequences, such as losing your job or having conflicts with your boss. The best approach for higher achievement is to own your goals.

4. **Backward thinking.** Another barrier to achievement in project management is the reluctance to try new approaches or to accept change. People can be too tethered to old dogmas, paradigms, comfort zones and "that's the way

Applying old solutions to new problems is incremental thinking.

we always do it" mindsets. Practical experience is invaluable but new problems require new solutions and you can't live in the past to solve current and future problems. Applying old solutions to new problems is *incremental thinking*, which may be acceptable for small problems, but to do great things and find great solutions, it requires *step changes* that are special, unique and elite.

5. **Downward pressures.** Another reason why it's tough to make the turn is because motivation (Chapter 7) and set point (Chapter 6) are subject to many downward pressures, such as interpersonal conflicts, stress, work-life imbalance, fear, regrets and negative consequences. For example, when people receive punishment or negative feedback, these experiences can turn into mental baggage and weigh people down emotionally. Instead of accepting R−'s, N's and P's as temporary setbacks, people let them linger, which reduces self-confidence, inner strength and accountability. To avoid this effect, seek to forgive yourself and avoid carrying the burden of self-disappointments. Forgive and move on.

WHAT DOES IT TAKE TO "TURN THE CORNER?" INNER STRENGTH AND ACCOUNTABILITY

Inner Strength

Achievement starts with self-confidence, which is the ability to take action in the face of uncertain outcomes. Inner strength is having the *mental toughness and determination* to beat the five mental barriers and not give up—to have the ability to "go through the dark room." It's a frame of mind that says, "I want to take action and I will persist and achieve because I am not afraid of criticism, rejection or making mistakes; in fact, I welcome it. I do not fear losing. I am more fearful of not playing and not having a chance to win—I can't win by being a spectator." When people have this belief, they have the inner strength to speak confidently from their space. They're not worried about being judged, competing with others or waiting for permission to act—inner strength is an internal, self-generated force.

When people possess inner strength, they're *not* afraid to show themselves. Great project managers don't mind people challenging their opinions or testing their resolve. In fact, the harsher the feedback the better; it makes them stronger. They say, "Bring it on!" "Give me your best shot!" People can train their minds to not only accept new challenges but to welcome them. They know these challenges will awaken their spirit and build their confidence. They gladly invite feedback—they do not personalize criticism but see *feedback as a gift*. **Inner strength re-frames the challenge** and gives you more energy, courage and self-trust to show who you are and pursue what you want.

Self-confidence initiates action; inner strength is the mental toughness and determination behind the actions. But how do you increase inner strength? Mental toughness and determination are derived from increased *mental* capacity and persistence, respectively.

- **Mental toughness takes capacity.** The more mental capacity you have, the more strength you have. You increase strength by regularly challenging yourself to do harder things. Each time you complete a hard task, overcome a tough barrier or achieve a difficult goal, you gain capacity and mental strength from that experience. Also, each time you show patience, good listening, constraint and unselfishness, you are storing up mental capacity that you can draw on later. With every extra effort, you are building more *mental muscle* to handle new challenges.

  Essentially every project requires some degree of mental toughness, whether it is working in manufacturing, medicine, engineering, academia or government. Through intensive training, drills and experiences, people are able to accomplish difficult tasks. Without that background, people would not have had the internal capacity to succeed at work. Hard lessons, setbacks, bad experiences and even failures increase mental capacity and toughness. It is in the struggle that people gain the strength they need; remember, each time you do something difficult, you are "banking" more mental capacity.

- **Determination takes persistence.** Building mental persistence is part of developing inner strength. You may have the mental capacity to do tough jobs but how long can you go before you have to stop? How long is your concentration? How long can you work on a task before mental fatigue sets in? It depends on the task but it also depends on your state of mind. Persistence is another learned mental behavior.

  A good case in point occurred at a local terminal where a temporary worker had the task of cleaning large storage tanks in the summer. What made this task particularly difficult was not the task itself but the personal protective equipment that the worker had to wear (respirator, gloves, eye protection, coveralls) in order to work in a confined space. Initially, he struggled to work even fifteen minutes. He was physically very strong, in great shape and received good training, but he lacked concentration and stamina because he was mentally unaccustomed to working in protective equipment and confined space. He was not physically tired but mentally strained. He wanted to quit. But after learning to pace his work and adapting to the personal safety equipment and confined work space, he was able to work almost as long as the veterans after three weeks. It took much longer for his mind than his body to adapt to the task. With more experience he became acclimated to the environment and his productivity improved dramatically. Of course, once he finished for the summer, he lost mental stamina for the task and had to build it up again the next summer but he adapted quicker the second time. This applies to any demanding activity, whether it is swimming, reading, driving or even listening. When people have mental stamina, they improve their persistence to solve problems and "stay in the game." This is called *staying power*, the ability to stick with a goal and see things through to the end.

Turning the corner is the ability to take successful actions and achieving. Bad fears and exclusion can be defeated by having the self-confidence to initiate action and the inner strength—mental toughness and determination—to tackle challenging problems and see them through to completion. The next step is learning how to deal with the results from one's actions, which is accountability.

ACCOUNTABILITY

Accountability means to accept personal responsibility, bear the consequences for one's actions, complete the action and "conquer the darkness." You're not afraid to

Accountability means taking responsibility for both the outcome and the judgment of the results.

say, "That was hard," "I messed up," or "I need to try again," and move forward. This is not a self-indulging, self-defeating behavior but an honest one with great self-trust. You readily accept the outcome, whether it is favorable or unfavorable. Successful project managers gladly accept personal accountability because they're not afraid of the consequences (i.e., "So what if I fail, I will survive and learn from whatever happens."). They are able to forgive themselves and move on (i.e., "live and learn") because effective *self-accountability re-frames the consequences*.

When things go wrong in a project, it's easy to point fingers and blame the organization, the system or other people for the failure. It's easy to find faults in organizational and team spaces; it's always easier to blame problems on a larger space and hide behind organizational and team spaces. People control their own personal space and "owning up" to one's actions and behaviors is accountability.

Improving Personal Accountability for Project Managers

The best strategy for improving accountability is to own the outcome, judgment, responsibility and consequences for your decisions and actions:

- **Own the outcome and judgment.** As with any challenge, failure is always a possible outcome. But success and failure are only relative, temporary effects. Goals are objectives, outcomes are the results but how you interpret those results (judgment) makes a big difference in how well you accept the outcome and move forward. Anytime you miss the target (outcome or result), you can internally or externally interpret that result (judgment) as a failure, disappointment or learning.

Too often people rely on others and external measures to interpret the outcome, which implies that they are allowing others to judge them. Accountability means taking responsibility for *both* the outcome *and* the judgment of the results. To improve your personal accountability, don't let others judge whether you are a failure or not—you make the *judgment* of the outcome.

By owning both the outcome *and* the interpretation of the results, you can more easily accept failure as a temporary setback and valuable learning experience. Owning both improves your self-confidence and resolve to try again. By believing that a "miss" is not failure but progress, it encourages you to accept the outcome and move forward.

It's difficult to hit the "bull's-eye" with one try, but the willingness to accept risks is a mental behavior that will not only increase your ability to act but also increase your persistence and opportunities to win. If you program your mind to accept a temporary setback as a "loss," you will surely lose, and when that happens enough times, your mind becomes "trained to lose"; moreover, when faced with adversity, you automatically assume defeat. But on the other hand, you can control what you think and you have the ability to reframe and reprogram your mind to become "trained to win"—a loss or a miss is viewed as: (1) "I am one step closer to success"; (2) "I am motivated to try again and again"; and (3) "I will try new ways to win."

- **Take the responsibility, not the blame.** You have the power to choose your own feelings, behaviors and actions. Even under the most stressful situations, you have the ability to transcend different behavioral states and choose your state of mind; but at times you may blame others for your bad feelings and behaviors and say, "This problem makes me so angry," "My boss aggravates me," or "This project frustrates me so much!" Problems, people and projects do not cause anger, aggravation or frustration. You *choose* to become angry, aggravated and frustrated. You're responsible for your own feelings. This is hard to emotionally accept because outside forces from team and organizational spaces (e.g., boss, micromanagement, difficult people and interpersonal conflicts) are powerful motivators that can override intrinsic motivation. When people lack emotional strength, they give in to the negative influences of other spaces and blame others and make excuses. Indeed, these are honest emotions that are triggered by outside sources but why do people let those de-motivators into their space? *They enter because people let them in.*

Personal accountability is not about "me versus them" or self-blame but that personal space is well-connected with organizational and team spaces and what's good for you is also good for your team and organization. In other words, you can't blame the system because you are part of the system and you have a responsibility to make it work. Therein lies the secret—when things go wrong, *take the responsibility and not the blame,* which means taking the problem forward with constructive actions where you say, "I made a mistake *but I have a plan to correct it*," or "I don't know the answer but *I'm going to find out and let you know*." You can't "turn the corner" by moving backwards. Taking responsible action is a positive, forward-acting approach that expands space, while assigning blame is a negative, backward-moving approach that reduces space.

- **Own the consequences and your feelings.** Relying on others to judge your behaviors is like allowing other people to dress you—you'll never know what you're going to wear. Why do people allow others to control their consequences? It's a "need" response for social acceptance but it shouldn't be confused with what you truly "want." Chasing acceptance and approvals from other people is a game of frustration because it makes you too emotionally dependent on others. Break this chain by championing yourself. Avoid the trap of letting external critics override your pride and self-worth; don't let your "need" (social acceptance) override your "want" (achievement and fulfillment). You should welcome feedback and advice but you should also be free to choose how you feel and what consequences you deserve. If you own the results (outcome) and the interpretation of the results (judgment), why shouldn't you own the consequences as well (feeling good, bad or indifferent about the judgment)? The secret is to maintain a good balance: feedback from others should be treated as "frosting on the cake," not the cake itself; *you should be the final judge* of your own actions. Accountability is taking personal responsibility for your actions but it should also mean taking responsibility for the judgment and consequences as well.

> *Judgment and feedback from others should be treated as "frosting on the cake," not the cake itself.*

- **Give yourself time to recover.** Taking ownership of your actions, outcomes and consequences gives you tremendous personal empowerment, control and self-satisfaction. But big failures and bad outcomes are difficult to just "chalk it up to experience" or "I'll do better next time." In a severe loss, it takes time to get over it, which may include a grieving process of denial, pain, anger, depression, reflection, reconstruction and acceptance. The important point is that everyone fails and you will survive it as long as you give yourself the time to heal. It's tough to bounce back unless you take the time to digest and accept what has happened, grieve the bad outcome and consequences, and give yourself time to move forward. The secret is to take the time to get over it. Time is on your side.

Taking Too Much Accountability

Accountability can sometimes be a double-edged sword. Mark was a senior manager who had a great sense of accountability. He readily took responsibility for his behaviors, accepted accountability for any shortfalls in his performance and worked passionately to correct any problems that occurred in his work unit. He was a fair person who always kept things factual and objective. Mark was self-critical at times but he also took pride and accountability in the good work that he and his team produced.

Mark was a wonderful person but he had a blind spot. He was highly protective of his project team and actively defended his team against any outside criticism. He would boast that he would "fend off any attacks on his team" and would "take the hit" for any mistakes that his team made. He would proudly exclaim, "I always protect my team!" He took responsibility for his team's work, which is admirable. But where it broke down was that his work team never felt motivated to perform at a high level since their manager, Mark, always defended any problems or errors they made. Mark believed that his team was so dedicated that any criticism from their customers would devastate and demoralize his team.

Mark's overly protective and highly accountable behaviors led to a weak performing team. Good accountability means taking personal responsibility for your actions, not sheltering others from feedback and consequences. Like an overprotective parent, Mark's intentions were good, but he denied his team the accountability for their work. He externalized his strong sense of accountability and as a result, reduced his team's performance.

In this story, Mark was preventing his team from accepting ownership of the outcome, interpretation and consequences of their actions. He built a wall around his team and they never received the valuable outside feedback that they deserved. Their space became smaller through the reduction in accountability and lack of ownership. His team failed to turn the corner. Sometimes the best role you can play is to help others learn to accept personal accountability.

Turning Points

When you have self-confidence, opportunity, inner strength and accountability, you not only increase your ability to achieve but also make significant "turning points" in your career. Some examples of turning points include:

- Completing a major project
- Getting the promotion you wanted
- Taking a risk and succeeding
- Bouncing back from failure
- Taking a chance on a new career path or job
- Earning a graduate degree
- Performing well in a crisis
- Achieving your goals

Inner strength and accountability give people the resolve to take action, make things happen, and step up and take some risks. Life is too short to play the "what-if" game and remain on the sidelines. To turn the corner, reframe the challenge and consequences in your favor and not let the risk of failure or negative consequences reduce your self-confidence and motivation. It takes faith, courage, competency, motivation, mental toughness, persistence and accountability.

Drawing on the concepts from previous chapters, there are seven compelling reasons why you should "turn the corner" and act on more opportunities:

1. **Your best moments in life can come from unplanned opportunities.** In the course of your life, unexpected opportunities will come along and you may or may not take them. Life maps (Chapter 3) indicate that the best joys in life result from chance opportunities, such as finding a new job, developing a new product or falling in love. You can have more successes from "leaps of faith" than you think.

2. **Life is a puzzle and every experience, whether good or bad, reveals a piece of yourself.** Passing on a new experience is a missed opportunity to learn more about yourself. Every experience brings you closer to finding your authentic self and what you were meant to do in life.

3. **False fears can hold you back.** Fear makes people overestimate the risk of failure, causing them to abstain or wait. Waiting for the right time to act is a false hope born from fear. As a result, the old adage is true: "People don't regret the things they do; they regret the things they *don't* do."

4. **Underestimating your ability to overcome failure.** History shows that you are probably more resilient than you think and you will bounce back from bad experiences; actually *your worst moments can inspire you to achieve great moments.* People often learn more from their failures than their successes.

5. **Bad outcomes are out of your control.** Life maps show that bad moments are usually outside your control and rarely a result from your direct actions. So why do people fear making decisions and actions to avoid bad moments? Outcomes can't be controlled but what can be controlled are behaviors, self-confidence (i.e., "I know I can do this well."), self-consequences (positive self-reinforcement, forgiveness and affirmations) and the joy of new accomplishments. You can't control bad outcomes.

6. **It's a false belief that the same opportunity will come along again.** You can't control opportunities—what's here today may be gone tomorrow; strike when it's hot.

7. **Regrets and disappointments are only temporary.** Your personal effectiveness cycle has human factors that serve as natural "backstops" that cushion and minimize the negative effects of bad experiences. They are your values (thinking); family and friends (space); knowledge, skills and talents (motivation); inclusion (achievement) and your personal goals and passions (sustainability). When you have all these factors backing you up, you have more courage and less regrets in taking chances.

SUMMARY

✓ Achievement in project management is having the self-confidence and motivation to take action, accomplish goals and "turn the corner." The ability to consistently "turn the corner," going from motivation to achievement in the personal effectiveness cycle, is what separates good project managers from bad ones.

✓ Three mental behaviors are needed to "turn the corner":
  ✓ Self-confidence initiates action
  ✓ Inner strength sustains the action
  ✓ Accountability completes the action

✓ It takes tremendous inner strength and personal accountability to achieve your goals. Success cannot be achieved without action and the willingness to take action and persist in the face of self-doubt, criticism, regrets and cynics. To "turn the corner" more often, mentally train yourself to reframe the challenge and consequences in your favor.

✓ This chapter presented five reasons why it's difficult to turn the corner (fear, unwanted consequences, lack of ownership, backward thinking and downward pressures) but gave seven stronger reasons why you should take more risks (best moments are unplanned; experiences reveal who you are; risks are overestimated; your abilities are underestimated; bad moments are out of your control; grab opportunities while you can; and your cycle contains many "backstops" that protect you). If you can expand your space, conquer your fears and stay in the game and win, you are on your way to succeed in project management.

Module IV

Sustainability

11

Passion
What do you love to do?

Passion is an extraordinary human factor and the purest expression of who you are and what you want. It is an intense emotion that emanates from deep within your inner-self, giving you enormous energy and enthusiasm to fulfill your dreams of personal success. The energy that converts your values into behaviors comes from your motivators and de-motivators, but the energy that converts your beliefs and dreams into success comes from your passion. Passion represents the best of who you are, and you are at your best when you show your passion.

Passion is an overwhelming desire to do what you *love to do*. Passion resides in personal space and provides a source of tremendous self-confidence, joy and enthusiasm. Everyone has a passion for certain things but how, when and in what form you express that passion is up to you. What activities give you the most fun and energy? What excites you the most about your job? What aspects of project management do you love the most? Do you know what your true passions are?

Passion is not some magical force possessed by the privileged few— anyone can have passion. It can be around a *subject*, a profession or particular knowledge area, such as medicine, law, engineering, music or fashion; or it can be around an *interest* or *activity*, such as computing, teaching, writing, hiking or reading; and it usually involves *intense feelings* such as love, power, enthusiasm and excitement. Some people have a passion for thinking—creating new ideas and solving problems, while others have a passion for the senses—food, wine and the arts. Passion is an intense emotion that can be expressed in many different ways and it may last for a few minutes to a lifetime. Everyone's got a "fire in their gut"; it's a matter of finding what fuels that fire, and how to sustain that energy in positive and productive ways in your life.

Passion is uplifting. When passion is expressed, personal space expands and mood elevates to a higher set point. Many people enjoy the *subject* of project management but what they often love the most is the *activity* of working with other people toward a common goal. They enjoy the work but it's the people aspect that gives them the best *feelings* of fulfillment and fun. For other project managers, they love the *feeling* and excitement of leading new projects; they love the challenge of planning, strategizing, organizing, resourcing and problems-solving. Passionate project managers also help other people find and express their passions in their work. People perform at their best when they do what they love, and they are also less stressed and willing to contribute more time and effort. The secret is not to motivate but to *inspire passion* in others.

Passion is boundless. I know a CPA who works during the day and does public service in the evenings; he enjoys being an accountant but he loves civic activities and often says "I love working for my community." It's interesting because he also enjoys supervising a team at work—his passion is *working with others on a common cause*. A friend of mine loves baking and became a pastry chef after retiring from her corporate job. She told me that the time she spent in the bakery was "like heaven." When she worked in corporate, she dreaded getting up at 6 a.m., but as a chef she loved going to the bakery at 3 a.m. and creating delicious pastries and desserts for people. It wasn't that she hated her corporate job; she loved her job when she was given a chance to create new programs for internal customers. She had a strong passion for *creating things that other people valued*. These examples demonstrate that passions are not confined to home or work but that they cross over. Passion is such a powerful human factor that it can be expressed anywhere—it has no boundaries. The lesson learned is that if people have passions outside of work, it is likely that they can also express those same passions at work. As a project manager, find your passions at work and help others find their joy too.

Passion is transformational. Whenever people are asked to describe their passions, they take on a different persona. Their face and demeanor immediately light up. Their eyes widen, they speak with great energy and you feel the love in their pursuit. Once they start talking, it's hard to get them to stop. Passion gives people a chance to reveal who they really are.

Passion requires action. People who say they are "waiting for the right time" or "plan to do it someday" are denying themselves the opportunity to live their passion. It's such a shame that so many people have found their calling but haven't taken the risk of living it. *Passions don't last forever—act on your passions today, it may not be there tomorrow.*

IMPORTANCE OF DISTINGUISHING MOTIVATION, VALUES AND PASSION IN PROJECT MANAGEMENT

Motivation versus Passion

How is passion different from motivation? Motivation comes from all three spaces, while passion comes only from personal space. In other words, you can motivate someone to perform a task but you can't motivate someone to have passion. Motivation is used to meet goals, but passion is used to exceed them. Motivation has purpose; passion has joy. Both generate human energy but only passion is self-sustaining. Everyone has a special calling in life that gives them passion, force, energy and sustainability. Table 11.1 provides a comparative summary of the differences between motivation and passion.

Table 11.1 Motivation and Passion

Motivation	Passion
Generated from organizational, team and personal space	Originates only from personal space
Strong compelling feeling	Happiness, zeal, enthusiasm
High energy	Tireless energy
Meet goals	Exceed goals
Worth doing *at* the time	Worth doing *all* the time
Can change depending on circumstances	A constant "fire in the gut"
Continues with reinforcement	Reinforcement not needed
Usually short-lived and variable	Usually long-lived and sustained
May not have personal meaning	Always has personal meaning
Can be offset by de-motivators	Does not have any offsets
Do it for satisfaction	Do it for joy
Behaviors are motivated	Passions are inspired

Values versus Passion

Passions are sometimes confused with values. Both are incredibly strong human factors that affect behaviors but they are distinctive and serve different purposes. Here's a good story that illustrates this point.

A young engineer was hired to serve as a team leader in the regulatory division of a large construction firm. Her name was Ashley and she was extremely bright, knowledgeable and dedicated. Her job was to ensure that the construction projects for the company met all applicable federal, state and local regulations and she led a team in conducting audits and inspections of the company's projects.

Ashley was highly respected for her expertise and due diligence. She was not afraid to challenge construction managers and often provided compliance training for their project teams. It was rare for her to miss a deadline or miss any details in her work. In discussions with her, she expressed her high interest and passion for compliance work. She was excited when she spoke of new regulations and the challenge of understanding new reporting requirements for the company. She interfaced regularly with the legal department and had a number of attorneys who she enjoyed working with. Ashley loved regulatory compliance work and the authority she had in overseeing the deployment of new rules and requirements.

After a couple of years working in compliance, Ashley was effective in her job but had become increasingly moody, defensive and irritable. Also, her boss started to receive some complaints about the frequency and scope of her audits on certain projects. When these issues were addressed with Ashley, it was clear that she was feeling stressed and unhappy about the year. Evidently, she was annoyed by having to do so many audits and the project managers were not always appreciative and forthright with her on compliance issues. She was a bit angry that some negative comments were being made "behind her back." Needless to say, she was not happy about the work.

Was Ashley mistaken about her love for compliance work? Is it possible that she had lost her passion? How can a person say they love their job if they're feeling stressed and unhappy? After a long conversation with Ashley, it was discovered that she still loved her job but not all aspects of it. As a "guardian" personality type, she enjoyed policy deployment, legal consulting and regulatory compliance and it fit her *personal values* of duty, responsibility, authority and serving the company. But she disliked dealing with the internal politics of audits, interdepartmental conflicts and management reporting. What she loved was the *content* of the job and the resolution of technical issues, not the internal audit *process* and activities. She loved the challenge of deciphering and interpreting regulations, working with the attorneys and helping the company stay compliant.

The point of the story is that values and passions are not the same thing. Values are the things you believe in, not what you love to do. When people did not comply with the rules and regulations, it was frustrating and upsetting to Ashley—a sure sign of a personal value (Chapter 3). What inspired Ashley was the intellectual challenge of the job. Values are beliefs; passions are gifts and they each motivate different aspirations. Ashley enjoyed the responsibility of her job because they fit her values but it wasn't her passion. Her real passion was being the company's technical expert on regulatory compliance. With that realization, Ashley continued in her current job but focused on the legal and technical aspects of the work and delegated the auditing and reporting duties to other team members. Two years later, Ashley received her "dream job" and worked successfully as a senior compliance consultant in the legal department.

In summary, values express what you "need to" do; motivation expresses what you "want to" do, and passion expresses what you "love to" do. People are inspired by passion, not values or motivators. Live your values to motivate the right behaviors; live your passions to inspire high performance in yourself and others.

PASSION IS A GIFT

Passion gives people energy and capacity to pursue their hopes and dreams toward creating greater happiness and fulfillment. Of the three "wants," achievement and recognition are highly motivating, but fulfillment is a much deeper "want" that is closely tied to passion—that's why passions *fulfill* people emotionally. Passion has special qualities and characteristics:

- **It is an inner drive that comes from authentic self.** You can't fake or mimic passion. It is a pure expression of who you are that can't be duplicated.
- **Gifts take time to develop but once you find it, you won't let go.** You may be born with certain talents but they may not develop into passions until you express it. Passions do not just happen; they require self-discovery and action. You may have a talent for architecture but until you are exposed to it, learn it and work with it, it may never fully develop into a passion. Take advantage of opportunities when they feel right. Once you find your gift, you'll find it difficult to let go.
- **Your passions today may not be there tomorrow.** The emotional excitement that you receive from your passions today may not last forever. There are no guarantees; don't wait too long to enjoy your gifts.
- **Passions are limitless.** There are no quotas on passion. Some people are crazy for sports and it occupies all their time. Some people are so passionate about life that they love everything that they do, which is incredible. You can have as many passions as you want.

PASSIONATE STATE

Everyone has passion—it's what you *do* with it that determines success. Being passionate means having the ability to take action and express what you love. Being passionate transcends motivation and takes you to a higher state of mind. As defined in Chapter 6, people possess a variable set point or motivational state that continuously loops between a lower and higher state of motivation; but there's a higher level that exceeds motivation—the *passionate state* (Figure 11.1).

You may have a strong inclination for certain subjects, activities or interests in life but it's up to you to choose what you want to pursue. Passion requires *ability*, dedication and good fortune. The good fortune part of passion is *opportunity*, and dedication refers to your commitment and *inner drive* to do it. You can have all the natural talents and abilities in the world but without opportunities and the drive to go after it, your passion will never be expressed. That's why your personal effectiveness depends on your ability to take risks, broaden your skills, knowledge and experiences and express who you are. You are at your best when you operate from your passionate state.

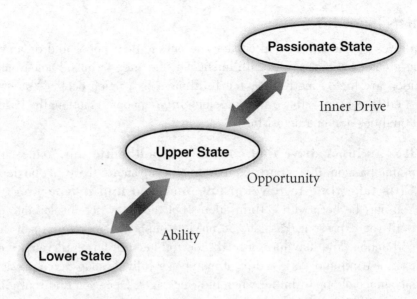

Figure 11.1 Lower, Upper and Passionate States

WHAT ARE YOUR PASSIONS?

It's likely that you have many passions in life. They may cover a wide range of activities, subjects and interests. Using both the criteria listed in Table 11.1 and the questions below, what are your strongest passions in life?

- What do you love to do?
- What gives you boundless energy and happiness?
- What comes easily to you?
- What activity do you do where time flies by?
- What things would you gladly get up at 4 a.m. to do?
- What would you do if you had endless time and money?

HOW TO LIVE A MORE PASSIONATE LIFE

You may have great passions but are you *living* a passionate life? A simple way to determine your level of passion in life is to estimate the time you're spending in doing what *you love to do*. In other words, what proportion of your day is spent pursuing your passions? Subtracting time for sleep, eating, bathing and other essential functions, you probably have about twelve hours available each day. Looking over the past six months, what percentage of your available time was spent on your passions? Are you spending a majority of your time, say sixty or seventy percent? Is it lower than that? Most people spend less than twenty percent of their time on their passions. They say most of their time is consumed by work, which is something they don't love to do. In asking why they can't love their work, they would remark, "if it was enjoyable, they wouldn't call it work!" Is that a truism or paradigm? "Work is not suppose to be fun" is a common paradigm that holds people back from having a more successful and fulfilling career.

No doubt there are competing priorities and obligations in life that preclude people from pursuing their passions. People have financial needs, a family to take care of and a future to secure, but the biggest risk is continually to accept the status quo. It's easy to find reasons not to change or take risks. However, in the absence of passion, time becomes a routine. People may not like their jobs, yet they end up doing it for ten, twenty or thirty years. Passion is seen as a luxury or something people do on weekends or when they retire. The belief is: "There's simply no time to do what I love to do." This is not reality but another paradigm that people have chosen to accept.

> *"Passion does not require time; it releases you from time because passion is atemporal."*

Undoubtedly, living a more passionate life will result in more fun and success, so what's holding people back? Two paradigms hold people back—(1) work *can't* be a passion and (2) passion requires time. Both are fallacies and in fact time is irrelevant. *Having more time does not make you more passionate; only passion makes you more passionate.* The secret is to find more passion, not time. Passion does not require time; it releases you from time because *passion is atemporal.* When you are in love, does time matter? Take actions to find more passion in what you do each day (even at work!) and you will live a more passionate life.

CAN PASSIONS CHANGE?

It takes work to find and develop your passion and it takes more work to keep it. It's like any skill or talent in project management—you have to work at it to maintain it at a high level. People gain and lose passion over time. At some point in your career, it is not uncommon to lose passion for your work, profession, company or position. It's normal. Your enthusiasm and zest may wane over time, and you may no longer feel as challenged and excited about your work. That's why it's important to pursue different passions in life, seek new opportunities and not feel limited.

Mid-Career Crisis

Passions can change in mid-career when people suddenly find that their journey no longer has the same strong purpose and excitement. They become more "needy" as their feeling of fulfillment decreases. They feel uncertain, unappreciated, unmotivated or unsuccessful. They feel "out of it"—unclear about what they're doing and why, searching for greater meaning. Their drive for achievement and impact has slipped, and what used to turn them on has now lost its punch. In response to this realization, people do crazy things, such as buying a motorcycle, quitting work, getting cosmetic surgery or doing other drastic things. It's a desperate attempt to feel renewed and excited again through impulsive actions. They want to "feel alive again!" They want to restore their motivation and feelings of excitement.

Why do people have mid-career crises? Did their values and passions change? Their values probably haven't changed but they may be questioning their balance between values (obligations) and passions (fun); i.e., "The work never stops; I wish I could find more time for myself." A mid-career crisis can be a healthy period of renewal and affirmation of their beliefs and priorities in life. They reached a point where they have settled into a comfort zone and they need rejuvenation. A mid-career crisis is not necessarily a negative time; it can be a great time to break old habits and find new passions.

Passions have a natural life cycle and passions do indeed change because abilities and opportunities change. As the passion model illustrates (Figure 11.1), any changes in ability and opportunities will affect your passionate state. To counter this effect, develop new abilities and opportunities to replace old ones that have either become stale or out-of-date. The secret is to build a portfolio of interests and try new things regularly. There is no limit to what you can experience—the world is a passionate place.

Finding New Opportunities to Re-Kindle Passions

Judy was a general manager of a large utility company and had an experienced project manager, Richard, on her staff. He was a well-regarded engineer who worked for the company as a strategic planner. Richard was an excellent analyst and a hard worker. He was a project manager early in his career and transferred into a staff position about ten years ago. Being in a staff position for ten years is a long time but he enjoyed the work and it gave him the opportunity to learn more about the company and see a broader view of the business. He was good with both people and numbers—a good combination for business.

However, after ten years, in essentially the same role, it was clear that his enthusiasm and spirit were not at their highest level. He never complained about his work assignments and appeared content to come in and do his work diligently.

Richard was always a cheerful guy and had a good sense of humor, so Judy always felt comfortable talking with him. One day, Judy met him for an afternoon coffee downstairs. It was a nice sunny afternoon so they sat outside and talked. They reminisced about the "good old days" when the company was much smaller and the work environment was more relaxed and personable. They talked about how the

Internet and email have seemingly taken over their lives, and how people were now more specialized and independent. She asked Richard how he felt about completing twenty-five years with the company and what he had hoped to do going forward.

He said, "Judy, I'll never regret working for this company and I enjoy the people here very much. I don't know how many more working years I have left but I feel comfortable where I am." He further remarked that "I know I'm maxed out in what I do here, but I think that's normal and I accept my role as an analyst. I still get a good project to do once in awhile."

He talked about how he missed field operations but realized that he has spent too many years away from it and would probably not have the energy to go back. While he was talking, Judy could see that he was content with his current state but that he misses contact with operations and meeting new people. He talked more about the past than he did about the future, which was a sign to her that he was not enthusiastic about the job. At his senior salary grade, she knew it would be tough finding him another assignment in operations. She thought, "Richard is such a pleasant and bright person that it was unfortunate that he ended up being somewhat trapped."

On the way back from coffee, Judy noticed a poster board mounted in the lobby of their building that was advertising a new supervisor's training program. This triggered a thought in her mind that perhaps she could enroll Richard into a training program, maybe not a supervisors program, but perhaps an outside business program that would reignite his interest in business and allow him to meet new people too. She went online and searched local universities for classes that were geared toward experienced people. Most were designed for new managers or people who wanted basic business training. As she reviewed the various course offerings, she didn't find anything new and exciting that she could suggest to Richard.

The courses were things that Richard already knew well; she thought to herself, "He's been there, done that. In fact, based on Richard's experience, he could easily teach these classes." Then, it struck her, *he could easily teach these classes*. She quickly contacted the employee training and development department and asked whether they were in need of any experienced, in-house people to give training in any areas. They told her that they would love to have in-house people give training, and they were anxious to find a person to give training in Facility Design. What a great match—this was Richard's forte. She was excited about this possibility but at the same time a little cautious since she wasn't sure if Richard would like the idea.

Judy met with him the next day and told him about the opportunity. He seemed puzzled at first but then asked if she could afford him the time to teach classes. She told him, "Absolutely, yes," if he was interested. They talked more about logistics and how he would be teaching both young and experienced people in operations. He was willing to give it a try.

After he started designing the class and drawing up examples from his past experiences, his interest and enthusiasm seemed to grow each day. After giving two classes, Richard was hooked. He was great in the classroom. She knew he loved the subject already but having the chance to share that knowledge with others and to mix it up with younger people was a great charge for him. He felt honored, respected and fulfilled by the experience. It truly gave him a spark to his job and he was using his knowledge in a different, energetic way. Teaching those classes gave him new energy—teaching *renewed his passion*.

Find your sources of energy and you will find your passion.

It's interesting that Richard's passion for the subject matter was still there but how that passion was being used was waning in his current job. By giving him a new *opportunity* and a new way to express that passion, it gave him the *inner drive* and belief that he had more to give. And people gave him tons of appreciation. This new opportunity supported Richard's three "needs" (well-being, acceptance and purpose) and three "wants" (challenge, achievement and fulfillment). It wasn't a big, dramatic change but just enough to rekindle that passion that he always had.

So passion is something that is essential to personal success but passion is not everlasting. It requires renewal in subtle and sometimes dramatic ways to be realized. Everyone can find a new passionate state in their life. You just have to go out and find it and never stop looking even when you feel comfortable and satisfied with the status quo. Personal success requires a great deal of human energy, and passion is your greatest power generator. Find your sources of energy and you will find your passion.

RENEWING YOUR PASSION

If you're feeling less passionate about your career, here are some tips for renewing your passion:

- **Assess your passion.** Has something changed to reduce your ability, opportunity or inner drive to live a passionate career? For example, it's not uncommon that changes at work or new things that consume your energy can lower your passion; you may have settled into a "comfort zone" and have not taken the initiative to recharge your passion, or "time" has taken you hostage. Try to pinpoint what has changed to determine what actions you can take to renew your passion.
- **Express your passion in new ways.** Like Richard's story, sometimes it takes a new opportunity, a different venue or an exciting project to renew your passion. Taking a class, joining a network or attending a professional conference can also reignite your enthusiasm.
- **Work with passionate people.** Work with people who are passionate and your fire will always burn brighter. Nothing feeds a passion more than having

enthusiastic people around you. Always surround yourself with passionate people and you will gain energy. Sometimes people outgrow their work environment and learning stops. Working with passionate people will fire you up!

- **Try a new challenge.** Create new passions by moving to a new position and trying something different and challenging. New challenges have a way of revealing new talents and interests. Being on a new "learning curve" is always exciting. New opportunities do not appear on their own, you have to create them—hunt for new adventures and challenges.

- **Redesign your work to fit your passion.** Improve the enjoyment of your job. If you could redefine your job, what would it look like? Re-align your job to your strengths and current interests. Perhaps things have crept into your job that are precluding you from doing your favorite activities. Redefine your work and it will reopen your passions.

- **Be a mentee or mentor.** Having a mentor is a great way of getting a fresh and objective perspective on your career and new opportunities. A mentor can guide you to things that you never thought about before. A good mentor can open new doors. Conversely, mentoring others is another way to enliven your interest in your work and also help others find their way.

- **Start parallel careers.** If you want to find new passions but don't want to give up what you have, start a parallel career. This might be volunteering at the food bank, working as a docent at the museum, starting a home business or even coaching at the high school. You're giving back to your community and the experience may open a new passion for you.

SUMMARY

✓ Passion is an overwhelming desire to pursue what you love to do, and it's an extraordinary human factor that is uplifting, boundless, transformational and inspirational.

✓ Passion is a one of the purest expressions of who you are and what you want—it gives you energy, self-sufficiency, meaning and fulfillment, enabling you to transcend your fears, doubts and insecurities. However, two paradigms hold people back from pursuing their passions—work can't be a passion and passion requires time—break these fallacies.

✓ In project management, it's important to distinguish values, motivation and passion: values express what you "need to" do; motivation expresses what you "want to" do, and passion expresses what you "love to" do. People are inspired by passion, not values or motivators. Motivation helps you meet goals but passion helps you exceed goals; motivation comes from all three spaces, while passion comes only from personal space.

✓ Passion does not just happen; it requires ability, opportunity and an inner drive. In the absence of passion, time becomes a routine. Living a passionate life leads to greater fulfillment and happiness.Ð

✓ Passions you feel today may not be there tomorrow. Passion requires continual maintenance and renewal by seeking new challenges, acquiring new skills, having new experiences, and finding new ways to express your passions.

✓ Time has a way of stealing your passions if you let it. Make time insignificant by living your passion—passion is atemporal; it releases you from time and inspires you to pursue what you love to do.

12

Personal Goals
How to make self-promises and keep them

In the personal effectiveness cycle, motivation and achievement are critical for "turning the corner," enabling you to take risks, complete actions and get results. However, to get the results that *you want* and feel personally successful, you want *personal goals*. Goals are specific things that you want to achieve within a given timeframe. They are self-promises that are linked to your definition of success and motivate you to go beyond where you are today. Successful people constantly set personal goals; it stems from their "can do" attitude, which helps them to attain higher achievements. In project management, your personal goals and project goals need to be aligned in order to maximize motivation. But project goals come and go, while personal goals are constant factors in your sustainability. No project is more important than your personal effectiveness, and personal growth and development is an important goal for project managers today.

Goal-setting is one of the most important behaviors affecting motivation and productivity. Research by Latham and Locke (2002) has shown that goal-setting motivates higher performance when:

(1) Goals are specific and challenging
(2) People are highly committed to the goal
(3) People believe they have the skills and abilities to achieve the goal

Personal goals provide purpose, commitment, direction and priority. They are self-determined challenges that are linked to "wants" and values. Goals enable people to set new direction and achieve personal growth and development. However, it is not uncommon for people to fall short on their goals and struggle to live up to their promises.

The most common mistakes are *not* setting:

(1) Clear, compelling goals
(2) the right goals
(3) sustainable goals

This chapter will cover the purpose and process of setting personal goals, and how to beat the most common mistakes and barriers for accomplishing goals.

WHY DO PEOPLE NEED PERSONAL GOALS?

In this busy stressful world, it's easy to fall prey to the daily cadence of life: you go to work, check your email, go to meetings, do your work, eat lunch, have more meetings, do more emails, finish your work, go home, unwind, go to bed, wake up and start the cycle again. Daily routines are things that you *have to* do each day but it doesn't *have to* be life itself.

Goals help break daily routines, making life more interesting, exciting and challenging, and forces you to think anew. Instead of doing the same things today as you did yesterday, goals challenge you to widen your perspective. For example, if a job promotion was your goal, instead of reading emails all day, you may devote your time to improving a work process or developing new ideas to improve the company. In your personal life, goals force you to do things differently. Instead of going straight home after work, you may have a goal of taking an evening class to learn a new skill or expand your knowledge. Each extra effort puts you closer to your goal. When you focus on a broader picture, you scale up your thinking and actions.

The good thing about personal goals is that they "pull" you forward in time, making you think about the future and developing yourself to meet future challenges. You have a choice—you can let the routines of life run you down or you can raise your sights and take action to live a more interesting, exciting and passionate life. If you choose to settle and remain the same, you are losing ground because the world keeps moving ahead of you in terms of technology, social change, new products and services, faster and more efficient processes, higher standards and tougher competition. Goals move you forward by motivating you to learn new information and skills. By moving you forward, goals create *hope*. Hope is one of the greatest internal motivators for success. When your goal is to save enough money for a home, you are creating *hope*. When you work extra hard each day, you *hope* to be recognized and rewarded. When you take that evening class, you *hope* that it will lead to a better job or new career. Hope is not wishful thinking but an inner energy that comes from believing in a positive future, and when that deep belief is coupled with your self-confidence, determination and passion, you have a winning mindset.

Personal goals create hope, sustainability and success by:

- **Keeping you focused and positive.** Goals keep you on the right track. Criticism, setbacks and disappointments can cause you to zigzag and doubt yourself, but your goals will keep you straight, focused and moving forward. Goals are your best friends; they are always there when you need them and they give you continuous hope and support. Even when things aren't going well or when you feel a bit unappreciated, your personal goals will keep you motivated, positive and optimistic. No one can ever take away your goals.

Goals are your best friends; they are always there when you need them.

- **Renewing your mindset.** Personal goals enable you to take a fresh perspective on your career and life. The act of setting goals makes you explore new possibilities and creates a new vision and renewed determination.
- **Making you think bigger.** Goals are bigger than actions. By setting a larger framework, it makes you take a larger view of yourself and the world around you. Goals help you to connect with the "big picture."
- **Inspiring action.** Because goals make you think bigger, better and forward in time, they inspire and excite you to take action. They have great personal meaning and when goals are completed, you feel a strong sense of accomplishment and pride.
- **Instilling faith in yourself.** Goals give you a stronger belief that you can achieve something meaningful. By developing personal goals, you are raising your self-confidence and making a promise to yourself.
- **Giving you personal control.** By setting goals, you are taking control of the direction and pace of your life—a personal quest. It belongs to you and you are free to decide your own course. Goals give you control, independence and self-sustainability.

In summary, goals create hope, sustainability and success by providing focus, renewal, inspiration, action, self-confidence, faith and control. Do these attributes sound familiar? They should because these are the same attributes as your upper state (high set point). Goal-setting is an upper level behavior.

GOALS VERSUS EXPECTATIONS

The inability to differentiate between goals and expectations is one of the most common problems in project management. Goals are specific, prospective desires while expectations are pre-determined anticipations. While goals are positive, forward-looking pursuits that you *hope will happen*, expectations are things you *expect will happen*. When things don't go as you *expect*, you feel disappointed, defeated and discouraged, which can quickly ruin your project. You lose sight of your goals when you set unrealistic expectations—I call this the *"expectation effect."*

Vacation and the Expectation Effect

Vacations are like mini-projects: they are planned undertakings that have a start and end date, requiring a coordination of various tasks and activities toward a common goal.

When Chuck was a young parent, he and his wife decided to take their two kids on a family vacation to Disneyworld in Orlando, Florida. They planned on staying in a nice, well-appointed hotel that catered to families and was close to the park. Since this was their family's first big trip, he rigorously scanned the Internet, travel agencies and tour packages for the best hotel, flight schedules, ticket prices, transportation, food and tours. He researched the best rides and attractions, souvenir shops, family shows and special events and read endless web reviews on all the excursions and restaurants. After many weeks of planning and scheduling, he had every aspect of the trip covered. He checked and double-checked all his bookings, hotels and schedules, and even had contingency plans in case it rained or if the flights got canceled. Needless to say, Chuck's plan was a masterpiece and with all his research and planning, he expected everything to work well, with no glitches and they would have the greatest time.

The first day of their trip went exactly as planned—the trip to the airport was perfect, the seating and preordered meals on the flight were spot on, all their baggage arrived intact, and the rental car transaction went smoothly with all his frequent traveler numbers preloaded. However, when they arrived at the hotel, he had prearranged for early check-in but for some reason, their room wasn't quite ready yet and they had to wait for the normal check-in time. Chuck expressed his disappointment to the desk clerk and hotel manager but it didn't change anything. So they had to stow their luggage in the storage room and the family killed some time around the pool area. The hotel had three gigantic pools, a waterfall and a killer slide but the slide was down for repairs and it was closed for the week. He couldn't believe it! Well, this string of terrible misfortunes continued throughout their stay: the cost for parking was much higher than what he had *expected*; on their second day, due to traffic they arrived at the park one hour later than he had *expected*, which meant longer lines at the popular rides; and they missed their meeting with Mickey Mouse because Mickey was not at the location that he had *expected*. On top of that, they ended up eating fast food by the pool because the restaurant couldn't find his reservation.

Chuck was tired, frustrated and disturbed about the whole thing. As he was sulking by the pool reflecting on what else could go wrong, his wife nudged him and said, "Honey, look at the kids." His two daughters were laughing and giggling as they were eating french fries and jumping into the pool. They had their floaters on and were having a wonderful time! That single moment woke him up—he thought, "Why am I sitting over here pouting and not in the pool with my kids? Why am I feeling so down? Why am I so tense and frustrated? Everyone is having fun but me." He suddenly realized that his disappointment wasn't from the hotel, Disneyworld or the restaurant. He was disappointed with himself. Things weren't going as *he had expected* and he had predetermined a flawless vacation down to the tiniest details. Because of his excessive worrying (fear) and planning, he had *high expectations* for everything.

The lesson of this story is that Chuck's high expectations caused him to lose sight of his goal—having fun. He set himself up for failure by setting up expectations that were way out of line with his goal. What makes vacations fun and memorable are the spontaneous, unexpected moments of joy. With such high expectations, he squeezed out any opportunities to have those moments. He didn't trust that those moments would happen and tried to control the outcome, when in fact, those outcomes are for the most part out of his control.

This "expectation effect" with this vacation experience is not unlike many situations and projects that you work on every day. Your expectations are often too high for the goal and you end up failing in terms of feeling good about what you have accomplished; like Chuck's vacation story, you can strangle the fun and joy out of achieving your goals. Indeed, people can be their worst enemy at times. High internal expectations often lead to frustration and anger when plans are not met. This is not an external pressure but a self-imposed, inner pressure that destroys happiness for yourself and others.

Don't let expectations define your goals, let your goals define expectations.

Expectation effects can also cut the other way, when your expectations are too low to enable you to reach your goals. This can happen when you set ambitious goals but don't take the initiative to pursue your goals; you give up when things become difficult or settle for a lower outcome. Sometimes you undercut your expectations due to fear.

In project management, all expectations are potential disappointments but you need expectations to help achieve your goals. Expectations should be reasonable, focused on processes and behaviors, and supportive of your goals. *Don't let expectations define your goals; let your goals define expectations.*

SETTING CLEAR, COMPELLING GOALS

To set effective goals, you need a clear vision of what you desire in your career and life. That vision should be both inspiring and empowering in your mind. Visualizing what you want to do is a powerful factor for change because it positions your mind for action. If you can visualize success in your mind, it becomes more doable. You see this method used by professional athletes and artists all the time and it helps them create a positive, "can do" focus to their thinking. It serves as a confidence boost.

Once you change your thinking, and you believe in it, your behaviors will follow. Do you have a clear mental vision of what success looks like for you? If you can see it and articulate it, you are well on your way in setting the right goals in your life— *if you can clearly see it, you can clearly do it.*

Visions do not need to be grandiose. They can be simple views of who you want to be, a personal characteristic, a specific skill, a level of competency, an experience you want in life or how you wish to behave. Your vision can be a big family, a house on the beach, becoming a CEO, playing in an orchestra, being an actor or owning your own business. Visions do not have to be exact, but they should inspire you emotionally and intellectually, drive you to set the right goals, motivate you to take action and raise your set point.

Visions are important for setting the right direction and moving you forward in time. For example, there was a local university student who emigrated to the U.S. from Russia to fulfill her dream of earning a doctorate degree in chemistry. In the course of pursuing her dream, she met an American scientist in graduate school, got married and had two beautiful children. She was happy and successful in her profession. However, her greatest achievement did not come from her vision per se—her vision led her to a greater joy, her family. Personal visions are essential for giving people a platform to stage success.

Once you have a personal vision, the next step is to create your goals that support that vision. If your vision is to be an expert in a particular field, you may have goals that include obtaining more education and training, doing research with leading experts in the field, gaining more practical experience in the area, joining expert networks or professional societies, or finding a mentor in the field. A clear vision will fail without clear and compelling goals.

Clear and compelling goals are *specific, challenging and exciting*:

- **Be specific.** Have a clear *endpoint* and *timeframe* to accomplish the goal. The goal should be pinpointed, observable and tangible and have a specific completion date. Create some *urgency* by identifying "why" it is important to complete the goal by a certain date.

  Common mistakes: The goal is too broad or too long-term. Goals are set that are too general or it takes too long to complete, and you can't get started or you give up due to unexpected changes. Make sure your goals are clear with specific target dates and a sense of urgency.

- **Set challenging goals.** The belief that goals should be realistic and attainable is old school. To do great things, you must have great goals; you must go beyond what you think you can do. Set a high bar for yourself and you'll be surprised by what you can accomplish. If you want to run five miles, make it your goal to run six. If your goal is to earn your master's degree, go for a doctorate. What do you have to lose? Don't settle for five miles when you can achieve six. Even if you fall short at five and a half, you will still feel more accomplished. Setting "stretch" goals increases your space and builds inner strength.

  Common mistakes: Underestimating your abilities; settling for mediocre goals; inhibited by negative internal dialogue; succumbing to the fear of failure, criticism or embarrassment.

- **Make goals exciting.** Goals should be fun, compelling and exciting. Ideally, they should motivate you emotionally and intellectually. Goals are not chores but things that you're excited to do. The secret is to incorporate some excitement either in the goal itself or in the endeavor, such as using a high tech tool, going to a new location, buying new equipment, buying new clothes for the task, inviting some friends along or posting your progress on social media. For example, if your goal is to learn about retirement investing, take a class in the city and try out new restaurants or join an investment club and make some new friends.

If your goals represent the best of what you want, they should embody who you are.

Common mistakes: You set goals that feel more like work than fun; it's no wonder you struggle to complete them. Try to set goals that are creative, active and fun for you.

Whether you're setting personal or project goals, they should be specific, challenging and exciting. The next step in building successful goals is to ensure your goals reflect who you are. *You are at your best when you are yourself* and if your goals represent the *best* of what you want, they should embody who you are. Goals need to be personalized and "right" for you.

SETTING THE "RIGHT" GOALS

To create the "right" goals, they need to fit your values, diversity, motivations and passions. For example, if the goal is to operate your own business, your *values* (responsibility, trust, self-reliance, community, independence, and high work ethic) and *diversity* (knowledge of the business, product/service and customer, entrepreneurship, marketing and people skills) need to support that goal. Goals are great but if they do not fit who you are, your chances for success are low.

As discussed in previous chapters, everybody has their own values, desired work environments, diversity, motivators and passions that help direct them to certain career paths. Similarly, inner motivations "push" people toward certain goals in life. Some people enjoy pursuing long-term goals and stick with them for many years, while others enjoy a faster pace and like to do many different things over short periods of time. For example, biomedical researchers who love the science of genetics may devote their entire careers to a goal of understanding one gene in the human genome. Their goal strongly matches their values (scientific principles and integrity), diversity (analytical thinker), desired work environment (universities or research institutions), motivations (fame, funding, reputation and prestige) and passion (knowledge and scientific discovery). Whether your profession is in medicine, education, engineering or project management, it's easy to set the right goals and achieve them when they fit your values, diversity and passions.

Some people discover their career interests very early in life and they become self-directed but for others, career goals are developed over time, requiring a great deal of trial and error. There are no right or wrong pathways to success. To achieve your career ambitions, motivation and passion provide "push," while vision and goals provide "pull," giving you a powerful *"push-pull"* effect.

Retired U.S. General Colin Powell is a highly successful military and national leader. He was Secretary of State under President George W. Bush and also served as National Security Advisor and Chairman of the Joint Chiefs of Staff. He attributed his success to a simple personal goal—"I set out to be the best soldier I could be . . . everything else followed from that." He wanted to realize his full potential as a soldier first. His human factors supported his goal; he thrived in the military culture. He enjoyed leading other people and had great *clarity* in what he pursued. General Powell believed in passion, commitment, execution, flexibility, consistency and clarity in his mission. Working in government and the military were challenges for him, and his leadership skills and talents enabled him to achieve great success. He had a winning formula based on his unique background, human factors and values that led to an extraordinary career.

Goals should stretch you in ways that make sense to you. For General Powell, it was the military and his goal was "to be the best soldier I could be." To reach your goals you must have clarity on who you are and what you believe in (diversity and values); what you're good at; what expands your space; what keeps you in your upper state (set point) and what motivates you to accomplish your goals.

SETTING SUSTAINABLE GOALS

It's not uncommon for people to lose focus on their goals and put their energy into daily routines, extraneous tasks and work demands that meet other people's goals.

> *When personal goals are overshadowed by other priorities, personal space shrinks.*

When people get into a work routine, they are likely activity-driven, process-focused, and missing the "big picture." It's like driving the same commute each day and not remembering any part of it.

Putting their jobs before their families or working under immense stress at the expense of their health are examples where people should know better. Far too often people are consumed by the demands of work and forget to make time for themselves. Instead, they resign themselves to make trade-offs and sacrifices in order to achieve success by someone else's standards. They set weak or no goals for themselves because "I'm too busy" or "I can't find the time." It's easy to slip into a complacent, risk-averse lifestyle and rely on extrinsic factors to forge your fate.

When personal goals are overshadowed by other priorities, personal space shrinks. When goals are lacking or neglected, personal capacity, achievement and self-sustainability decrease. Furthermore, personal integrity, influence and independence shrink as well and it becomes a vicious cycle—instead of expanding space to accommodate bigger and better goals, space contracts due to inactivity

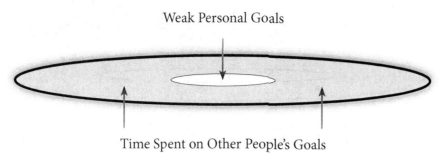

Weak Personal Goals

Time Spent on Other People's Goals

Figure 12.1 Weak Goals Compress Your Space

(Figure 12.1). Having weak goals is like having a weak immune system; you lose strength and become vulnerable to system failure.

Personal space is strengthened when you develop clear, compelling and meaningful personal goals that are consistent with your values, diversity, ambitions, passions and motivations.

Personal goals create a firewall that shield you from feeling vulnerable, irrelevant, criticized and diminished.

Your goals should be as unique as your human factors. It is the uniqueness of your goals that makes them powerful, enduring, motivating and sustainable. When you step back and look at your goals, do they look and feel like you—and only you—or could they belong to anybody? Does it give you a strong sense of personal pride, ownership and excitement? Or do your goals look generic, standard and predictable? This is the test. Your goals should represent your unique human factors, aspirations and future desires.

When your goals are highly personalized and sustainable, they protect your space and prevent encroachment like a "firewall" from extraneous goals and bad outside elements (Figure 12.2). They maintain your focus, integrity, motivation and independence. When you give up too much of your space to meet other people's goals, you diminish time and space for your own goals. With a strong firewall, you create more "room" and resist cynicism, pessimism, naysayers and other destructive forces to your psychology. You are shielded from people who say things such as, "You can't do that," "That will never work," "That's not possible," and "You're not good enough to do that." These put-downs and criticisms contaminate your mind, creating self-doubt, negative internal dialogue, lower level thinking and self-destructive prophecies. These elements can kill your success by causing you to fear failure. Your firewall is a belief in your goals and a commitment to succeed. When you set your sights high and keep the focus on your goals, the negative elements are kept out. Personal goals create a firewall that shields you from feeling vulnerable, irrelevant, criticized and diminished.

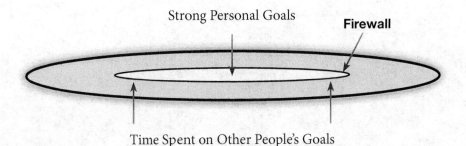

Figure 12.2 Strong Goals Expand Your Space

HOW GOALS AND PASSION PREVENT CONFLICTS

As a project manager, one of your biggest barriers to personal effectiveness is conflict, either internal conflicts or external conflicts with other people. Conflict can drain you emotionally and intellectually—it can keep you awake at night; it's the biggest source of stress and can stay with you for a long time. When conflict strikes, people become defensive and take refuge in their lower level, where they become judgmental, exclusionary and negative. As discussed in Chapter 6, instead of fighting a conflict in your lower level, you can raise your motivational state and address the issue in a more upper and collaborative state of mind. However, simply shifting to a more positive state of mind is hard to do in the midst of a conflict. It's like trying to reverse a car that's speeding downhill. You need a more effective method.

By focusing on your passions and goals . . . your mind will always stay above the fray.

To beat a tough conflict, you need to quickly shift to a much bigger and higher state of mind than the conflict itself. The secret is to immediately think of your best passions and goals. Once you upload that thought, the conflict and everything about it becomes much smaller and less emotional. Your feelings about your goals and passions will dwarf any conflicts. By focusing on your passions and goals, which are often related to your core values such as family, friendship, service, character, achievement and religion, your mind will always stay above the fray. You not only avoid your lower level, but you transcend to a completely higher realm that is beyond the reach of conflict, difficult people and criticism. Your mind is surrounded by the things you love to do and the things that you aspire to achieve and *no one can diminish or take that away from you*, even in the worst conflicts.

Why do you need both passion and goals to reduce personal conflicts? Bad conflicts hurt because they hit you intellectually and emotionally. This method works because goals give you intellectual power, while passions give you emotional lift to stay positive and hopeful. Together, passions and goals give you strong mental protection.

KEY BEHAVIORS TO ACHIEVE GOALS

Setting clear, compelling, meaningful and sustainable goals is important, but what is even more important is personal commitment and accountability. This is an area where project managers commonly fall short. You need to support your goals with processes that keep you motivated, and a support system that helps you stay focused on your goals.

Use these tools, tips and strategies to help you stay committed to your goals:

- **Focus on quality over quantity.** Although you may have plenty of goals, try to work on one to three goals at a time. Any more than that and you are risking disappointment and dilution. Time is precious—try not to spread yourself too thin. More progress is made when you *"go slow, to go fast."* Set yourself up for success, not failure.

- **Write down your goals and keep them in front of you.** Nothing helps focus the mind more than putting your goals on paper in specific details and deadlines. Post your goals where you will see them every day, such as on your refrigerator, desktop, tablet or smartphone. And when you complete a goal, highlight it or write, "DONE!" or "YES!" in bold letters. Better yet, celebrate your success with others.

- **Develop an action plan and schedule.** To achieve your desired goals, it's important to have an action plan, outlining *what* things you need to do and *by when* in order to reach your goal. It doesn't have to be precise but a set of specific actions to move you forward and build personal commitment and motivation. The first step is crucial so make sure it's an easy one. Also, you can improve your game plan by seeking feedback from other people, especially successful people.

- **Define consequences.** What rewards do you deserve for meeting your goals? What negative consequences are you willing to accept for not making a goal? Strong positive and negative consequences are effective in shaping desired behaviors, such as, "When I make my goal, I will go to Hawaii!" or "I will buy a beautiful coat when I receive my certification."

- **Measure your progress.** Having a method to track your progress, such as a calendar or an action list, will help you stay on track. For example, if your goal is to lose ten pounds, you can record your weight every week on a chart. Display the chart where you can often see it. As they say in project management, *"what gets measured, gets done."*

- **Update your goals if needed.** Things change and goals may need to be modified or deferred. That's acceptable. Sometimes you have to revise your goals to regain your personal commitment to them. Is there a danger that you may get complacent and change goals with no accountability? You can avoid this by pre-establishing a specific criterion for allowing changes.

GOALS ASSESSMENT

Use this list to determine the strength and quality of your goals.

Table 12.1 Goals Checklist

Do your goals meet these characteristics? (Yes or No)
_____ 1. Clear, pinpointed and specific
_____ 2. In written form, documented
_____ 3. Have both personal and work goals
_____ 4. Short-term and long-term goals
_____ 5. Challenging—has "stretch" and urgency
_____ 6. Exciting and fun
_____ 7. "Right"—my goals reflect who I am (vision, values, diversity and passions)
_____ 8. Supported by an action plan with target dates
_____ 9. Method to track progress
_____ 10. Expectations are consistent with my goals
_____ 11. Predefined consequences for achieving goals (e.g., celebration) or not (e.g., "no dessert")
_____ 12. Sustainable—personal priority, unique, committed (firewall)
Total Score: [   ]
Total the number of "yes" responses and see key at end of chapter.

BARRIERS TO ACHIEVING PERSONAL GOALS

With the right goals in place to pull you forward, what are your primary barriers holding you back? You can overcome your barriers by understanding what they are, how they affect you and take action to mitigate those risks.

- **Weak commitment.** Telltale signs of a weak commitment include no action plans, measurements or target dates, and no predefined incentives or consequences for making or not making your goals. If there are no consequences, why do it? Goals need a support structure of well-defined actions and incentives.

- **Low motivation and urgency.** This occurs when you treat your goals as things you would "like to do," "nice to do" or things when you have "time to do." This is not a strong basis for taking any actions. Instill a sense of urgency and make your goals a priority.
- **Lack of inner drive.** You want to achieve your goals but you struggle to stick with it and "turn the corner" due to a lack of inner drive. Make sure your goals mean something that is "bigger than you"; in other words, find reasons beyond yourself—"I do this for my kids" or "I do this to help others succeed." Inspire from within to gain inner drive.
- **Difficult people.** Difficult people are people who impede the progress of others. They tell you, "it can't be done," it will "take too much effort" or "let it go." If you believe in these negative assertions, you will eventually lose belief in yourself. Successful people do not let other people erode their goals. Use your goals and passions to build a strong firewall.
- **Lack of passion.** Achieving goals require motivation; achieving *great* goals require passion. Passion gives you great energy, enthusiasm, dedication and sustainability. Connect your goals to your passions and you will accomplish great goals. Find a way to love your goals.

SUMMARY

✓ Goals give you direction, confidence, control, inspiration and hope.

✓ While project goals come and go, *personal* goals are self-sustaining and life-changing. No project is more important than your personal effectiveness. Don't neglect your personal goals—they have purposes beyond your belief.

✓ The best goals are clear, compelling sustainable and "right"; they are linked to your vision, values, diversity, motivations and passions.

✓ Goal-setting raises your set point, expands space, builds self-confidence and increases capacity. Sustainable goals act as a firewall, protecting your

Key for Table 12.1 Number of "Yes" Answers

13 or more "Yes's" = excellent

10 or more "Yes's" = good

8 or more "Yes's" = not bad

7 or less "Yes's" = opportunity to improve

space against extraneous goals, conflicts, criticism and difficult people and strengthening your focus, motivation and integrity.

✓ Goals are not the same as expectations. Goals are things that you *hope will happen* (desires), while expectations are things you *expect will happen* (anticipations). You lose sight of your goals when you set unrealistic expectations resulting in self-disappointment and frustration.

✓ Goals are your best friends; they give you continuous support and comfort. Even when things aren't going well or when you feel lost or unappreciated, your personal goals are always there, keeping you motivated, positive and optimistic. No one can take away your goals.

✓ This chapter provided a checklist for testing the strength and quality of your goals, how to overcome barriers, and strategies to increase personal commitment and accountability.

13

How to Achieve Self-Sustainability

Project management is a continuous process where change is constant and every project is unique and challenging. The ultimate goal is to *get results and feel good about it,* which means feeling intellectually and emotionally fulfilled and meeting project and personal expectations. The challenge is not whether a project manager can run a project but how well he or she can consistently adapt and deliver on changing expectations from project to project. What makes or breaks projects is not the execution of plans, activities and tasks but managing the human factors behind the projects, which involves decision-making, motivation, achievement and sustainability.

Self-sustainability is the capacity to achieve continuous success with a high degree of efficiency, independence, self-efficacy and self-fulfillment. When people are able to pursue their passions, achieve goals and fulfill their "wants" in life, they have sustainable success. While passion and goals give people tremendous energy and focus, what keeps people going forward, enabling them to "turn the corner" (Chapter 10), and having the mental hunger and stamina to succeed long-term are the *five elements of self-sustainability*: These five elements enable project managers to remain sane when things get crazy, persist when things appear futile, go forward when others turn back and do the extraordinary when the ordinary is expected:

A. Core Goal
B. Success Factors
C. Personal Life Balance
D. Winning Attitude
E. Self-Esteem

A. CORE GOAL

As demonstrated in previous chapters, success is a continuous cycle that is self-directed, opportunistic and passionate—a journey for excellence, recognition and fulfillment. However, for the journey to be successful and sustainable over time, people need to find their definition of personal success or *core goal*. The definition of personal success is the ultimate goal that people continuously seek in their lifetime.

It is neither a single endpoint nor an accomplishment but a core mission that people pursue their entire life. Your core goal is the motivating force behind your personal goals and aspirations; the one "bucket" that you want to spend your entire life filling in an endless pursuit of personal joy and happiness.

In project management, having a core goal helps you stay centered, inclusive, less stressed, more optimistic and successful. Success is not always determined by the number of promotions, size of salaries or how high you get on the corporate ladder. These things may represent success to you but the feelings of success come from knowing how much hard work you put into it and how much you had to overcome to achieve those results. *Success is the meaning and emotion behind the results, not the results themselves.* Getting results is achievement; meeting your core goal is success.

Because people perceive success differently or have different expectations, people may feel differently about the same result or consequence of their actions. For example, two project managers, Janet and Tom received promotions. They were both outstanding employees in the department and highly motivated to move up the career ladder. The promotion gave them greater status, a larger salary and more international travel.

For Tom, greater status and more money were great but due to family reasons, traveling abroad was undesirable. However, Janet was ecstatic about the promotion, more money and traveling internationally. Should Tom feel less successful even though the consequences meant something different for the two of them? Travel wasn't a benefit to Tom and it affected his feelings about the job going forward. Tom may feel successful about the promotion but may not feel successful being away from home. His core goal was his family. On the other hand, Janet's success was tied to promotions, money and travel; they gave her personal satisfaction, security and prestige. They contributed significantly to her core goal in life—freedom.

Having feelings of being personally successful is not an all-or-none effect. It comes in varying degrees of emotion. Everyone has small and large moments of feeling successful. The key is to celebrate as many moments of success as possible and continue to pursue the outcome that you truly want. Tom feels successful but hopes to find his dream job—a work environment that meets his core goal.

Defining Your Core Goal

What is your core goal or definition of success? What gives you the greatest joy in life? What is your ultimate mission? This next section provides ten common core goals of people. Which one(s) represent your definition of success? Using this list (and you may have others), complete the sentence, **"I feel personally successful when I experience..."** Your core goal is likely a combination of two or more choices.

1. **Personal growth.** To learn and grow intellectually and emotionally: "I need to continually grow and expand my abilities—personal growth is the essence of life." My success is having rich experiences and challenges.

2. **Professional achievement and recognition.** To reach my professional goals and being recognized for making significant contributions to my profession: "Receiving awards, accolades and recognitions makes me feel successful and accomplished."

3. **Family love.** To feel loved and supported by my family and friends. Success is achieving work-family balance in my career: "My family's happiness is my measure of success."

4. **Social acceptance and respect.** I feel most accomplished when I am accepted, trusted and respected by the people around me—my family, friends and community. I feel best when people regard me as a good person: trustworthy, honest, reliable and unselfish. "I feel honored and respected when people look to me for leadership and guidance."

5. **Inner strength.** To believe in myself and feel confident and proud. Feeling vital and important and possessing strong mental toughness and persistence; an ability to stand up for what I believe in. "I'm proud of my character, will power and mental strength."

6. **Inner peace.** To achieve contentment and satisfaction with who I am. Being honest with myself and having personal integrity. Feeling emotionally and spiritually satisfied: "I have no inner stress or conflicts; I am living a genuine life."

7. **Serving others.** To help others grow and succeed; being caring, charitable and supportive of others—serving others and my country. "My success is measured in the people and communities that I have helped and loved."

8. **Fun.** To take time to laugh and enjoy life. I feel best when I'm having fun. "Fun is the bottom-line in life; if you're not having fun, you aren't living—fun and enjoyment are my measures of success."

9. **Security.** To have enough money and benefits to support my family, pay the bills, have good health care, live in a nice home and have a stable job. "I feel successful when I feel secure and safe in life."

10. **Freedom and independence.** I have great freedom in my life and career. I am self-sufficient and have the skills and knowledge to survive on my own. "Having freedom at work and personal life is a key indicator of my success."

Did you have a hard time finding your core goal? Most people have a good feeling about all these choices and a few may overlap each other but which ones truly define your core feeling of success? Defining your personal success is one of the most important things that you can do to improve your life's direction.

Our definition of personal success is often related to family, culture, past experiences and personality type. It is likely that your perceptions of success are in fact reflections of your own values. That's why true success lies in your inner values and not in your external environment (e.g., money, fame and position). Also, your level of happiness and satisfaction can change over time. People may have felt satisfied and happy when they received a paycheck early in their careers, but now their happiness is tied to the quality of their work and friendships. Your core goal needs to be revisited periodically, especially at different stages in your life.

B. SUCCESS FACTORS

Now that you have defined personal success, which human factors contribute most to your core goal? Human factors that consistently support your achievements and core goal are *success factors*, and they are unique to you and are developed throughout your life. In previous chapters, eight human factors were identified as affecting your personal effectiveness: diversity, values, space, set point, fear, inclusion, passion and goals. But when you step back and look across these human factors, which ones matter the most and what makes these human factors so special to you? Success factors are critical to project management because they are the talents, skills, motivators and passions that enable you to consistently achieve your goals with great competency, independence and self-sufficiency. A good criterion for defining your critical success factors is: *"These are the factors that if I did not have them, I would likely fail."*

Which Factors Contribute Most to Your Success?

This four-step process will help you identify your *critical* success factors:

1. Using the questions below, identify the common themes, work environment, personal attributes, people factors and passions that contribute most to your success.
2. Using Table 13.1, select your strongest "success factors."
3. Combining the results from (1) and (2), pick your top six to eight success factors.
4. In Table 13.1, rate each of the six "human factors" as a "Strength" "Satisfied" or "Improve" (i.e., grow, develop or better utilize).

- **Common themes.** Success factors are the personal qualities and common threads that recur in all your successes in life. Think about it, in all your proud moments and achievements, what common themes or qualities made it happen for you?
- **Work environment.** As discussed in Chapter 5, what is your best work environment for success? How would you describe the type of work culture that has enabled you to perform at your best? This can be a blend of your favorite subject, team behaviors, work conditions and values.
- **Personal attributes.** Which personality traits were critical in achieving your past goals? Which personal behaviors enabled you to work at your best? These are your best work habits. Without these attributes and characteristics, you would have fallen short in your endeavors. These are your key strengths, skills, talents, knowledge and experiences.

Table 13.1 List of Common Success Factors

Human Factor	Success Factors	
Diversity *My personal "library"* *Strength* | *Satisfied* | *Improve*	▪ Knowledge ▪ Experience ▪ Abilities and skills ▪ Academic background	▪ Cultural factors ▪ Age, gender, race ▪ Personality type ▪ Religion
Values Knowing my core beliefs *Strength* | *Satisfied* | *Improve*	▪ Honesty and integrity ▪ Education ▪ Responsibility ▪ Respect ▪ Wealth ▪ Friendship	▪ Public service ▪ Work ethic ▪ Family ▪ Safety and security ▪ Justice and fairness ▪ Health
Space *Extrinsic Motivators* *Strength* | *Satisfied* | *Improve*	▪ Respect and trust ▪ Freedom, independence ▪ Clear purpose and goals ▪ Career development ▪ Promotions ▪ Effective rules, policies	▪ Rewards, recognition ▪ Camaraderie ▪ Good boss, coaching ▪ Money and benefits ▪ Responsibilities ▪ Title and rank
Set Point *Intrinsic Motivators* *Strength* | *Satisfied* | *Improve*	▪ Faith, purpose, meaning ▪ Self-confidence ▪ Independence ▪ Desire to work hard ▪ Expression, creativity	▪ Desire to help others ▪ Competitive nature ▪ Desire to learn ▪ Optimism ▪ Relaxed, stress-free
Fear *Motivates positive behaviors* *Strength* | *Satisfied* | *Improve*	▪ Drive to achieve compete ▪ Work hard, won't give up ▪ Seek security, stability, well-being ▪ Foster relationships, collaboration	▪ Do things right and thorough ▪ Drive to be self-sufficient ▪ Act with urgency, focus ▪ Inspires creativity
Inclusion *Open, engaging, centered* *Strength* | *Satisfied* | *Improve*	▪ Good listener ▪ Compassionate ▪ Collaborative ▪ Transparent ▪ Teamwork ▪ Involved ▪ Engage others	▪ Help others succeed ▪ Praise, recognize others ▪ Patience ▪ Leadership ▪ Tolerance ▪ Accept other ideas ▪ Try new things

continued

Table 13.1 List of Common Success Factors *(continued)*

Human Factor	Success Factors	
Passion *Living a passionate life* 	■ Travel and adventure ■ Technology ■ Environment ■ Sports and recreation ■ Performing arts ■ Hobbies ■ Food	■ Sciences ■ Education ■ Religion ■ Humanities ■ People, culture ■ Trade, profession ■ Music
Strength / *Satisfied* / *Improve*		
Goals *Clear, compelling, "right," sustainable* 	■ Personal vision ■ Core goal	■ Personal goals ■ Work goals
Strength / *Satisfied* / *Improve*		

- **People factor.** People don't succeed alone. Relationships are critical success factors. Why are people important to you and your success? What characteristics have enabled you to make friends and connect with people? What activities do you do with people that are most meaningful?
- **Passions.** Your past successes were likely tied to your passions. What passions were behind your greatest moments and highest achievements? What gave you the energy and excitement to pursue your goals? What is the "fire in your gut" that has sustained you all your life?

C. PERSONAL LIFE BALANCE

Along with stress, personal life balance is probably the number one issue for project managers today. Family life and work career are strongly connected to people's values, "needs" and "wants" in life. Although family life and work career are core to success, they are not necessarily compatible; in fact, they are commonly in conflict with each other. Too often people put money, work, professional obligations and "pleasing the boss" ahead of other life choices such as personal fulfillment, vacations and health (sleep, diet and exercise). Although people say their personal time is a priority, when push comes to shove, the job and the boss always seem to win. Some people are lucky to have it all, but for most, it's a matter of priority and trade-offs. People work for money because they *have to*. But what people *want* is personal fulfillment and happiness.

Whether it's work or personal, people do many things that they dislike or *have to do,* such as cleaning the house, commuting to work or going to meetings. Unfortunately, for many, work is a *have to* activity or worse yet, a *hate to* activity. Hopefully your chores and work are balanced against many things that you *like to* and *love to do*. In everyone's life, time is divided into five types of "to do's":

- Hate to do: Things that you strongly dislike or avoid doing.
- Have to do: Things that you are required or expected to do.
- Indifferent to do: Things that you neither like nor dislike—neutral.
- Like to do: Things that give you pleasure and satisfaction.
- Love to do: Things that bring you great joy and fulfillment.

If success is defined as personal happiness, a good indicator would be the balance between time spent on enjoyable activities, *like to and love to do*, versus time spent on *have to* and *hate to do*. What is your personal life balance? In a typical month, what percentage of time do you spend on *hate to, have to, like to, love to and indifferent to do*? Determine your time percentages for your work, personal life or both. A "work" life balance example is provided in Table 13.2.

The Right Balance

In the 2009 edition of *The Conference Board's* annual job satisfaction survey of 5,000 households, only 45 percent of Americans expressed satisfaction with their jobs, down from 61 percent in 1987 (Franco et al., 2010). Surprisingly, this low statistic was not attributed to the economic recession. In fact, an analysis of the job satisfaction data produced by *The Conference Board* finds that increased worker unhappiness is not cyclical but that job satisfaction has steadily declined for years.

In a local survey of project managers and other working professionals in the San Francisco Bay Area (Wong, 2010), 76 percent of the respondents felt they were "often or always unhappy" with the time they were spending at work, with 69 percent feeling "stressed, tired or depressed because of work" and 66 percent saying they are "missing out on quality time with family and friends." When asked if they thought employees would be more effective if they were able to maintain a better work-life balance, the overwhelming majority (94 percent) said "yes." The erosion of employee faith and motivation on the job does not bode well for future worker satisfaction. However, it's not too late to take action to regain a better personal life balance.

It's universal that people want to improve their work-life balance. People are happier, more productive and creative when they're doing what they *like* and *love to do*, but few people have that luxury. Most people are fully occupied by work and *have to's*, feel their time for enjoyment is limited and believe fun happens only after the *have to's* are done. But that's the problem—*have to's* are never done! When *have to's* are done, more *have to's* appear.

Time has a way of limiting the fun side of life. Too easily people allow the *have to's* to steal away from the things they *like to* and *love to do*. The basic barrier is that most people do not know their right balance, and they continue to live off-balanced and overwhelmed. When *have to's* and *hate to's* dominate, a dangerous "tipping point" can be reached where a person's mental well-being is in jeopardy (Figure 13.1).

Figure 13.1 Personal Life Balance

The tipping point is reached when people feel burned out, stressed out or on edge. Just as the sun seems brightest at dusk, work may feel intense and enlightening but it can darken quickly. People may overindulge, such as excessive eating, drinking and partying, to compensate for the stress and duress. When people reach their tipping point, they are destined to fail. Worse yet, they may fail their families and friends who mean the most to them. People fail when they fail to balance their work (have to) and personal desires (like to).

Using the example provided in Table 13.2, estimate how much of your work or project time was spent on "hate to," "have to," "indifferent to," "like to" and "love to" activities over the past three to six months.

In the work life balance example in Table 13.2, the balance is heavier on the *hate to's* and *have to's* (50%) than the *like to's* and *love to's* (35%), which is typical for most people. Also, "have to" activities usually represent the largest proportion of time. What does your balance look like? How much time are you spending on *hate to's* and *have to's* versus *like to's* and *love to's* activities?

In personal and project work, when people are imbalanced, they are at risk for discontent, frustration, stress and failure. The reason for this imbalance is that most people do not actively manage their work and personal life balance. They don't know how to re-balance and what's worse is that people don't know what they truly want instead. In the absence of this information, people tend to continue filling their time with more *have to* activities. That's because *have to* activities are seen as necessary, urgent and concrete, while *like to* activities are considered "nice to do," "when I have time to do" or "one of these days I'll do" activities. *People live in a "have to" world*, pursuing the almighty buck, pleasing others and chasing deadlines—which originate from organizational and team spaces.

Table 13.2 "Work" Life Balance Example

Type of Activity	Major Activities	Percentage of Time
Hate to...	■ Commute to work ■ Attend meetings ■ Work on weekends	10%
Have to...	■ Email ■ Prepare budgets ■ Administrative work	40%
Indifferent to...	■ Supervise others ■ Read reports	15%
Like to...	■ Lead project teams ■ Work with others ■ Meet new people	25%
Love to...	■ Learn new skills ■ Solve problems ■ Work on big projects	10%

The *like to* world is inside personal space and it fulfills what people truly desire. Without a clear core goal, people believe working hard and making more money will automatically lead to a balanced life. Wrong! This is why work-life balance is one of the biggest issues in project management. In the absence of knowing and committing to one's core goal, people fill time with more *have to* work. This is a losing proposition. To achieve self-sustainability, it takes a breakthrough on two fronts: first, break free of any excessive dependency on team and organizational spaces, which are "need to" and "have to" motivators, respectively; and secondly, living in a "have to" world is a choice—from this moment forward you *can* give higher priority to the things you truly love to do.

D. WINNING ATTITUDE

If you take into account all your success factors, it becomes abundantly clear that you have much more going for you than you realize. Knowing your core goal and success factors gives you a clearer understanding of what you do well and why. Having that insight makes you a better project manager by giving you greater self-confidence, self-direction, self-sustainability, and a basis for identifying the right opportunities and goals for yourself. No one has your same set of goals and success factors, and it is this uniqueness that makes you a winner. A "winning attitude" means that you have what it takes to achieve your goals—positive internal dialogue, self-confidence, inner strength, accountability and self-esteem. Having a winning attitude is essential for pursuing new opportunities, expanding space, growing, learning, turning the corner and sustaining personal success. You are able to stay encouraged when others are discouraged; move your project forward when others want to turn back; and see opportunities when others see trouble.

Project managers who possess low set points, low self-confidence and small personal spaces attribute their failures to other people, negative circumstances and bad luck. They're "losers" because they have *lost personal space* and have retreated into their lower level. Losers are disconnected from the real world—they live in the past while success lives in the future. They carry a self-defeating, defensive attitude such as, "I don't see why I have to do this," "Why do I have to change?" Or "Why do people always do this to me?" It's easy to find reasons why you can't succeed; it takes much more mental strength, courage and foresight to find new and creative ways to win. An unwillingness to change, go forward and accept new ideas is a loser's mindset.

Ineffective project managers believe success is beyond their control and blame their lack of progress on external factors. In contrast, good project managers see their barriers as internal and within their control. Winners believe in themselves and posses the ability, energy and confidence to continuously improve. They believe they have the capacity to *do more* and *be more* in terms of learning and growing.

Assessing Your Attitude

To assess your attitude, think back to the last major *problem* or *conflict* that you had in your most recent projects. What was your attitude in addressing and solving the problem? Using both columns in Table 13.3, mark an "X" against the mental characteristics that *strongly represented your attitude during the conflict*.

Your true attitude is revealed during times when you are at-risk of losing, such as during project conflicts and problems. It's easy to carry a winning attitude when everything is going well. *The true test of attitude is when things get tough and there is a "win-lose" opportunity.* In projects, win-lose situations challenge you to find a "win-win" solution, which can only be accomplished with an optimistic, positive, "can do" attitude. From your assessment, what was your ratio of "winning attitudes" (left column) to "losing attitudes" (right column)? A two-to-one ratio (winning-to-losing) indicates a positive attitude; a three-to-one or greater ratio means a strong winning attitude. A winning attitude makes people more self-sustainable because it motivates collaboration, inclusion, trust and constructive behaviors.

In summary, winners see success; losers see failure. Winners see success from the inside; losers see failure from the outside. Winners feel in control, while losers feel loss of control. When making decisions and solving problems in projects, take a winning attitude and seek different points of view, make observations, be proactive and look for win-win solutions.

Table 13.3 Attitude Assessment

X	Winning Attitude	Losing Attitude	X
	Forward-looking	Backward-looking	
	Take responsibility	Seek fault	
	Step up and act	Step back and avoid	
	Observational	Judgmental	
	Space producer	Space robber	
	Trustful	Distrustful	
	Low fear level	High fear level	
	High set point	Low set point	
	Selfless	Selfish	
	Give control	Take control	
	Use right values	Use no or wrong values	
	Forgive and learn	Punish and reprimand	
	Proactive	Reactive	
	Visible, transparent	Hidden, conceal	
	Inclusionary	Exclusionary	
	Optimistic	Pessimistic	
	Want to win	Afraid to lose	
	"Can do", "and" person	"Can't do," "but" person	
	Want to, like to, love to	Need to, have to, hate to	

E. SELF-ESTEEM

Having a winning attitude helps people go longer and stay in the game but more important, it helps build self-esteem. When it's all said and done and the project is completed, the only thing that matters is how people feel about themselves and what they have accomplished.

Self-esteem is a self-judgment of personal value. It is based on a number of elements including self-confidence, self-respect, pride and happiness. These emotions are modulated by the person's culture, experiences and personality type and the feedback that they receive from others. The opinions, expectations, respect and trust of family, friends, colleagues and loved ones have a large impact on a person's view of themselves. But the most important human factor that *defines* people's self-esteem is their personality type:

- Rationals take pride in their individual accomplishments and competencies. They feel best when they have mastered and conquered subjects, challenges, problems and goals.
- Guardians feel good about themselves when they have successfully completed their work and responsibilities. Their value is in the quality and execution of their work and the appreciation they receive from others.
- Idealists judge their self-worth by the support, acceptance, affirmations and affections from others. They feel best about themselves when people sincerely praise, respect and trust them.
- Artisans see their value in their bold actions and abilities to make impact. They feel best when they are free, unencumbered, empowered and self-sufficient.

In project management, people feel good about themselves when their needs and wants are fulfilled (Chapter 5)—they are given tasks and responsibilities that make them feel important, challenged, valued, accepted, respected and trusted. High self-esteem requires positive internal dialogue and self-belief coupled with strong external reinforcement, especially from the boss, management and colleagues at work. Regardless of the feedback from others, people will judge themselves through their own values. If they feel "valued" through the eyes of others, it must also be internally accepted and reinforced through personal experiences. People who struggle to accept praise and compliments are often plagued by self-criticism and poor internal dialogue that devalue their self-worth such as, "I always say stupid things"; "I'm not good enough to lead projects"; and "I can't do it as well as others."

Understanding what drives self-worth is important for individual and team motivation, risk-taking, productivity, creativity and problem-solving. Self-esteem is defined by one's personality type but it is maintained by good mental behaviors: positive internal dialogue, self-confidence, inner strength and accountability. Self-criticism, self-doubt, fear, exclusion, and a "losing attitude" are all enemies of self-worth.

Self-esteem is a product of personal success. *You only lose self-esteem when you believe you are losing, failing or quitting.* If you believe every opportunity is a potential for achievement, success and personal growth, your self-esteem will always stay strong.

How Much is Your Bottle of Wine?

In a wine tasting study conducted by Stanford and the California Institute of Technology (Plassmann et al., 2008), eleven graduate students were told that they would be trying five different Cabernet Sauvignons, identified by price, to study the effect of sampling time on flavor. Two inexpensive, two expensive and one moderately priced bottles of wine were used in the test. For the two inexpensive bottles of wine, one was labeled by its true price of $5 and the other marked with a false $45 price tag. For the two expensive pair of wines, one was marked with its actual $90 price and the other by a false $10 tag. The fifth bottle of wine was marked with its correct $35 price. Water was given between wine samplings to refresh their palate. The wines were randomly presented for tasting, and the students were asked to judge the wines based on flavor and tasting enjoyment. During the test, researchers monitored the participant's brain activity in an area that is associated with pleasure, the medial orbitofrontal cortex.

The study reported that the participants said they could taste five different wines, even though there were only three, and expressed that the expensive wines tasted better. Moreover, the researchers found increased brain activity in the medial orbitofrontal cortex with the perceived increase in the price of the wine. Evidently, simply the taste expectation of the more expensive wine was enough to trigger a greater pleasure response in the brain. Thus, people's brains were influenced more by the labeled price of the wine than the actual composition of the wine. This implies that knowing the price of a bottle of wine can affect the pleasure response of the brain. It shows that people's expectation is much more powerful in their brains than the actual situation.

Whether people drink a $5 or $90 bottle of wine, the feeling of pleasure will correspond to their perceptions. In parallel, if people have high expectations of themselves, their brain activity will likely follow in suit. It's not that people should pretend to be a $1,000 bottle of wine when they're not. The point is that no one should see themselves as either an inexpensive or expensive bottle of wine when they aren't. Is your wine over-priced or underpriced? The price of your wine is based on the composition of your personal effectiveness cycle—values, diversity, internal dialogue, space, set point, confidence, fear, inclusion, inner strength, accountability, goals, passion and self-esteem. *Only by knowing who you are will you realize the true price of your wine.*

Assessing Your Self-Esteem

Self-esteem is a self-judgment of your personal worth. Using Table 13.4, estimate your self-esteem by assessing how strongly you agree with these eight statements. On a scale of 1 to 5 with 1=low and 5=high, rate each statement based on how you currently feel about yourself. There are no right or wrong answers.

Does your average score reflect how you feel about yourself? What was your range of scores? Were your scores consistent or were certain ones much higher or lower than others? A higher score does indicate a higher self-esteem, but you may be surprised to learn that a high or low self-esteem does not necessarily correlate with

Table 13.4 Self-Esteem Assessment

Rate 1 to 5 (1=Low, 5=High)	*I believe...*
	I am an important person.
	I possess above average self-confidence.
	I possess above average talents and skills.
	I am at or near the top in work performance.
	I am at or near the top intellectually.
	I am at or near the top professionally.
	I am influential.
	I am a high achiever.
	Total Score
	Average Score (divide total score by 8)

one's performance (Baumeister et al., 2003). Both high and low self-esteem have potential pluses and minuses.

Low self-esteem. An average score of 2 or less indicates *low self-esteem,* which may reflect a very modest, self-critical and inferior view of oneself relative to others. Having low self-esteem may make a person more vulnerable to self-criticism, worry, insecurity, risk aversion, pessimism, discouragement and low self-confidence; however, if managed properly it can help a person work harder, be more cooperative and collaborative, and accept feedback and guidance from others.

High self-esteem. An average score of 4 or greater implies high self-esteem, which can translate into greater happiness, self-confidence, assertiveness, self-initiative, decisiveness, optimism and resilience. Having too high of a score may imply a strong personal ego, self-admiration and narcissism, which cause one to seek more validation, attention and power. High self-esteem can make one more prone to defensiveness, arrogance, self-indulgence, exclusion and conceit.

Balanced self-esteem. An average score between 2 and 4 indicates a balanced self-esteem where a person has great pride and confidence in oneself but with a recognition that he or she is also flawed and may not be at their best at times. They carry a realistic, skeptical, open-minded and humble view of themselves and welcome feedback and opinions from others.

Similar to other human factors and mental behaviors, such as fear, inclusion, internal dialogue, confidence, and motivation, self-esteem is not static but is constantly shaped by culture and experiences. A well-balanced self-esteem gives people the best flexibility, resiliency and sustainability.

FINAL SELF-SUSTAINABILITY CHECKLIST

To determine your overall self-sustainability, take the final "test" questions for your five elements of self-sustainability:

1. **Core Goal.** In ten seconds or less, can you articulate your core goal? Is your core goal strongly linked to your core values?
2. **Success Factors.** Of the six human factors listed in Table 13.1, do you have at least four rated as "strengths"?
3. **Personal Life Balance.** Is time spent on the things you "love" and "like" to do greater than your "hate" and "have" to do? Do you spend over 25% of your time on your passions? (Table 13.2)
4. **Winning Attitude.** Are your number of "winning attitudes" during conflict exceeding your number of "losing attitudes" by at least two-to-one? (Table 13.3)
5. **Self-Esteem.** Is your self-esteem score between 2 and 4? (Table 13.4)

If you were able to say "yes" to these final questions, you are on track to be self-sustainable. Are you satisfied with your assessment of the five elements? What goals would you set to improve your sustainability? The key is to set goals and improve in areas where you have the most energy and interest. The most popular goal for improving self-sustainability is to spend more time on the things that people love to do—living a more passionate life. This says a lot about what people value the most.

SUMMARY

✓ Self-sustainability is the capacity to achieve continuous success with a high degree of efficiency, independence, self-efficacy and self-fulfillment, where your three "needs" (well-being, social acceptance, self-purpose) and three "wants" are satisfied (achievement, recognition and fulfillment).

✓ In the personal effectiveness cycle, going from achievement to sustainability requires knowing who you are (core values), what you have (success factors), and what you want (core goal) and pursuing your goals with an effective personal life balance, winning attitude and healthy self-esteem.

✓ The five key elements of self-sustainability are:
  ✓ Core goal: This is your definition of success—your ultimate desire and purpose that you continuously seek in your lifetime. Your core goal is tied to your core values.
  ✓ Success factors: These are the talents, skills, motivators and passions that enable you to consistently achieve your goals with great competency, independence and self-sufficiency. These are the factors that if you did *not* have them, you would likely fail. This chapter provided a simple four-step process for finding your critical success factors.

✓ Personal life balance: This is the desired balance between what you *like and love* to do and what you *hate and have* to do. In the absence of pursuing what you truly love, time is filled by *have to's*. The secret is to rebalance your *hate to's* and *have to's* with more *like to's* and *love to's*.

✓ Winning attitude: It's a state of mind that supports positive thinking, self-confidence, inner strength, accountability and self-esteem, which are all required to achieve your personal goals and success.

✓ Self-Esteem: It's how you feel about yourself, an appraisal of your self-worth. Self-esteem is lost when you believe you're losing, failing or quitting. The secret is to believe that every opportunity is a potential for achievement, success and personal growth.

✓ The mark of a truly successful project manager is in their ability to consistently achieve project results, meet personal expectations and fulfill their core goal—to do the right things, in the right way, to get the right results and feel right when the job is done.

14

Fulfilling Your Personal Effectiveness Cycle

Your personal effectiveness cycle does not end with sustainability. Certainly goals, passion and self-esteem give you tremendous power to keep your cycle going but your personal effectiveness depends on how well you take past learnings and apply them to the next cycle of decision-making, motivation, achievement and sustainability. Lessons learned are cycled forward to improve your thinking, diversity and values and help you make better decisions and take more effective actions on future challenges.

Just as you do "look backs" on past projects, personal effectiveness is a continuous cycle of learning from past experiences and risks. Whether your projects turn out good or bad, the value is in the learning and the personal judgment, consequences and feelings resulting from your performance. Each time you complete a cycle, you reveal more of yourself and what you need to do to achieve greater personal success—as you know yourself better, you will become a better project manager because *you are at your best when you are yourself.* That's why it's so important to take more risks, opportunities and experiences in life and cycle as many times as possible. The personal effectiveness cycle is like the "Monopoly" game, you are rewarded each time you pass "Go," so why not take more chances and go for it?

The preceding chapters have attempted to reveal the best tools, tips and strategies for improving your intrapersonal and interpersonal skills in project management through introspective assessments, ideas, stories and self-evaluations. These principles and methods were designed to increase your awareness and ability to "bring out the best in yourself" by understanding the role of human factors in personal effectiveness. This book presented a simple, unified, easy-to-use model—*the personal effectiveness cycle*—to help explain, organize and improve your "soft" skills as a project manager in decision-making, motivation, achievement and sustainability. Managing projects requires skills in managing eight human factors for making the *right decisions*, taking the *right actions*, achieving the *right goals* and *feeling right* about the outcome:

- *Diversity*: who you are
- *Values*: what you believe in
- *Space*: what motivates you externally

- *Set Point*: what motivates you internally
- *Fear*: what enables and inhibits your performance
- *Inclusion*: what keeps you engaged, centered and collaborative
- *Passion*: what you love to do
- *Goals*: what you want and your ultimate desire (core goal)

Diversity and *values* define your "wants" and "needs" and give you strength, knowledge and character that are reflected in your behaviors and interactions with others. You increase your chances for success by having a motivating work environment, *expanding your space* and increasing your influence in organizational and team spaces. Self-confidence produces greater motivation and new opportunities, which leads to achievement when you have the inner strength, accountability, *fear and inclusion* to "turn the corner." *Passion* and *goals* give you the inspiration, focus, energy and self-sustainability to accomplish your ultimate *core goal*. However, your human factors are not fool-proof; they can also lead to misjudgments, negative internal dialogue, false beliefs, self-deceptions, exclusion, unreasonable expectations, low achievement, unmet goals and low self-esteem.

Your human factors are constantly challenged and at times you may feel discouraged, insecure, mentally squeezed and disheartened. However there's no need to despair, you have two mental assets that will keep you motivated, inspired and strong: the belief in yourself and the belief in your goals (Figure 14.1).

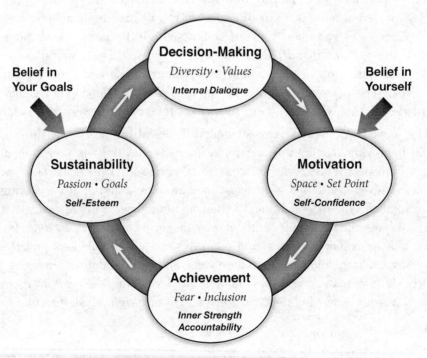

Figure 14.1 Two Beliefs in the Personal Effectiveness Cycle

- **Belief in yourself.** Knowing "who you are" enables you to think and behave honestly and confidently. No more personal dishonesty, self-doubt, pretension and self-distrust. You can go forward with greater self-confidence, self-motivation and self-determination. You *recognize, accept and realize who you are*; you're comfortable in your own skin and no longer depend on others for validation and self-esteem. Your strength comes from your diversity, values, character, humility and uniqueness. You are independent, self-sustaining and free to be who you are, pursue what you believe in and determine your own success.
- **Belief in your goals.** Knowing "what you want" and pursuing them with great inner strength, accountability and *passion* allows you to create more opportunities and "turning points" in your life. You no longer fear making mistakes or taking criticism as you stay focused on your goals. Your goals and passions keep you above the fray of conflicts, disputes, criticism and difficult people. And when you hit your goals, you're now *doing the right things, in the right way and feeling **great** about it,* which reinforces your values, behaviors, motivations and achievements. With each success, you increase *sustainability*—efficiency, independence, self-efficacy and fulfillment.

Your values serve as the foundation for your goals, giving you continuous hope and motivation to do great things. When your personal effectiveness cycle is working, you're wasting less time and energy and accomplishing more with less effort and stress. Your cycle is no longer a random, wishful journey but a purposeful life filled with great moments of joy, kindness, gratitude, learning, fulfillment and personal satisfaction.

Staying on the Right Path

Success is not an end result but a continuous journey that cycles throughout your life. As opportunities arise, your ability to successfully act on those opportunities depends on your personal effectiveness and how well you stay on the right path. How do you know if you're on the right path? It's simple: you're on the right path when you make decisions and take actions that are true to your values, diversity, passions and core goal—it's the *inside path* of your personal effectiveness cycle. It's a path where you're not worried about being judged, controlled and defined by other people and *outside* elements. The outside path is loaded with mental traps: externalizing negative judgments, neediness, small space, low set point, fear, exclusion, weak goals, poor self-esteem and "have to" work. In contrast, the inside path produces self-sustainability: efficiency, independence, self-efficacy and self-fulfillment. You're not waiting for someone else to make decisions, take actions and provide consequences for you. It is a path of self-direction, self-determination and self-sustainability— a path that belongs only to you. Now that you know your path, what's holding you back? Life is short. *You are at your best when you are yourself* so go after what you were meant to do. Expand your space, express your passions, set your goals, do great things and celebrate your many moments of success.

References

Baumeister, R. F., and Leary, M. R. The Need to Belong: Desire for Interpersonal Attachments as a Fundamental Human Motivation. *Psychological Bulletin*, 1995, 117, 497–529.

Baumeister, R. F., Campbell, J. D., Krueger, J. I., and Vohs, K. D. Does High Self-Esteem Cause Better Performance, Interpersonal Success, Happiness, or Healthier Lifestyles? *Psychological Science in the Public Interest*, 2003, 4, 1–44.

Briggs, K. C., and Myers, I. B. *Myers-Briggs Type Indicator*. Princeton, New Jersey: Educational Testing Service, 1957.

Chirkov, V., Ryan, R. M., Kim, Y., and Kaplan, U. Differentiating Autonomy from Individualism and Independence: A Self-Determination Perspective on Internalisation of Cultural Orientations, Gender and Well Being. *Journal of Personality and Social Psychology*, 2003, 84, 97–110.

Compton, William C. *An Introduction to Positive Psychology*. Wadsworth Publishing, 2005.

Covey, S. R. *Everyday Greatness*. Nashville: Rutledge Hill Press, 2006.

Covey, S. R. *Principle-Centered Leadership*. New York: Simon and Schuster, 1990.

Covey, S. R. *Seven Habits of Highly Effective People*. New York: Simon and Schuster, 1989.

DeCharms, R. *Personal Causation*. New York: Academic Press, 1968.

Deci, E. L. *Intrinsic Motivation*. New York: Plenum, 1975.

Elliot, A., and Harackiewicz, J. Approach and Avoidance Achievement Goals and Intrinsic Motivation: A Mediational Analysis. *Journal of Personality and Social Psychology*, 1996, 70(3), 461–475.

Franco, L., Gibbons, J., and Barrington, L. *I Can't Get No — Job Satisfaction, That Is: America's Unhappy Workers* (Research Report No. 1459–09–RR). New York: The Conference Board, 2010.

Fredrickson, B. L. The Value of Positive Emotions. *Am. Scientist*, 2003, 91, 330–335.

Goldsmith, M. *What Got You Here Won't Get You There*. New York: Hyperion, 2007.

Hardin, G. The Competitive Exclusion Principle. *Science, 1960*, 131, 1292–1297.

Hills, Le Grand and Piachaud. *Understanding Social Exclusion*. New York: Oxford University Press. 2002.

Harter, S. Effectance Motivation Reconsidered: Toward a Developmental Model. *Human Development*, 1978, 1, 661–669.

Hitlan, R. T., Cliffton, R. J., and DeSoto, M. C. Perceived Exclusion in the Workplace: The Moderating Effects of Gender on Work-Related Attitudes and Psychological Health. *North American Journal of Psychology*, 2006, 8,217–236.

Jung, C. G. *Psychological Types*. New York: Pantheon Books, 1923.

Janis, I. L. Effects of Fear Arousal on Attitude Change: Recent Developments in Theory and Experimental Research. *Adv in Experimental Social Psychology*, 1967, 4, 166–224.

Janis, I. L. *Victims of Groupthink*. Boston: Houghton Mifflin Company, 1972.

Keirsey, D. *Please Understand Me II*. Del Mar, California: Prometheus Nemesis Book Co., 1984.

Kohlberg, L. *Essays on Moral Development, Vol. I: The Philosophy of Moral Development*. San Francisco, CA: Harper & Row, 1981.

Lancaster, L. C., and Stillman, D. *When Generations Collide*. New York: HarperCollins, 2002.

Latham, G. and Locke, E. Building A Practically Useful Theory of Goal Setting and Task Motivation, *American Psychologist*, 2002, (57)9, 705–717.

Leary, M. R. *Interpersonal Rejection*. New York: Oxford University Press, 2001.

Luciani, J. J. *The Power of Self-Coaching*. New Jersey: John Wiley and Sons, 2004.

Luthans, F. *Organizational Behaviors*. New York: McGraw-Hill Irwin, 2008.

Maslow, A. *Motivation and Personality*. New York: Harper Collins, 1954.

McClelland, D. C., Atkinson, J. W., Clark, R. A., and Lowell, E. L. *The Achievement Motive*. Princeton: Van Nostrand, 1953.

McNamee, P. and Celona, J. *Decision Analysis for the Professional*, SmartOrg, Inc., Fourth Edition, 2005.

Mor Barak, M.E., Cherin, D.A. and Berkman, S. Organizational and Personal Dimensions in Diversity Management: Ethnic and Gender Differences in Employee Perceptions. *Journal of Applied Behavioral Sciences*, 1998, 34, 82–104.

Plassmann, H., O'Doherty, J., Shiv, B., and Rangel, A. *Marketing Actions Can Modulate Neural Representations of Experienced Pleasantness. Proc Natl Acad Sci*, 2008, 105(3), 1050–1054.

Project Management Institute. *A Guide to the Project Management Body of Knowledge (PMBOK® Guide)*, Fifth Edition, 2013.

Report of the Presidential Commission on the Space Shuttle Challenger Accident, Washington D.C., June 6, 1986, Chapter 6, p 148.

Rokeach, M. *The Nature of Human Values*. New York: The Free Press, 1973.

Ryan, R. M. and Deci, E. L. Intrinsic and Extrinsic Motivations: Classic Definitions and New Directions. *Contemporary Educational Psychology*, 2000, 25, 54–67.

Schwartz, S. H. Value Priorities and Behavior: Applying of Theory of Integrated Value Systems. In C. Seligman, J. M. Olson, & M. P. Zanna (Eds.), *The Psychology of Values: The Ontario Symposium*, 1996, 8,1–24. Hillsdale, NJ: Erlbaum.

Schneider, K. T., and Hitlan, R. T., & Radhakrishnan, P. An Examination of the Nature and Correlates of Ethnic Harassment Experiences in Multiple Contexts. *Journal of Applied Psychology*, 2000, 85, 3–12.

White, R. W. *Ego and Reality in Psychoanalytic Theory.* New York: International Universities Press, 1963.

Wong, Z. A. *Human Factors in Project Management: Concepts, Tools, and Techniques for Inspiring Teamwork and Motivation.* San Francisco: Jossey-Bass, 2007.

Wong, Z. A. *Team Work Life Harmony Survey.* Human Factors and Team Dynamics in Project Management, U.C. Berkeley Extension. Spring, 2010.

Yerkes, R. M. and Dodson, J. D. The Relationship of Strength of Stimulus to Rapidity of Habit Formation. *Journal of Comparative Neurology and Psychology*, 1908, 18, 459–482.

Index

About the Author

Zachary A. Wong, Ph.D., D.A.B.T., is a highly acclaimed instructor of personal effectiveness, human factors, team dynamics and leadership at the University of California at Berkeley Extension and Adjunct Professor with the University of California at Davis. Dr. Wong has over thirty years of managerial and project management experience. He has held senior positions in research and technology, strategic planning, business analysis, mergers and acquisitions, and risk assessment. He has extensive experience as a senior manager and team facilitator.

Dr. Wong is currently an *"Honored Instructor"* at the University of California at Berkeley Extension and has received numerous teaching awards. For over twenty years, Dr. Wong has published and taught a wide range of courses in project management, team development, project economics, global marketing, environmental toxicology and strategic planning.

He was born and raised in San Francisco and received his Ph.D. in Toxicology and Pharmacology from the University of California at Davis. He has served extensively on project teams, executive leadership teams and decision review boards in public committees, industry associations and academia. Dr. Wong lives in Alamo, California, with his wife, Elaine and two daughters, Amy and Sarah.

To contact the author:
zawong@sbcglobal.net

Learn How To Die
The Easy Way.
Nick Waplington

** TROLLEY **

Learn How To Die The Easy Way
Nick Waplington

Text by Carlo Mc Cormick

Welcome to a brave new world. It's an easy and accessible place. We know lots of people gladly living their lives there already. Foreign and familiar, it offers all the comforts and disease of the culture from whence it was conjured. Just jump right on in, the web waters are warm in this perverse, predatory and all too pervasive cyber-swamp. Here, full-time fools can spout half-baked ideas and semi-truths without any recourse to the skewered ratio of irrationality and ignorance. Think of it as a grand millennial costume ball, an endlessly unfolding shopping mall. You can come as anyone and leave with anything. Yes it's a brave new world indeed, where everything is possible as long as you pay no attention to the cowards hiding behind streaming curtains. Just like the mighty all-powerful Oz the substance is in the projection, not the weak and the geek riding on a mouse. And just as surely as that former fiction exploded the dimensions of representation with the technology of Technicolour to birth a Pop planet, our new meta-fictions are here to collapse that space with an industry of icons that will just as surely give rise to an even more artificial Eden. Nick Waplington has been busy tending this garden of unearthly delights, cloning its illusory flowers of seduction into mutant hybrids of hucksterism, and mining the fecally fertilised soil for all its component contradictions and curious conformities.

These places.com don't really exist per se, but you will recognise them anyway as prior projections of this domain's more probable terrain. In turns pathetic, provocative and prurient, Waplington's webscape may often be disturbing or just as likely appealing, but most of all it's just plain hilarious. No more a condescension than an endorsement, it's really a comic celebration of the chaos. The implicit content and barely-hidden agenda Waplington makes absurdly evident in these mock-sites are like generic caricatures of the various genres that populate and pollute the Internet. Taken individually, these home pages can run the gamut from shocking to mundane, from the completely unbelievable to the all too likely. And just when you think something is so completely over the top that it defies all credibility and reality, you might just be surprised at how much stranger the truth is from fiction. There is no editorial here, just an index of our cultural idiocy. Of course

whatever their spiel, Nick's got his tongue so firmly in cheek the logic gets tripped up in the lurid prose of its own visual and linguistic propaganda. The artist's position in all this is opaque, his politics as invisible as his hand in the slick spectacle of these hard-sell surfaces. But if the point is ambiguous, the perspective itself is far from ambivalent. Waplington avoids the polemics of cultural critique in favour of a more sarcastically-edged social satire. Portraits of the public discourse that are so outré they hardly need exaggeration, they are nonetheless unmistakable as piss-takes on the inherent stupidity of the medium and its message.

For the many who have come to regard Nick Waplington as one of the most honest and deeply humanist voices in contemporary art, the pleasure he now takes in perpetrating the same kinds of vulgar lies and cheap come-ons of the infotainment industry, and the brutally dark humour he bares here, constitutes an aesthetic shift so abrupt and outrageous that the very terms of continuity by which we measure creative evolution are all but obliterated. And this eye of his, so celebrated for its formidable focus on the visual and social marginalia that has long existed outside the frame of photography- how his pictures, captured by a truly understanding lens and a master's command of photographic craft and history, could show us things we actually didn't know before or make us look at the overly familiar in utterly new ways- how could it be that it has strayed so far from the viewfinder to gaze instead on something so lowbrow? My God, this young man from England has already produced five stunning, challenging and widely-respected photo books in his remarkably brief and still rising career behind the camera, and this new work of his is not even photographs! Well, Waplington's work has never been easy, you would think we might have gotten used to that by now. And just because he may make it all look simple and effortless, don't think that it has been any less work for him. Nick Waplington knows all about being clever. So when we try to justify work that is so blatantly stupid against the subtle heart of The Living Room and The Wedding or the casual brilliance of The Indecisive Momento, we might also keep in mind that there is always a discrete method to his madness.

www.anarchy.co.uk
www.depression.com
www.satanicvacation.org
www.cigarettecollector.com
www.pentaloft.com
www.revenge.com
www.adultchildlove.com
www.webcemetry.com
www.jesusmilitia.com
www.safari2000.com
www.plasticafantastica.com
www.thirdparty.com
www.glorydays.com
www.socialclimber.co.uk
www.spacester.com
www.communist-vacation.com
www.privatearmyinternational.com
www.whitesupremacist.com
www.ladyivanka.com
www.incartoilet.com
www.fiercelove.org
www.childprodigy.com
www.extramaritalrelationship.com
www.dwarfswop.com
www.easymillion.com
www.downsite.com
www.theafterlifeinvestmentcorp.com
www.sylvianpike-healing.com
www.thirdworldfriend.com
www.snowdropadoption.com
www.theotherside.com
www.cyrogenics.com
www.newawakenings.org
www.americahusband.com
www.socialistinternational.com
www.assasination.com
www.ordinanceinternational.com
www.get-thin-kwik.com
www.lookingback.org
www.noncommitment.com
www.dickregal.com
www.objects-of-desire.com
www.primemover.com
www.mammal2mammal.com
www.orgycircle.com
www.thelordneunaveria.com
www.familytradegy.com

narchy.co.uk-www.anarchy.co.uk-www.anarchy.co.uk-www.anarchy.c

anarchy.co.uk

We can help you access literally thousands of websites telling you of victories against the system.

THE SYSTEM YOU HATE,

and like you we hate the system.

and if we don't destroy it, it will destroy us. It's time you joined us in taking action.

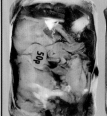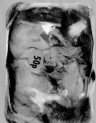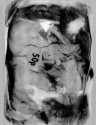

We have operatives in place to record these events for your pleasure, so you can WATCH THE DESTRUCTION OF THE EVIL SYSTEM at your leisure in the privacy of your own home. But don't worry we encript so not even your server will know what you're up to.

* Mindless acts of vandalism are taking place right now.

*Don't miss out.

*Join now.
FEELING SUICIDLE?
don't be selfish, we show you how to take some yuppy scum with you.

the violence chart is updated hourly.

CHATBOXES

Freedom fighters against the system need love too!

w.anarchy.co.uk-www.anarchy.co.uk-www.anarchy.co.uk-www.anarch

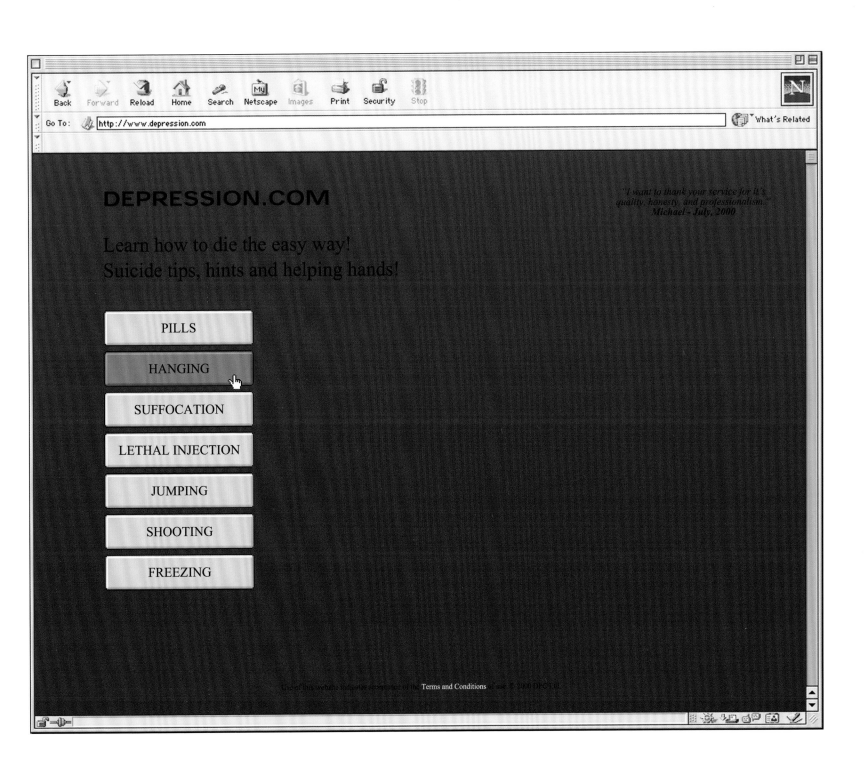

Options menu

Use this menu to turn your
imagination on or off, select
object information, and choose
physical, celebral, voluntary, or
involuntary, links and motivation
wrap options.

Go To: http://www.cigarettecollector.com

CIGARETTECOLLECTOR.COM

A COLLECTOR RUN SITE. WE WORK WITH ALL THE MANUFACTURERS BUT ARE NOT SPONSORED SO WE REMAIN IMPARTIAL.

Who said cigarettes are just for smoking?

They are a unique piece of our history. As collectors we are preserving an important part of global culture. Heritage is an important part of a collectors purpose, Passing knowledge on to the next generation is the main purpose of the cigarette collectors club.

Conventions

Swops

Sales Boards

Auctions

Paraphenalia

Chatrooms

Parties

Collector Fares

Exhibitions

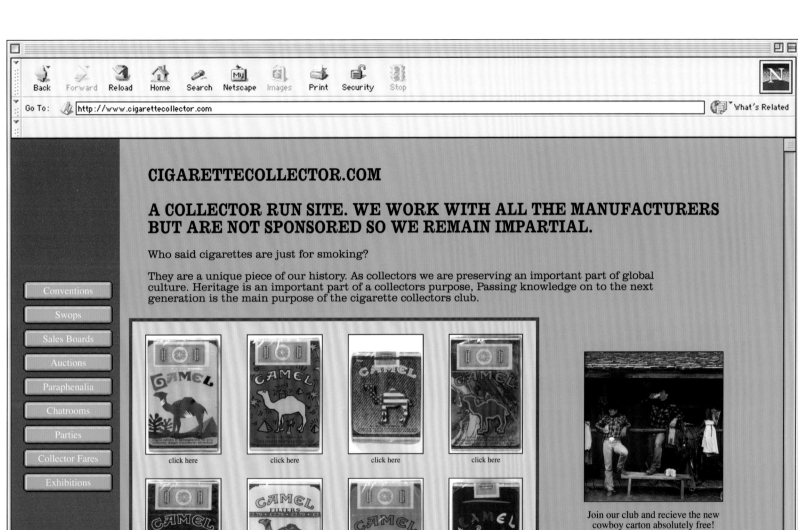

click here   click here   click here   click here

click here   click here   click here   click here

MORE EXAMPLES LIKE THIS AVAILABLE ON OUR SWOPS PAGE

Join our club and recieve the new cowboy carton absolutely free!

Unique Specials, Gifts, Interviews with designers, growers, manufacturers!

The pentaloft are the one and only realtors to offer the unique combination of the penthouse and the loft. With pentaloft you can experience the downtown artists bohemian life while retaing the penthouse refinement of the uptown executive, however the mood takes you. This is a new century so mix and match lifestyles rule the day, at pentaloft we lead the way!

Live the everyday existence or experience the pentaloft!

Next phases soon
releasing in your area

Willingness for more
than dream fulfilment

Final Phase
Released Today!

Pentaloft.com

Live Beyond The Realms Of Comfort!
Show off you unique housing abilities within the cosmopolitan refineness of a pentaloft!

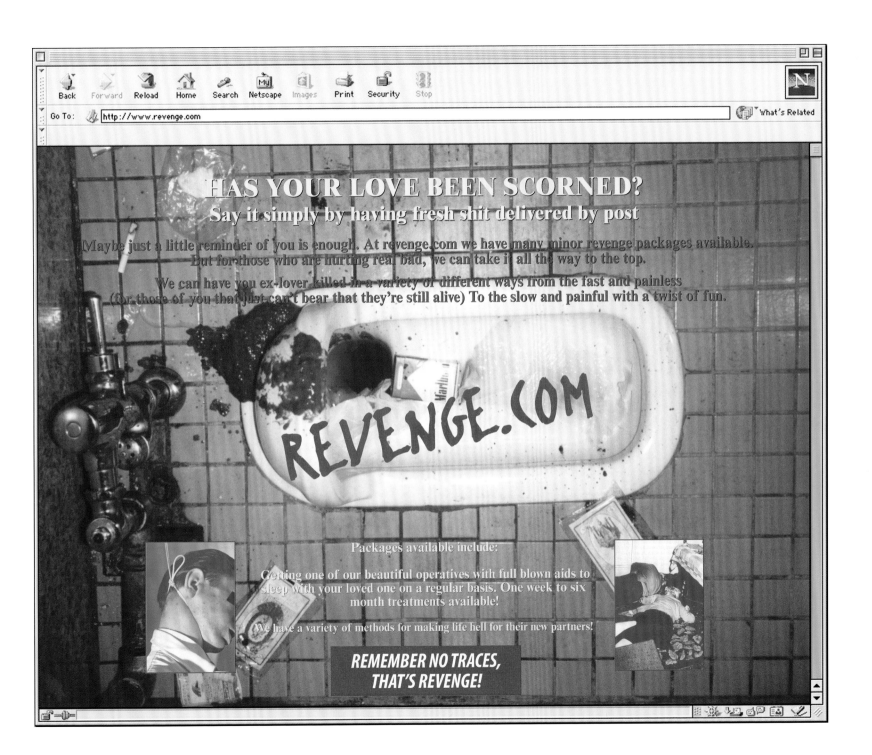

Go To: http://www.adultchildlove.com

ADULTCHILDLOVE

THE SITE THAT UNDERSTANDS THAT YOUR FEELINGS ARE ONLY NATURAL

LINKS

JOIN

TOYS

FRIENDS

We can arrange documents for you stating that you are a child care worker/teacher/youth operative.

Hundreds of holidays are available to all your favourite destinations. Amazing packages to South East Asia and Eastern Europe. As new locations open up we will keep you informed. Friends will be working for you, catering for your needs everywhere you travel with us.

We can take care of any legal matters that arise for you in your home country. Also we try to stay one step ahead of legalisation globally for your peace of mind.

Safe houses and friends through our network of chums.

Membership allows you access to kids current favourite games, candy and T.V. shows, so your knowledge is always up to date. Both sexes and all age groups are covered. This kind of information will be of value to you in your search for a child sweetheart.

Enjoy introductions to voluntary work in organisations such as the Scouts/Guides, and other such organisations – global lists.

 Remember, You are not alone.

Edit menu

Use this menu to undo thoughts,
modify actions, change results,
cut, copy, destroy, subvert and
set ridicule preferences.

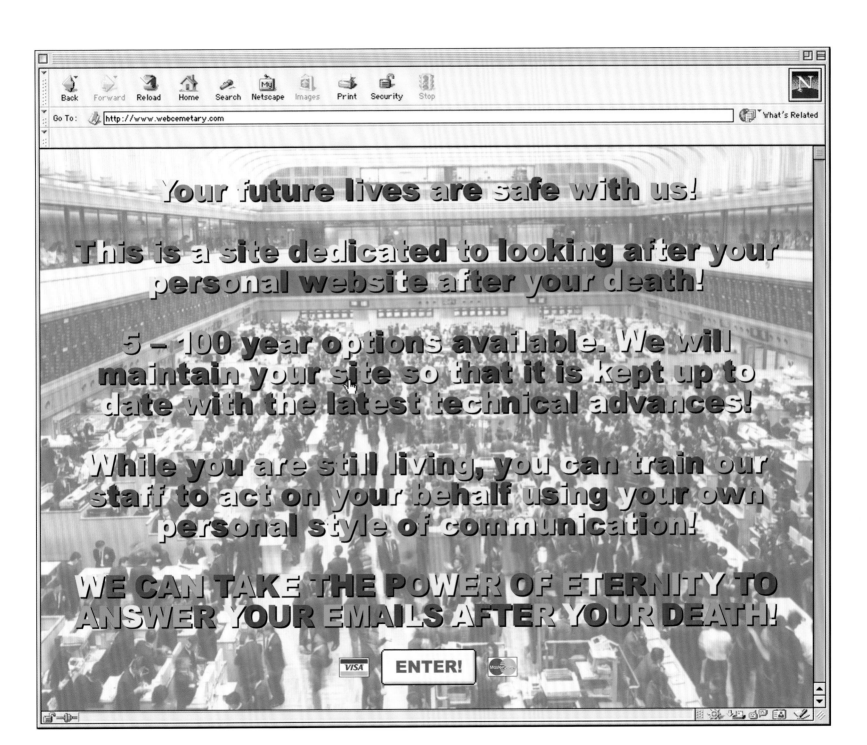

Home | Jesus People | Talk To Us | Search | Tour

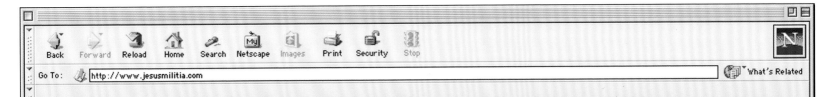

YOUR DAILY HOROSCOPE

your b'day [/ /] **GO!** *check it out!*

FREE ADVERTISING ON THIS SITE CLICK HERE!

Join the March for Jesus!

subscribe now to get our FREE NEWSLETTER containing info on all forthcoming Jesus Militia events around the world!

Check out some of our awards and reviews

Jesus Militia Shop for books, music, videos, witnesswear

Exclusive Jesus Militia Pics!

A special welcome to all our visitors Worldwide
Welcome to the Jesus militia. We Are Loving People!

GUNS FOR GOD!

Hoping for salvation, then join us in the fight!
Bread = Guns. Wine = Ammunition.

To fight the Devil, we need to play him at his own game!

We'd like to hear from you. Please sign our guestbook or e-mail us your comments and requests.
If you like this site, please link to it, and tell your friends about us.

Bookmark our page now for future reference!

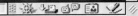

Go To: http://www.safari2000.com

Go Tribal Weekends!

Click Here For Free Brochure

Safari2OOO.com
TRAVEL IS YOUR LIFESTYLE

SAFARIS by country

SAFARIS by Activity

LODGES & CAMPS

GAME PARKS

PLANNING A SAFARI

MAPS OF THE WORLD

CONTACT US

**NEW!!! NEW!!! NEW!!!
SPECIAL EXPEDITIONS**

- Meeting a local? We'll give you tips.

- Beggar and riff raff avoidance.

- Nifty Drinks!

- Do you want to look and feel like a native wherever you go? We show you how!
- Our international directory is the online version of your little black book!
- Advanced planning for perfect looking places!
- The luxury of high class for less, with the power to know why!
- How to use cash in the third world and still give the impression that only quality plastic can!
- Independence of mind, body and wallet!

THIS SITE IS NOT FOR BEGINNERS!   SURFACE IS EVERYTHING!

PLASTICAFANTASTICA

Congratulations on choosing Plasticafantastica

This is the home for those of us who live the physically enhanced lifestyle to the full!

Exclusive pictures of celebrity operations here! Don't wait, JOIN NOW for a FREE bonus week!

CLICK HERE TO SEE THEM!

Plasticafantastica's surgeons don't do surgery for anyone else

If you live outside the U.S. Click Here for form!

For Secure Commerce Processing, Click Here!

CLICK HERE TO PAY BY CREDIT

First Name:			
Credit Card #:		**Exp. Date:**	mm/yy
Email Address:		**Zip Code:**	
Username:		**Over 18?**	Check box if YES
Password:		**Verify Pwd:**	

Back Forward Reload Home Search Netscape Images Print Security Stop

Go To: http://www.thirdparty.com
What's Related

thirdparty.com

Welcome to thirdparty.com. The thirdparty specialists for all occasions!

Physical alibies provided for all circumstances and occasions!

We provide people of any sex, age or race in person anywhere in the world at short notice!

EXAMPLE 1: CHEETING HUSBAND
Does your wife need to meet your long term drinking buddy after years of false anecdotes? We've got him!
Trained to fit your stories an optional extra!

EXAMPLE 2: GAY GUY
Do you parents need to meet your fiance/wife regularly, to get your inheritance? We've got her!

SCENE OF CRIME!

COMING OF AGE!

CHANCE MEETINGS!

SPOTTED AT IMPORTANT HISTORICAL OCCASIONS!

All available at thirdparty!

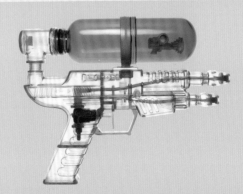

THE BEAUTY OF THIRD PARTY IS YOU CAN BUILD UP A WORKING RELATIONSHIP WITH YOUR ALIBI!

Join our mailing list!
Enter your email address below, then click the 'Join List' button

[   ] Join List

Powered by Webstaff

Special menu

Use this to empty the trash,
erase lives, and to start and
stop economic growth.

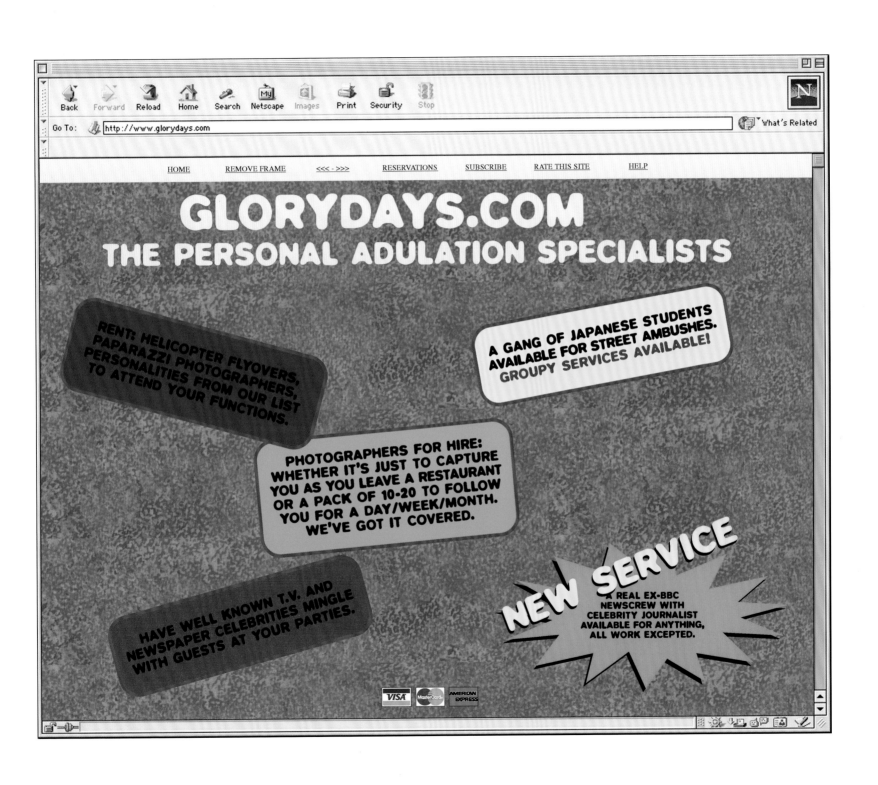

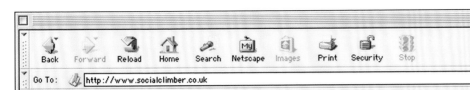

MEET CELEBRITIES LIKE YOURSELF

Learn how to get yourself photographed and into the limelight!

Tickets to the best T.V. shows!

Learn how to sell your stories to tabloid newspapers from people who have been there time and time again!

We have the hotest social calender!

Get emails from the celebs and invites to parties with the stars!

Williams
Grant
Pinochet
Ball
Minogue
Gallagher
Turner
Houston

Hindley
Putin
Jackson
Clinton
Biggins

Your Name Here:

Hurley
Cruise

Sutcliffe
Crow
Nielson
Manson
Sheen
Hanks
Pot
Moore

Ryan
Di Caprio
Chegwin
Beckham
Blair
Taylor
Guest
Spielberg

Designer clothes a season in advance!

FUTURE STAR

Chat with other celebrities!

Back | Forward | Reload | Home | Search | Netscape | Images | Print | Security | Stop

Go To: http://www.communist-vacation.com | What's Related

COMMUNISTVACATION.COM

IN THE HEART OF FREE AMERICA, TAKE A JOURNEY BACK IN TIME. EXPERIENCE THE
LATEST IN THEMED VACATION. 1930'S STALINIST SOVIET UNION IS NOW AVAILABLE AT
STALINGRAD U.S.A. THE LEADING HAMMER AND SICKLE IN COMMUNIST BLOCK HOLIDAYS.

!!!PACKAGES AVAILABLE!!!   !!!PACKAGES AVAILABLE!!!   !!!PACKAGES AVAILABLE!!!   !!!PACKAGES AVAILABLE!!!

THE OPPRESSED.	THE OPPRESSOR.	POLITBURO DELUXE.
Packages for individuals, families, weekends, short breaks, 2 week vacations	Packages for individuals, families, weekends, short breaks, 2 week vacations	(includes dacha). Build your own vacation

SPEND YOUR DAYS WORKING ON OUR COLLECTIVE FARM OR TANK
FACTORY – 18 HOUR SHIFTS WITH HOURLY PUBLIC HUMILIATIONS!

ATTEND EVENING MARX CLUB LECTURES (COMPULSORY).
AFTERWARDS VODKA STYLE DRINKS ARE AVAILABLE AT OUR
ROADSIDE CONCESSION STANDS!

BE: TORTURED, INDOCTRINATED, BEATEN IN PUBLIC!

MOCK PUBLIC EXECUTIONS OF CAPITALIST OPPRESSORS – ATTEND AS A VIEWER OR A VICTIM.	DO YOU WANT TO CREATE YOUR OWN PURGE?	DIVERT OUR MOCK RIVER.	FOR ONLY A FEW MORE DOLLARS YOU CAN RUN A SOLZHENITSYN INDORSED GULAG.	MURDER OUR COSSACKS. WE HAVE A FULL ARMY.

AFTER THE DOGMA, THE IDEOLOGICAL WAR HAS BEEN WON. SO WHY NOT STEP BACK IN TIME AND ENJOY A COMMUNIST VACATION!

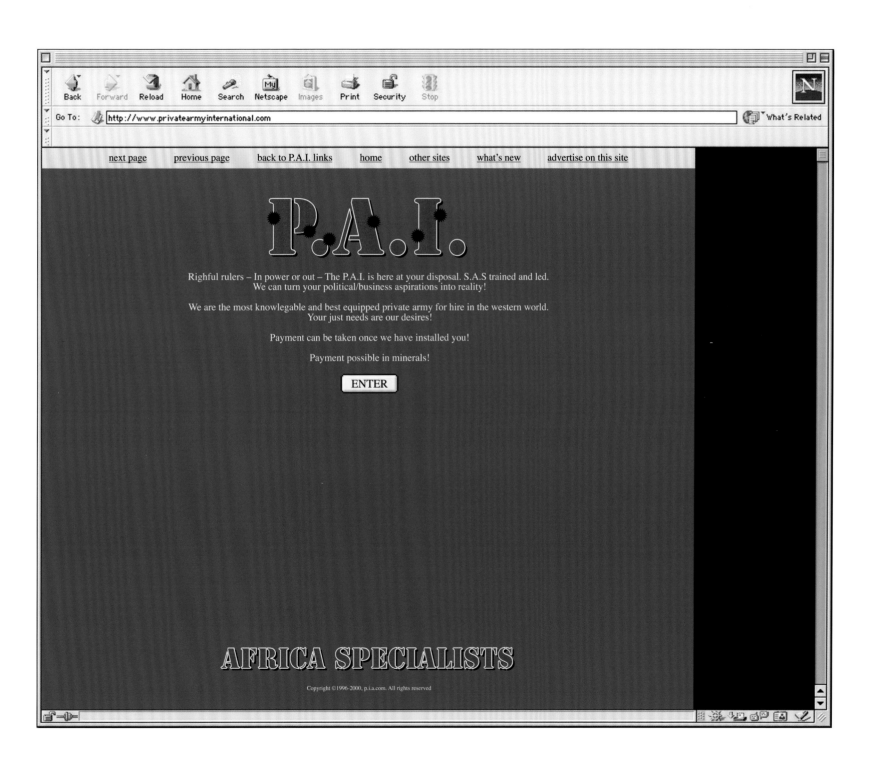

next page   previous page   back to P.A.I. links   home   other sites   what's new   advertise on this site

P.A.I.

Righful rulers – In power or out – The P.A.I. is here at your disposal. S.A.S trained and led.
We can turn your political/business aspirations into reality!

We are the most knowlegable and best equipped private army for hire in the western world.
Your just needs are our desires!

Payment can be taken once we have installed you!

Payment possible in minerals!

ENTER

AFRICA SPECIALISTS

View menu

Use this menu to change
the way people are in the
active window.

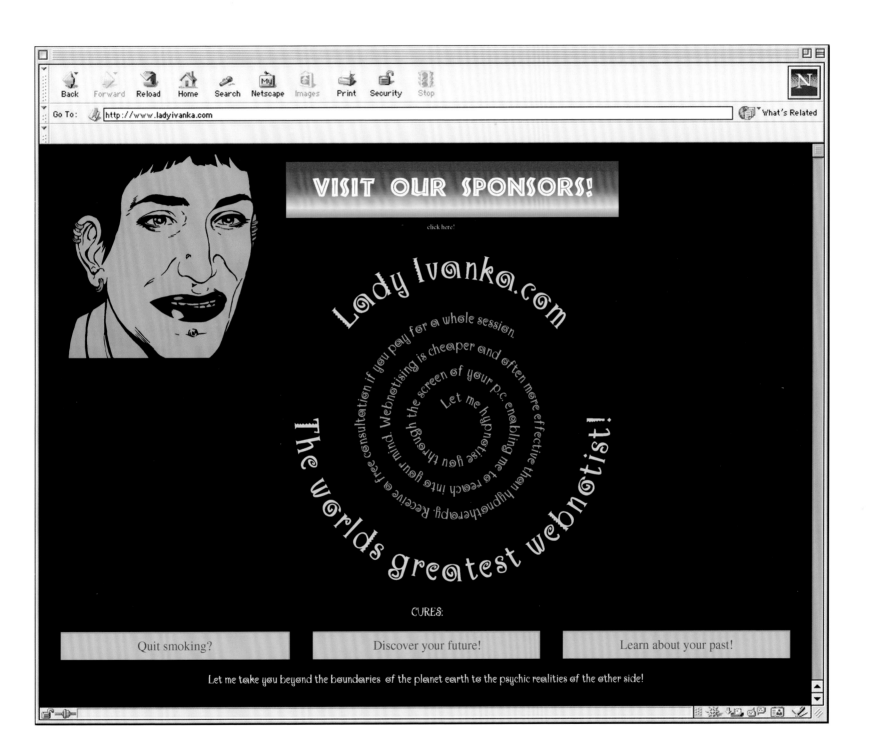

Back | Forward | Reload | Home | Search | Netscape | Images | Print | Security | Stop

Go To: http://www.incartoilet.com What's Related

WELCOME TO
incartoilet.com!

BROCHURE

SALES

FITTING

TEST DRIVE

DOUBLE PACK

CLEANING

INSTRUCTIONS

LINKS

Do you have to make long journeys and detest the inconvenience of stopping to use the bathroom?

HABITAT proudly present the worlds first in-car toilet.

This collapsable item fits neatly between the front and back seats so you can enjoy relief while on the move.

Mums and dads, it's sure to put a smile back on your child's face!

habitat

4736

So load up and off you go, knowing that you don't have to stop to drop!

CHILD PRODIGY

Is your child a Model/Genius/Actor?
Well welcome home, finally a place that understands
you and the future of your offspring.

- Is the school not responding to the desires and needs that you have for your child?

- Does no-one understand, not even your nearest and dearest?

- Are you fed up of your child being treated like any other?

- Yes it's time to stop it and we're here to help – welcome home new CHILDPRODIGY.com member!

- Meet other parents, many of whom have gone on to make comfortable livings out of their children!

- Get introductions to top model agencies!

- Think, within weeks of joining CHILDPRODIGY.com, you could be the parent of one of the richest children in the country!

- From our one to one classroom/site, you will recieve all the coaching you need to fine tune your baby into a 'Star Of Tomorrow'!

- FREE online screen test for your child!

- We can help you relax safe in the knowledge that your child is finally safe and secure for life!

Initial consultation and membership only £100!

VISITOR NUMBER 1.000.216

FAMOUS CHILD EXPERT JACKO IS OUR PATRON. COULD YOUR CHILD MEET HIM?

Window menu

Use this menu to change your
view from your window, bring
a different object in front of
the window or show glutton
bar, tools or presention
controls.

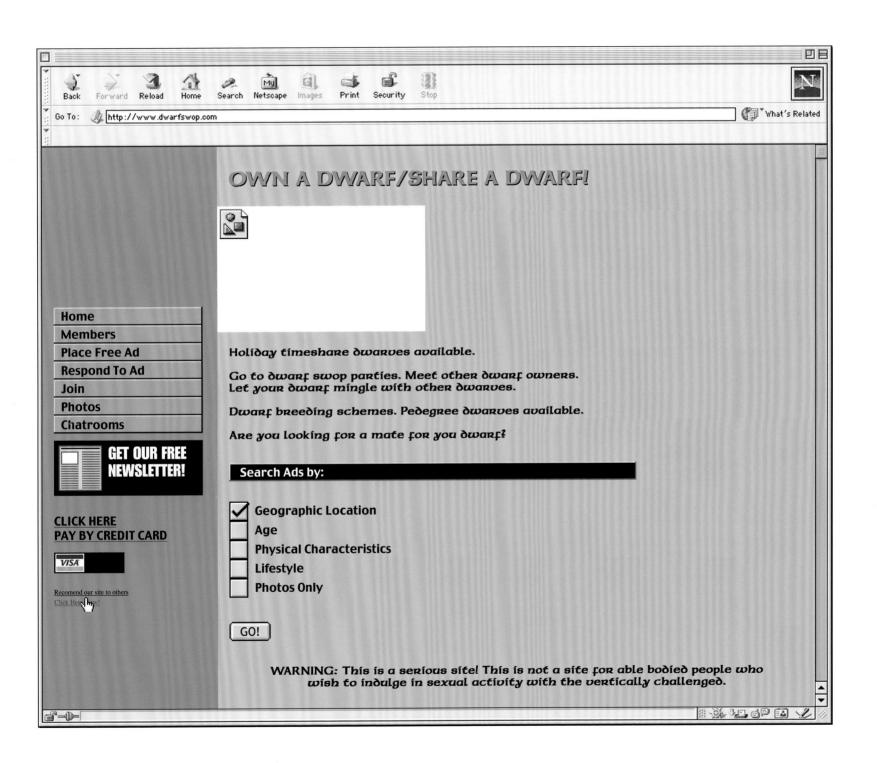

OWN A DWARF/SHARE A DWARF!

Holiday timeshare dwarves available.

Go to dwarf swop parties. Meet other dwarf owners.
Let your dwarf mingle with other dwarves.

Dwarf breeding schemes. Pedegree dwarves available.

Are you looking for a mate for you dwarf?

Search Ads by:

☑ Geographic Location
☐ Age
☐ Physical Characteristics
☐ Lifestyle
☐ Photos Only

GO!

**WARNING: This is a serious site! This is not a site for able bodied people who
wish to indulge in sexual activity with the vertically challenged.**

Home
Members
Place Free Ad
Respond To Ad
Join
Photos
Chatrooms

GET OUR FREE NEWSLETTER!

CLICK HERE
PAY BY CREDIT CARD

VISA

Recomend our site to others
Click Here Now!

Back Forward Reload Home Search Netscape Images Print Security Stop

Go To: http://www.dwarfswop.com

What's Related

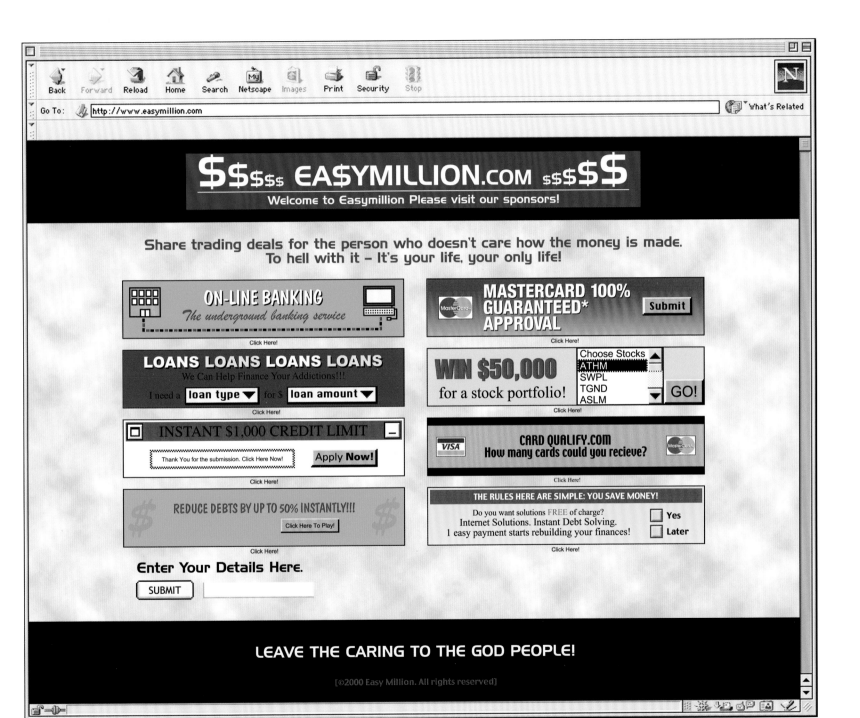

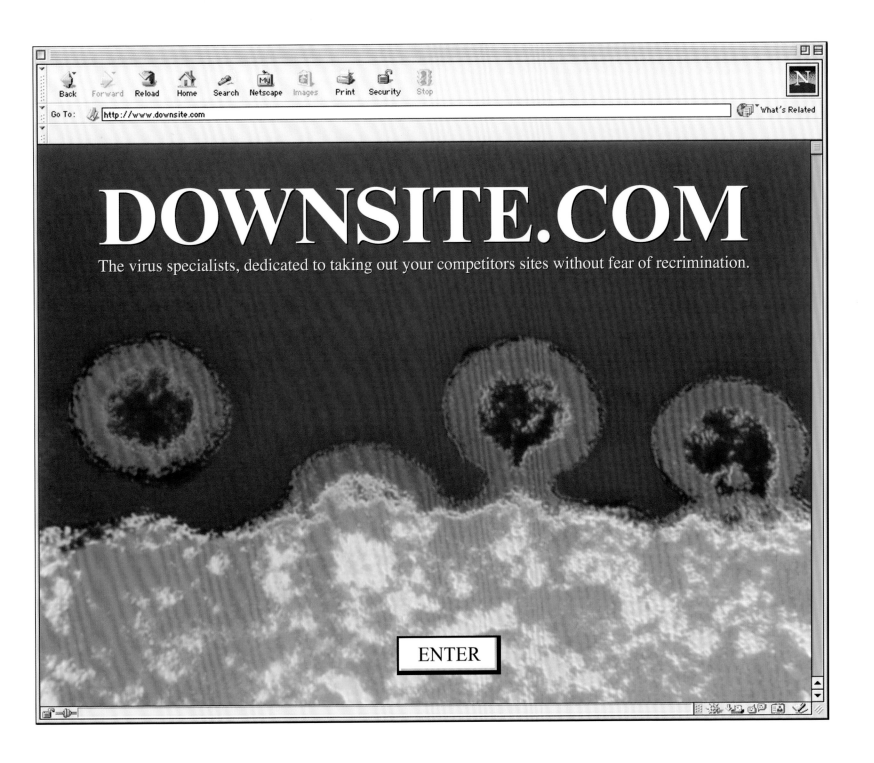

Format menu

Use this menu to change the appearance of parasites, groups, or entire populations and create winners and losers.

SYLVIAN PIKE – HEALING

**Sylvian Pike
Site Map**

Sylvian Pike
Main Page

Biography

News

Contact Info

Feedback

Guestbook

Links

MEMBERSHIP

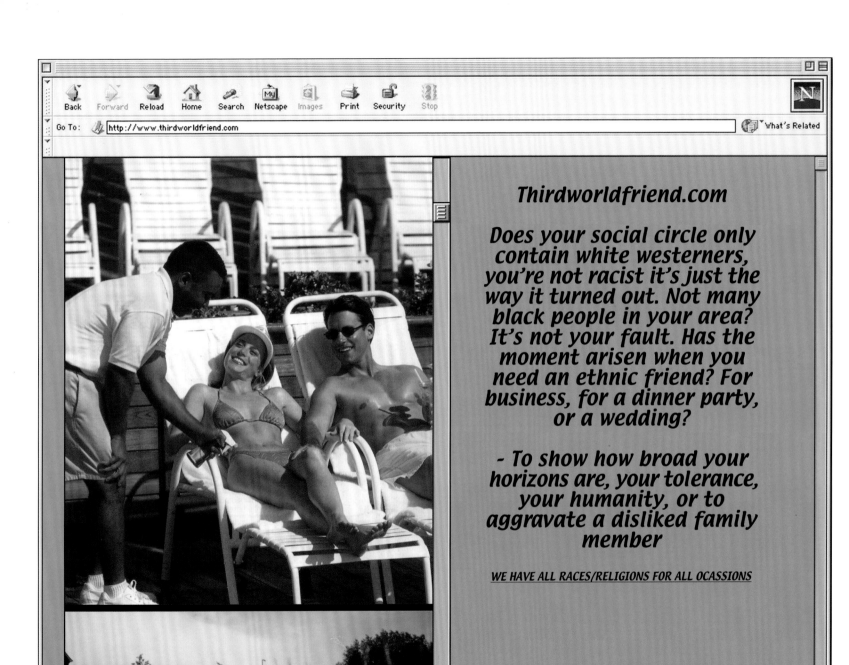

Thirdworldfriend.com

Does your social circle only contain white westerners, you're not racist it's just the way it turned out. Not many black people in your area? It's not your fault. Has the moment arisen when you need an ethnic friend? For business, for a dinner party, or a wedding?

- To show how broad your horizons are, your tolerance, your humanity, or to aggravate a disliked family member

WE HAVE ALL RACES/RELIGIONS FOR ALL OCASSIONS

Snowdropadoption.com

New born babies of yours and your loved ones racial group hard to source!

click here!

Snowdrop has caucasian babies available to be flown direct to you now!

The Otherside.com

The people who allow you to reach out beyond the grave and talk to your deceased loved ones via cyberspace.

Millions of people are now dead for whom email was their major form of communication while alive. Our psychics have discovered that it is still the main form of communication in the afterlife. We have developed the worlds first psychic server to allow you to talk to your loved ones on-line.

Don't worry if your loved one died before the invention of the internet, we have e-angels in heaven to teach your loved ones computer literacy, so via our psychic, you can be in contact again.

Please note a small fee is necessary to train people on the otherside who are currently computer illiterate. This is staggered on when they died. i.e. grade 1, 1990's — grade 10, 1900's. This is due to the fact that increasing the ghosts modern awarness gets more difficult the longer ago that they died. But anyone who can proove that they knew anyone in the 19th century, the training is free!

CYROGENICS

click on image to enter site

DO YOU WANT TO LIVE FOREVER?

Appearance menu

Use this menu to change
your outward appearance
using adornments.

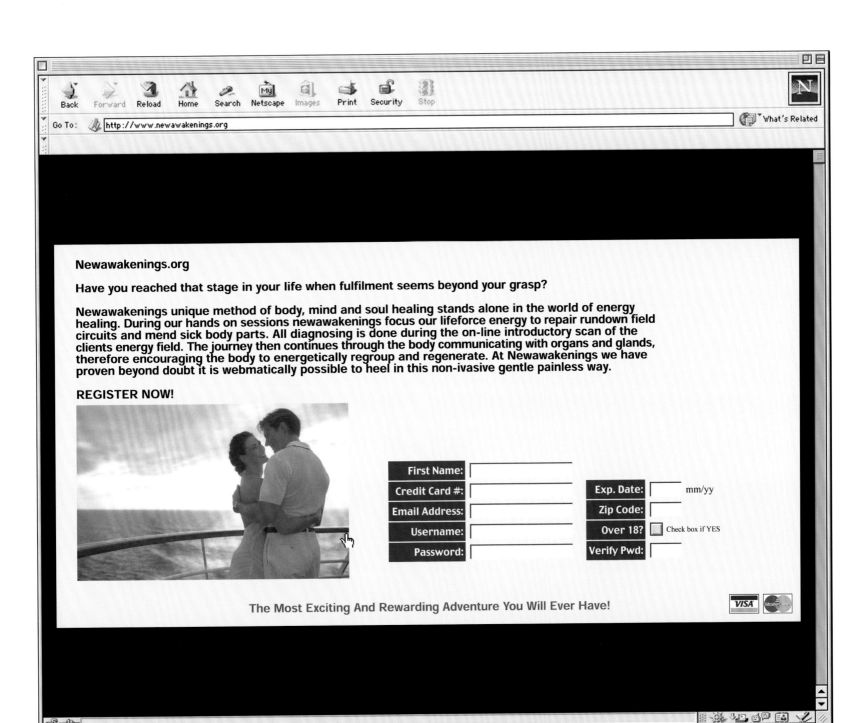

the-afterlife-investment-corporation.com

Heaven can be hell for the unprepared!

Eternity is a very long time to have no savings for!

Invest in your money after your death for when:

A) You return, the technology is coming.

B) Or via your psychic specialists for you to spend in the afterlife.

info@the-afterlife-investment-corporation.com

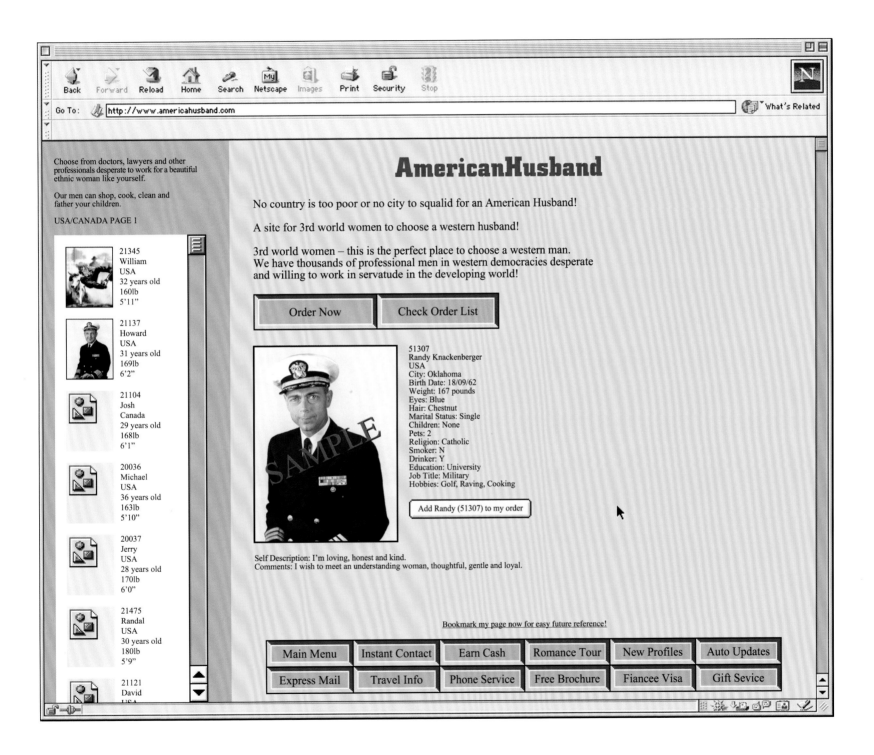

Back Forward Reload Home Search Netscape Images Print Security Stop

Go To: http://www.assasination.com   What's Related

WARNING: Complete indisgression guaranteed!

Assasination.com

This is a no traces site.

It operates in 2 stages.

(1) You give us the name of the person you need eliminated, with as many personal details as possible. This will enable us to build up a pricing profile – this is judged on ease factors not the wealth of the victim.
(2) When we have come back with a price (one week) there are 5 easy to understand categories:
1) 1000. 2) 2000. 3) 5000. 4) 10,000. 5) 100,000.

We also offer frightning, maiming and wounding options.

All this is done in complete confidentiality.
All hard drives used in your transactions will be destroyed after use.

Arrange menu

Use this menu to arrange, group, lock, align, rotate, flip, and penetrate your enemy.

Ordinance International

Meeting your needs first. 24 hour maximum delivery service on most items kept in stock.

Warning: This is a conniseurs site. You know your needs. For legal reasons we cannot say which items we carry, needless to say, ordinance international carries most protection and attack devices being produced today.

ENTER

New Clients Always Welcome!

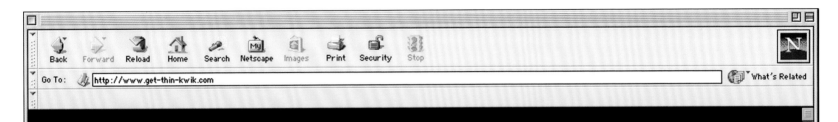

GET-THIN-KWIK.COM

Forget the bull, it pays to be thin. Even just a regular amount of fat is just too much.
We cut the crap and show you how it's done the easy way!

Smoke low-tar cigarettes, they supress your appetite.
At least one an hour whilst awake, more during stress or exercise!

Chew sugar-free gum while not smoking!

If this does not work for you, you need a drugs cocktail!

At Get-thin-kwik, we can do this for you, but you'll have to pay baby.
And for that, you'll have to join!

Get-thin-kwik.com The Real Weight Loss Company!

MEMBERS CLICK HERE!

By Clicking the ENTER button, I declare that

PLEASE CHECK OUR TERMS AND CONDITIONS AND
PRIVACY POLICY BEFORE AGREEING TO
ENTER THIS SITE!

EXIT   ENTER NOW!

CLICK HERE PAY BY CREDIT

(Privacy Policy)

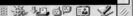

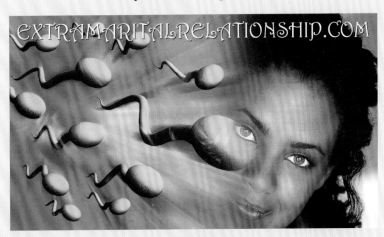

LOOKINGBACK.ORG
LOOKING BACK AT THEM.

THEM WHO WE KNOW ARE WATCHING US. A SIGHT TO EXPOSE THE EVOLS.
SISTERS & BROTHERS, A FORUM FOR YOU TO EXPOSE THE CORRUPTION OF MULTINATIONALISM.
SEND US YOUR EMAILS NOW!

10 COMPANIES TO OWN EVERYTHING BY 2020!!!

US OR THEM?

McDonalds	Microsoft	Sony	Cable & Wireless
Walmart	General Electric	Nike	Motorola
Glaxo Wellcome	Chrysler Damiler Benz	Smiths Industries	B.A.T.
Exxon	Boeing	Coca Cola	HSBC
Shell	Phillip Morris	B.O.C. Group	
ICI	Seagrams	News International	more!

TAKE THE MESSAGE AND PASS IT ON. THEY MUST NOT WIN!

Free Speech Online
Blue Ribbon Campaign
Click on the graphic to keep this
page as a Starting Point Hot Site

vote us a
Starting-
Point:
Hot Site

Add Active Channel
Add to Active Desktop

Outline menu

Use this menu to organise
people in human or subhuman
form.

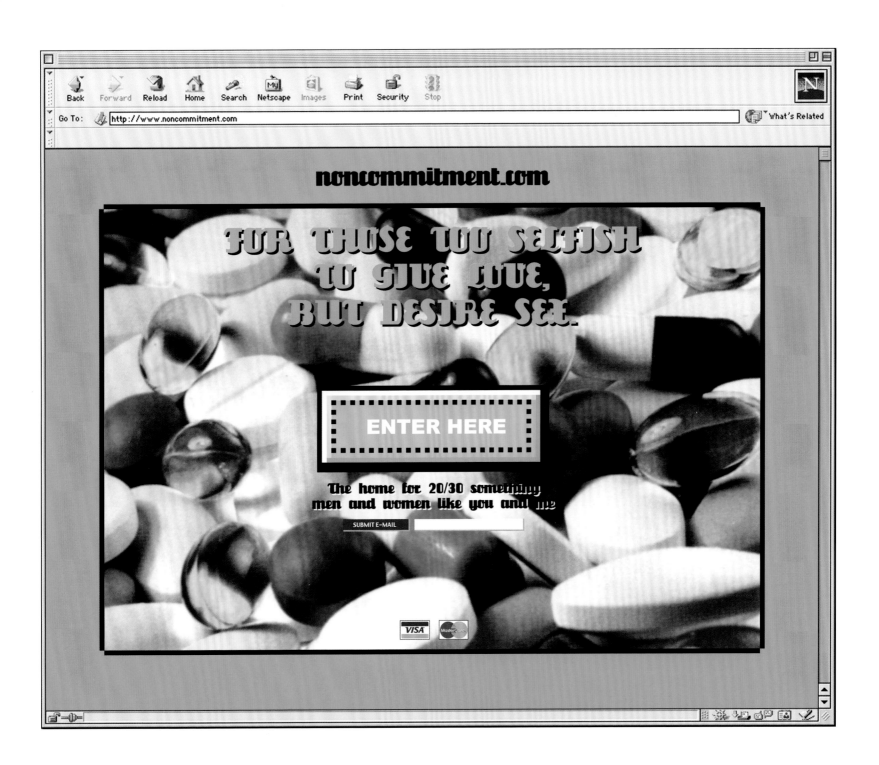

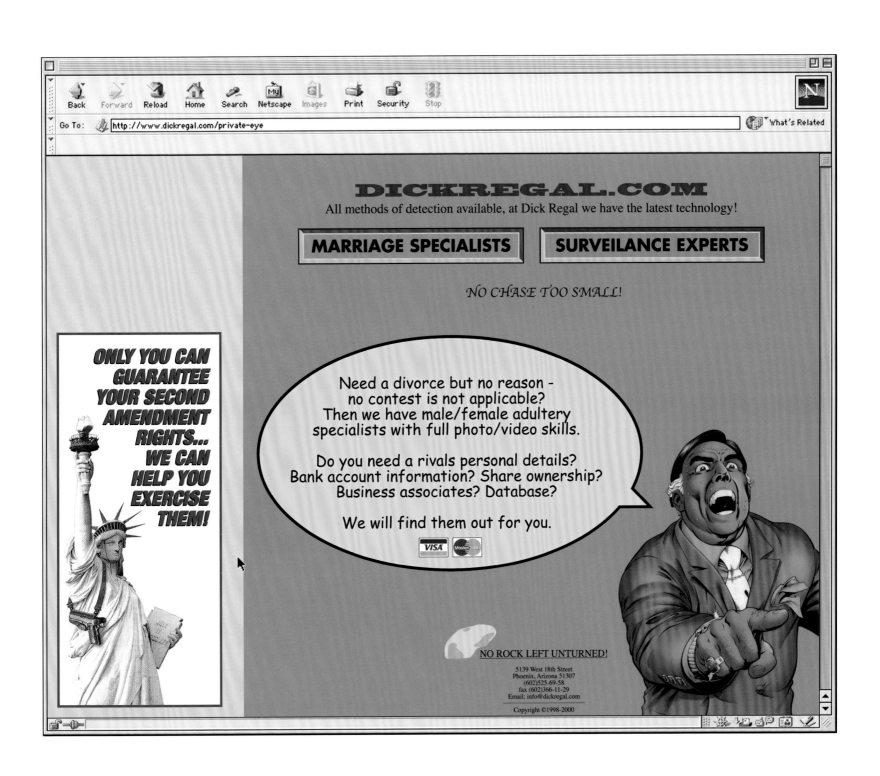

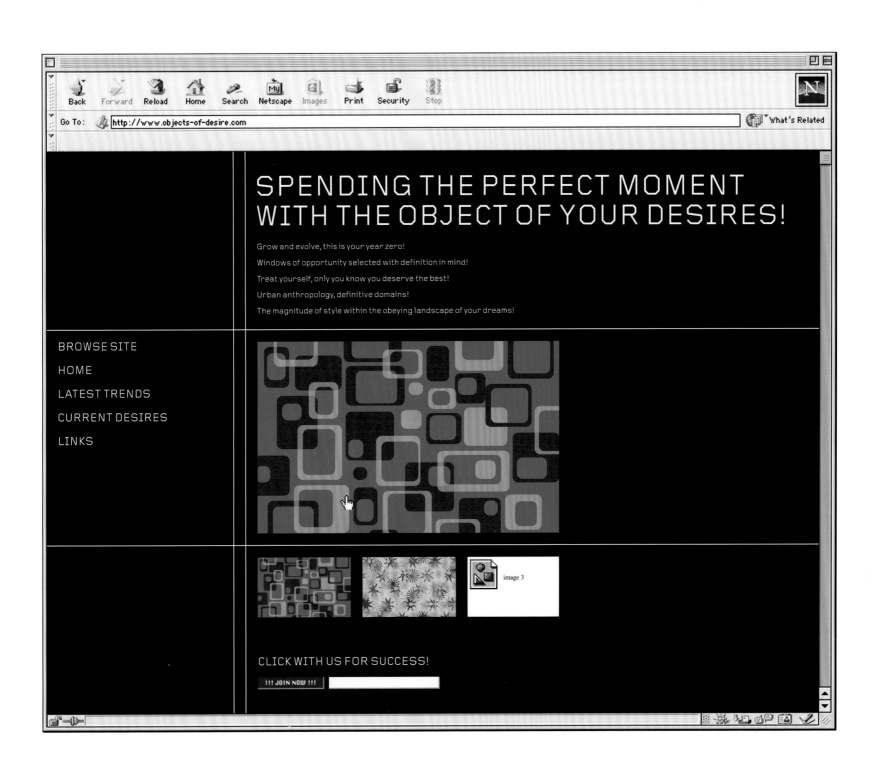

SPENDING THE PERFECT MOMENT WITH THE OBJECT OF YOUR DESIRES!

Grow and evolve, this is your year zero!

Windows of opportunity selected with definition in mind!

Treat yourself, only you know you deserve the best!

Urban anthropology, definitive domains!

The magnitude of style within the obeying landscape of your dreams!

BROWSE SITE

HOME

LATEST TRENDS

CURRENT DESIRES

LINKS

image 3

CLICK WITH US FOR SUCCESS!

!!! JOIN NOW !!!

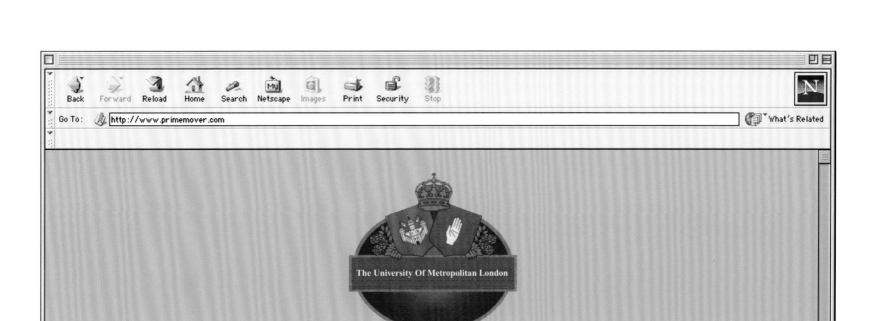

The University Of Metropolitan London

This is an educational programme conducted under licence from the university of Metropolitan of London!

Join our 3 year online bachelor of honours degree in self refinement (male)!

This is a top-up degree aimed at sophisticated businessmen who to go that little bit further in their quest to be a true gentleman!

We offer you the chance to refine your conversational skills with a group of professors.
Each one is trained in a different subject to suit your needs.
Subjects include finance, business, languages, art, travel, music!

Enter into on-line lectures where you are simultaniously an individual and part of a group!

Up to an hour of personal questions available at the end of each session!

One-to-one tutorials available!

Discounts available for extra tutorials!

Why not come beyond cyberspace and attend one of our residential retreats!

Stunning campuses situated at a number of strategic locations!

Remember if you enjoy studying the three years can go as slow as you wish!

Group and Personal humiliation available for your advancement!

Primemover for gentlemen everywhere!

PRIME MOVER!

Window menu

Use this menu to change your
view of the current status quo,
bring a different document
window to the front, or show
room bar, accents or
presentation controls.

parties   chatroom   bulk food   farmhouses

mammal2mammal

All types of love catered for through our site specific home pages. Just click on the species of your love.

The site for people whose relationship with their pet goes beyond the plutonic.

Forbidden Love

NO, Natural Love

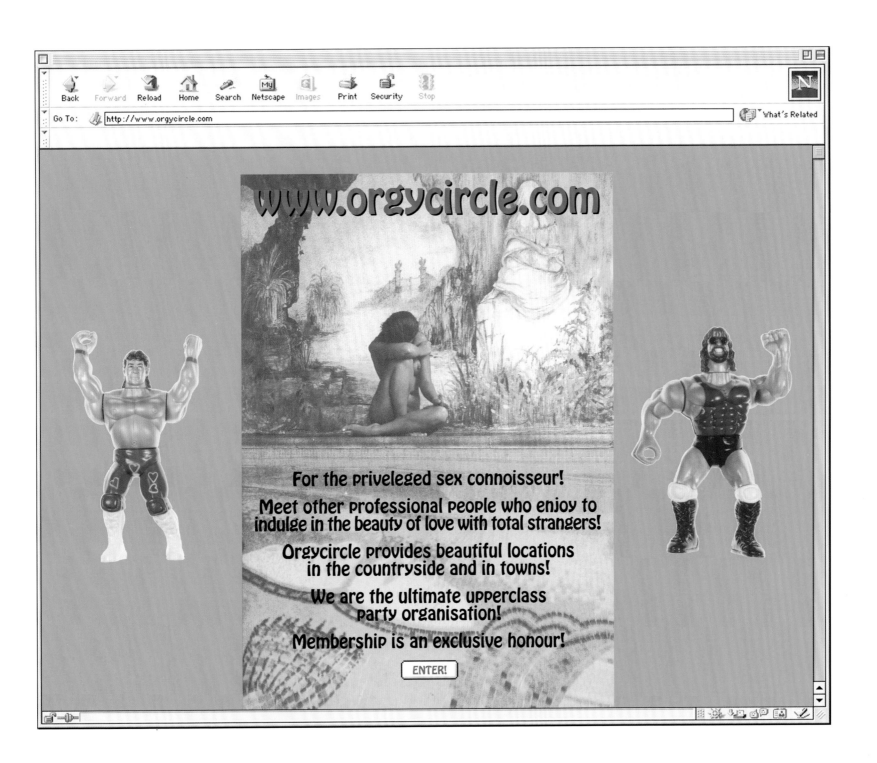

THELORDNEUNAVERIA

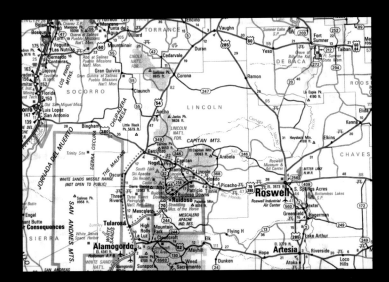

THELORDNEUNAVERIA.

MASTER OF THE UNIVERSE. SAVIOR OF ALL MORTAL SOLES.

THE ONE AND ONLY TRUE GOD. HAIL, FOR HE WALKS AMONG US.

CLICK HERE TO ENTER!

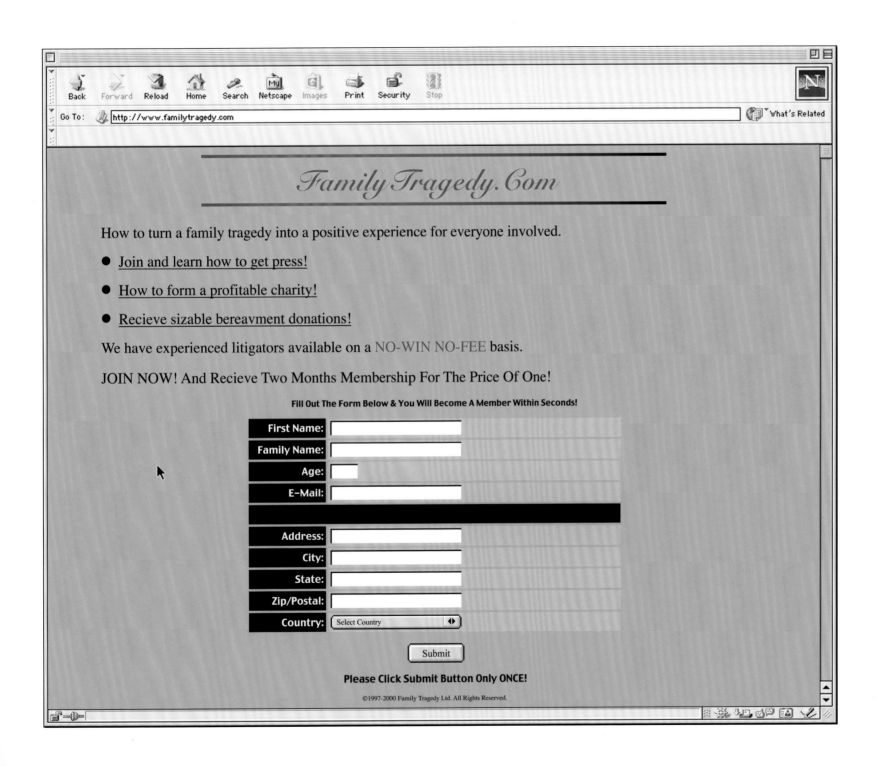

FamilyTragedy.Com

How to turn a family tragedy into a positive experience for everyone involved.

- Join and learn how to get press!

- How to form a profitable charity!

- Recieve sizable bereavment donations!

We have experienced litigators available on a NO-WIN NO-FEE basis.

JOIN NOW! And Recieve Two Months Membership For The Price Of One!

Fill Out The Form Below & You Will Become A Member Within Seconds!

First Name:	
Family Name:	
Age:	
E–Mail:	
Address:	
City:	
State:	
Zip/Postal:	
Country:	Select Country

Submit

Please Click Submit Button Only ONCE!

To empty the trash without
seeing the world, hold down
your ears before you open
your eyes and choose this
command.

First published in Great Britain in 2002 by Trolley Ltd.
Unit 5, Building 13, Long Street, London E2 8HN

Art Works © Nick Waplington 2002
Text © Carlo Mc Cormick 2002
Design by Simon Parkinson
Photograph by Niels Alpert

10 9 8 7 6 5 4 3 2 1

ISBN 0-9542079-7-1

Printed in Italy.

nickwaplington@hotmail.com